Short-Term
Therapy for
Long-Term
Change

A Norton Professional Book

Short-Term Therapy for Long-Term Change

Marion F. Solomon, Ph.D.
Robert J. Neborsky, M.D.
Leigh McCullough, Ph.D.
Michael Alpert, M.D.
Francine Shapiro, Ph.D.
David Malan, D.M., FRCPsych

W.W. Norton & Company

New York • London

For information about permission to reproduce
selections from this book, write to
Permissions, W. W. Norton & Company, Inc.,
500 Fifth Avenue, New York, NY 10110

Composition by Techbooks
Manufacturing by Haddon Craftsmen
Production manager Leeann Graham

Library of Congress Cataloging-in-Publication Data

Short-term therapy for long-term change/Marion F. Solomon. . . [et al.].
    p.   cm.
  "A Norton professional book."
  Includes bibliographical references and index.
  ISBN 0-393-70333-9
    1. Brief psychotherapy. 2. Psychodynamic psychotherapy. I. Solomon, Marion Fried.
RC480.55 .S556   2001
616.89'14—dc21   2001030684

W. W. Norton & Company, Inc., 500 Fifth Avenue, New York, N.Y. 10110
www.wwnorton.com

W. W. Norton & Company, Ltd., Castle House, 75/76 Wells Street, London W1T 3QT

1 2 3 4 5 6 7 8 9 0

Contents

Foreword

Lewis L. Judd

AT THE TURN OF THE TWENTIETH CENTURY a small group of physicians began to report that talking and interacting with emotionally troubled patients, in a specifically prescribed manner, could ameliorate psychopathological symptoms. From these few early anecdotal clinical reports the enormous health-care effort that encompasses the psychotherapies has evolved. Today literally tens of thousands of psychotherapy clinicians are responsible for the treatment of millions of people worldwide. The compelling and consuming goals of psychotherapy scholars and clinicians have always focused on how to increase the therapeutic efficacy of psychotherapy and at the same time decrease the duration of treatment time needed to achieve "a cure." In essence this volume describes the theory and the methods that have been developed to increase psychotherapy effectiveness in as brief a period of time as is feasible. As such there is much to recommend here to psychotherapy researchers, practitioners, trainees, and students.

Despite its very widespread practice, psychotherapy has remained primarily a clinical art rather than emerging as a legitimate clinical science. Until recently most techniques of psychotherapy had not been subjected to credible rigorous empirical scientific testing. This had been a particularly telling indictment of the practice of dynamic psychotherapy. However, with the pioneering efforts of Habib Davanloo and David Malan, along with an emerging group of dynamic psychotherapy scholars, many of whom are authors of this book, systematic attempts have been made to address this vital issue.

My first contact with short-term dynamic psychotherapy came when I accompanied my wife (a psychotherapist) to one of the early international symposia organized by Davanloo in the mid-1970s. It was not the usual meeting I attended, since I was an empirically trained clinical scientist focused on the biological roots of mental illness. However, I came away from this symposium impressed by these efforts to shorten and increase the effectiveness of inter-personal psychotherapy. I was particularly intrigued by Davanloo's and Malan's willingness and openness in sharing their ideas and techniques by way of the liberal use of videotapes recorded from ongoing psychotherapy sessions and by their recognition that results needed to be documented scientifically.

While organizing and leading what proved to be one of the more impor-tant modern scientific departments of psychiatry in the country, I invited Davanloo and Malan to conduct annual symposia in San Diego over the next several years. These symposia, where they presented their ideas and tech-niques to my faculty and the mental health community at large, created substantial excitement and enthusiasm among some of the clinicians in our community, who organized their own intensive short-term dynamic psy-chotherapy study group under Davanloo's direction. From this study group, one of the authors of this volume (Neborsky) was introduced to and trained in Davanloo's technique, and he has now studied, practiced, and written about it extensively.

Over the years, because of the steady accumulation of responsibilities, in-cluding serving as the director of the National Institute of Mental Health (1987–1990), I had little contact with the short-term therapy movement. However, in the interim and in parallel, psychotherapy research per se be-gan to evolve as a legitimate empirical science, however with a somewhat different focus than short-term dynamic psychotherapy. Clinical scientists be-gan to develop disorder-*specific* psychotherapies, such as cognitive behavioral panic control or interpersonal psychotherapy of depression. The disorder-specific psychotherapies, designed to treat *specific* mental disorders, stood in opposition to broad-spectrum approaches, where a single approach is used for all types of disorders. These newer psychotherapies have been described in detail in how-to manuals, and rigorous training programs have been established to maintain quality control of their practice. Most importantly, these new disorder-specific psychotherapies are being subjected to objective, carefully designed outcome studies to establish effectiveness. This has re-sulted in a number of large-scale clinical studies focusing on these techniques, either alone, in comparison to psychotropic medications, or in combination with them, in which effectiveness is being proven in a scientifically accept-able manner.

On March 11 and 12, 2000, I participated in a symposium with a number of the authors of this book, which gave me an opportunity, after some

20 years, to assess the current state of short-term dynamic psychotherapy. One of the major questions I have had about short-term dynamic psychotherapy as practiced by Davanloo is whether it can be successfully generalized and practiced with a high degree of effectiveness by clinicians other than Davanloo. There is little doubt that Davanloo is a gifted, creative, and perhaps uniquely effective psychotherapist, but can others learn this technique and practice it as well and with the same results as the master? Further, can the technique be elaborated and modified to make it both easier to teach and also more effective in treating patients? In reading this volume, I would say that the answer to these questions is yes—but with qualifications.

There is a growing body of empirically established evidence that there is merit to short-term psychotherapies based upon psychodynamic principles. I believe that a number of issues must be resolved before there will be broad acceptance and practice of these approaches. The apprenticeship is long, and a student must have the motivation or willingness to undergo lengthy training. The concepts of short-term dynamic psychotherapy should be broken down into more easily measurable hypotheses that can be empirically tested. Malan and Davanloo were groundbreakers in this area. McCullough and Shapiro have made significant scientific contributions to the identification, isolation, and testing of specific therapeutic factors in their approaches. However, much more work needs to be done before it can be demonstrated with scientific rigor that (1) short-term dynamic psychotherapies can produce results superior to those of disease-specific therapies, or (2) therapists can be trained in these techniques as readily as they can in the disease-specific approaches.

This compendium of chapters covering short-term therapies based upon psychodynamic principles is an excellent beginning and also a testimony to the fact that serious scholars are addressing these issues, which augers well for the future of short-term psychotherapy. I look forward to more from this excellent and productive group.

Introduction

Marion F. Solomon and Robert J. Neborsky

THIS IS A TIME OF RAPIDLY CHANGING expectations of psychological treatment. Instead of claiming that there is the *one true path* to psychological healing, the authors of this book have made a substantial effort to integrate disparate perspectives and develop a unified theory of effective treatment.

This book originated out of a series of conferences sponsored by Lifespan Learning Institute in Southern California. Lifespan, founded by Mathew and Marion F. Solomon, is an organization dedicated to teaching psychotherapy to the professional community. In 1994 the program committee brought Habib Davanloo to Los Angeles. The next year Davanloo asked one of his former students, Robert J. Neborsky from San Diego, to discuss his work. This generated considerable enthusiasm in the community, and Neborsky formed a Los Angeles study group to teach Davanloo's technique of intensive short-term dynamic psychotherapy. When grassroots interest in the whole field of short-term dynamic psychotherapy exploded, Lifespan sponsored a series of conferences by Neborsky on Davanloo's technique. The community was impressed with the therapeutic results achieved in the cases presented.

To satisfy the demand for training in short-term dynamic psychotherapy, Solomon brought Leigh McCullough from Boston to present her approach to the community. McCullough's work also generated excitement, so it was natural to put together a conference of active short-term practitioners. Solomon asked David Malan from England and Michael Alpert from New York to present alongside Neborsky and McCullough. Convergences and divergences in techniques became apparent, and the idea for this book was born.

Later, at a Lifespan conference on trauma and traumatic attachments, Francine Shapiro gave a magnificent audiovisual presentation of her treatment with an earthquake victim who had been molested as a child, and we discussed the convergences and divergences between the dynamic view of the unconscious and Shapiro's information-processing view of the memory system. After all, what is meant by unconscious if not memory that cannot be accessed? *The fit was natural, and new conceptualizations of psychopathology and technique evolved.

In this book six senior clinicians bring together overlapping ideas that focus on underlying causes of neurotic disorders and character pathology. Each of the authors outlines the exact methods he or she uses with patients to create emotional reintegration.

For years, each of us has been searching for the best ways to approach patients whose pain persists despite many attempts at prior treatment. David Malan, practicing in England, was part of the initial search for effective short-term dynamic treatments. A peer of and collaborator with Habib Davanloo, he has been open to new ideas of treatment while insisting on their scientific validation. Neborsky attended each training available with Davanloo for over twenty years. Leigh McCullough originally trained in behavioral and cognitive models of treatment, studied IS-TDP with Davanloo, and has been researching the effectiveness of various methods of psychotherapy for over twenty years. Her current research at Harvard University, presented at two conferences at UCLA, led our group of short-term pathfinders to explore the effects of treatment on the brain. In her chapter, as in her book, *Changing Character*, McCullough presents an anxiety-regulating therapy designed to overcome the patient's resistance to emotional truth. Michael Alpert, after studying with Davanloo, developed a method of accelerated treatment that is compatible with Heinz Kohut's theories of empathic attunement. Alpert is relentless in his exploration of the patient's reactions to the caring responses of the therapist. Francine Shapiro independently developed a new model of treatment, EMDR, that uses eye movement to process communication between different parts of the brain. Solomon applies dynamic theories of treatment to relationships in the patient's life—marriage and other intimate partnerships.

As the six of us came together over a period of several years to present to each other and conference attendees on various models of treatment, we refused to pit theory against theory. We were more interested in observing how different theories affected direct treatments with patients. Using videotapes of treatment sessions, we received feedback from each other and the therapists in the audience and began the process of integration that has resulted in this book.

By expanding the range of speakers, we assimilated new knowledge of how the brain develops, how early attachment affects the developing mind, how trauma blocks processing of emotions, and how emotional reprocessing can be expedited and advanced in ways that enable us to achieve the goals that go back to the early therapeutic goals of Sigmund Freud. In this process, we continue in the tradition of Freud, who suggested that: "We must recognize the limitations of current knowledge, be prepared to continuously learn new things and alter treatment methods in any way that can improve them" (1918).

During our conversations several important points have emerged as significant commonalities. We all recognize that early trauma can cause lifelong emotional blocks. All models describe intense reactions in primary attachment relationship and the damaging effects of the failure of significant attachment figures to acknowledge the painful and frightening emotions felt by a developing child. This failure results in intense affect, reactive anxiety, guilt and shame, and protective defenses. We agree that understanding and focusing on the transference is an important part of effective treatment of neurotic disorders and character pathology. What the child initially experiences is later recreated in the transference and in the current life situation of the adult patient.

We agree that increasing the capacity for emotional closeness by healing damaged attachment bonds is central to the therapeutic endeavor. Despite our various emphases, we all make extensive use of the therapeutic relationship to both assess and work through emotional blocks and achieve a greater capacity for closeness.

We acknowledge that, just as each patient is unique, each clinician has unique attributes, clinical training, and areas of specialty. We know that there are different ways to achieve the goal of overcoming resistance to awareness of painful affect and to guide patients toward emotional reintegration, thereby increasing freedom to feel emotion within the self, decreasing symptomatology, and increasing the ability to maintain boundaries. The result is enhancement of self-directed compassion, empathy for and attunement with others, and the blossoming of a capacity for intimacy. Shapiro talks about emotional reprocessing, McCullough speaks of desensitization of affect phobia, Alpert describes accelerated empathic attunement, Malan and Neborsky stress accessing genuine repressed feeling, and Solomon emphasizes empathy and interdependency in intimate attachments. Each is a piece of an emerging model of treatment that might be called ADP, *accelerated dynamic psychotherapy*. This model takes into account the societal changes since Freud's time, including the transitions in family structures and their effects on child development that have made attachment failures endemic in our culture. It considers core conflicts and disturbances that result from the loss of secure emotional bonds for many children. It recognizes that responses to the trauma of attachment failure that are utilized to cope with this painful state during the first two years of life become imprinted in the brain, mind, and body of the child. This painful state rigidifies into defenses that are resistant to change. Our work is designed to alter the way these defenses cripple the adult and continue to affect the child who resides within every adult.

The six of us have been engaged in the process of developing treatments that can be proven scientifically valid, taught to others, and reliably reproduced by effectively trained psychotherapists with a wide variety of patients. Our goal is to provide accelerated methods of dynamic psychotherapy in as effective a way as humanly possible. This model takes into account important developmental and neurobiological research that provides evidence for the effects of early trauma and deprivation on brain growth. Finally, this model expands on the research of the last fifty years, which confirms that effective psychotherapeutic treatment is *not a function of length of time* but a direct correlate of *depth of emotional experience*.

This is a work in progress, and we hope to continue to integrate the burst of new scientific research that is coming out of various related fields in the coming years. A generous donation to the Lifespan Learning Institute Foundation for Research and Training has been essential in expediting this process and enabling us to expand our learning potential. The Lifespan Learning Institute is attempting to shape and influence the direction that psychotherapeutic treatment takes in the twenty-first century. This book is a first step, reflecting that emerging vitality. The foundation's support provides the opportunity for clinicians from various parts of the world to continue a series of ongoing meetings and dialogue in a quest to both improve and scientifically evaluate the treatment efficacy of accelerated dynamic psychotherapy.

Reference

Freud, S. (1918). From the history of an infantile neurosis. In J. Strachey (Ed. and Trans.), *The standard edition of the complete psychological works of Sigmund Freud* (Vol. 17). New York: Norton, 1955.

Acknowledgments

THERE ARE MANY PEOPLE whose support made this book possible. First, we want to acknowledge Habib Davanloo, M.D., whose unique genius opened a path that made our journey possible. Next, we thank Lewis Judd, M.D., who brought Davanloo to UCSD, supported his methodology, and brought the authors of this book to UCSD 20 years later.

We thank our patients and our families. This book could not have been written without the partnership of patients who worked with us to find solutions to their problems. We also owe a debt to our families for their encouragement as well as their patience when our writing made us unavailable. We especially thank Matthew Solomon for his consistent support and ability to turn preliminary ideas into action, and Joanna Neborsky for skillfully transcribing the "The Woman Who Blamed Herself."

We owe a debt of gratitude to our editor, Susan Munro, who insisted that we create narrative consistency in a multi-author text. She brings to editing both an in-depth knowledge of the field and a remarkable attention to detail that made this as good a book as it could possibly be. We also want to thank Caron Broidy for reading the manuscript in its early form and giving feedback that helped add clarity to complex ideas, and Emanuel Peluso, MFT, for his lucid input and advice.

The ideas in Chapter 2 evolved from teaching Davanloo's Method of IS-TDP in Lifespan Symposia and in the Los Angeles study group. Thanks to Drs. Reimer, Kupper, Koch, Gilbert, Teets, White, Carmalt, Green-Pae, Kay, Brod, and again Emanuel Peluso for their participation and questions.

The ideas in Chapter 7 rely heavily on the writings of Allan Schore, Ph.D. and Daniel J. Siegel, M.D. We thank them for their willingness to not only share their ideas, but also for their thoughtful editorial advice.

Finally, we wish to thank Ruth Steckdaub for her dedicated and patient compilation of this multi-author effort.

1

The Challenge of Short-term Psychotherapy

Robert J. Neborsky and Marion F. Solomon

An Ideal Therapy

IN 1980, DAVID MALAN wrote about *a wish fulfillment fantasy* of brief psychotherapy based entirely on psychodynamic principles. He stated:

1. It would be applicable to a high proportion of the psychotherapeutic population.
2. Therapeutic effects would begin to appear within the first few sessions.
3. At termination no traces of the original disturbances would remain, and this position would be maintained at follow-up.
4. Adverse phenomena that complicate ordinary therapy—sexualized or dependent transference, acting out, and difficulties over termination—would not appear.

The purpose of this book is to describe the work of six short-term clinicians who aspire to these lofty outcome goals. The authors of this book have dedicated their careers to the goal of delivering to their patients the promised results of dynamic psychotherapy in as effective a way as humanly possible.

A Definition of Short-term Dynamic Psychotherapy

Short-term dynamic psychotherapy (STDP) has its theoretical origins in psychoanalysis but at the same time has a mutually ambivalent relationship with psychoanalysis. The major conflict between the two treatment modalities revolves around the issue of time and efficacy. STDP ambitiously purports to treat the same disorders as psychoanalysis but in a shorter period of time. STDP uses the scientific method to evaluate outcome whereas psychoanalysis rarely does. Naturally, many psychoanalytic practitioners feel threatened by the emergence of STDP—a treatment that can comprehensively treat neurotic patients in less than 40 hours of therapy compared to between 250 and 600 hours for a "complete" psychoanalysis. Traditionally, psychoanalysis has ignored the findings of the short-term group, hiding from the implications of the research behind the superficiality hypothesis.

Technically, psychoanalysis requires the establishment of a transference neurosis between the patient and the analyst. This means that the analyst *becomes* the parent to the patient and the patient *develops symptoms* in order to deal with unconscious feelings toward the analyst. The analyst uses resistance interpretation and dream symbol analysis to uncover the patient's repressed feelings and impulses. Eventually, the unconscious transfer ends, and the patient ideally terminates analysis with a reconstructed personality. Outcome research by Malan and others questions whether, in fact, this really occurs.

Short-term dynamic therapy also uses the transference to a great extent. However, the development of a transference neurosis is discouraged by the intense focus on the affective relationship between patient and therapist in the session, and all emotions are identified and acknowledged before the patient leaves the session. The therapist is more a catalyst or guide to help the patient face unacceptable feelings, rather than a figure to attach to in order to slowly emerge from the suffering of symptoms. Transference is seen as a ubiquitous phenomenon that occurs in all intimate relationships. It is explored on an affective level in the first session and all subsequent sessions until the neurosis is resolved by discovery of genuine feelings, affect desensitization, corrective emotional experience, and insight into one's unconscious process. The specific techniques of short-term dynamic psychotherapy have been developed to accelerate the working through process in order to restructure psychic balance between id, ego, and superego (dynamic) forces in an attempt to (1) reduce symptoms, (2) change character, and (3) improve the relational capacity.

Now, within this camp there are emerging schools represented by each of the authors, as well as active debate among the practitioners of each subgroup. Those in the Davanloo group, represented by Neborsky, Patricia Della Selva, Allan Kaplain, Allen Abbass, and others, work along the lines in which they were trained and largely adhere to the central dynamic sequence as the key to their approach. For this reason, they place heavy emphasis on bringing self-punishment trends into consciousness in the initial moments of the first therapeutic contact. McCullough and her followers organize their treatment around a flexible approach, which includes psychoeducation about defenses, mild pressure to feeling, persistent pressure not to self-punish, and encouragement to feel emotion in the session. McCullough believes that the experience of affect is essential to character transformation, but she goes one step further and adds what she calls "self-other restructuring," wherein she explores the transference-countertransference distortions that occur in treatment of patients with low self-esteem and negative self-images. She actively encourages "self-directed compassion" when patients are self-critical. Michael Alpert, Isabel Sklar, and Diana Fosha (2000) represent a school of short-term dynamic psychotherapy centered in the New York area that emphasizes the healing aspects of affect and empathy. They work exclusively in the area of self and other by focusing in minute detail on what the patient experiences in the moment between the patient and therapist. This approach evolved when Alpert noticed the affect of one of Davanloo's patients deepen when Davanloo commented on the patient's courage. In the process of the relational work, remarkable associations to the patient's past spontaneously appear and past traumas are worked through in a short time.

In summary, short-term dynamic psychotherapy takes place in three to forty hours of therapy. The initial contact is two to three hours. The length of the therapy within the range is defined by the degree of psychopathology that the patient demonstrates: low resistant neurotics with one focal conflict (e.g., Oedipal focus) can be treated in three hours; patients with diffuse pathology and multiple foci may need closer to forty hours.

Confusion About Short-term Dynamic Psychotherapy

There is considerable confusion about "short-term" in the term short-term dynamic psychotherapy. The term originated because psychoanalysis and long-term, open-ended therapy was the gold standard of treatment from the post World War II years until the 1960s. This was the form of therapy that was taught in academic centers throughout the country. In fact, most chairmen of academic departments of psychiatry from 1946 to 1960 were psychoanalysts. Thus, the curriculum presented their biases to generations of psychiatrists and psychotherapists. So the term "short-term" was an attempt by Malan, Sifneos, Davanloo, and others to distinguish their efforts from the traditional therapies of the time. Ironically, in our age of managed care, and with the authorized treatment of complex problems with the "three-session limit," short-term therapy of up to forty sessions seems like a luxury!

In addition to the time distinction there is also confusion about the term
"dynamic." Dynamic has both general and specific meanings. The term dynamic has its roots in the Victorian concept of the mind as a closed system
in which psychic energy flows were generated by human libido. The new science of psychoanalysis hoped to influence these energy flows away from pathogenic foci that created anxiety, depression, conversion disorders, etc. The
force of libido was, of course, infantile sexual drive, which was influenced by
early childhood events, which were later repressed into the unconscious. Distinct from this formulation is the structural theory of the mind, that is, the
tripartite organization of the psyche into id, ego, and superego. In this context "dynamic" refers to the interplay of these three sections of experience,
part of which may be unconscious. So, dynamic has multiple meanings from
history and metapsychology. It is also used in one other important way. In
the late 1950s and early 1960s there was considerable controversy between
the schools of analytic treatment and the behavioral therapists. The behav-
iorists were entering territory that was the exclusive domain of psychoanalysis:
phobias, compulsions, anxiety disorders, and ultimately depression. They
were getting documented results and challenging the stranglehold analytic
therapy had on the academic and professional training centers. Plus the treatments were scientifically conducted and results—outcomes—were measured
and published in refereed journals. So the term *dynamic* became a modifier
that distinguished treatment from the behavioral approach. Finally, a new and
important meaning has become attached to the term *dynamic psychotherapy*: it
refers to the deeply therapeutic process of accessing repressed feelings. This
is a newer usage of the phrase, but it has become synonymous with STDP.
Let's now explore the development of this specific approach from a historical perspective.

The Evolution of Dynamic Short-term Psychotherapy

Early History

Psychoanalysis began with Breuer's "talking cure" of Anna O (Freud, 1893).
Soon thereafter, Freud struggled with the hysterical symptoms of Emmy Von
M, Lucy R, Katharina, Elisabeth von R, and lastly Dora (1900). As Breuer's
young associate, he was given cases of hysterical psychopathology to treat.
Intrigued, Freud began to investigate the psychological causes of these
women's symptoms. To do so he had to invent a technique. He first gravitated
to hypnosis but became disenchanted with its results. Later, he discovered

free association as a technique, and this led to the discovery of transference and then resistance. Each of these cases was treated in months, not years. Soon Freud became enamored with dream analysis. This change in interest naturally caused the process to lengthen. Freud's initial concept of psychopathology was that of direct or actual molestation trauma as the origin of hysterical pathology. He later revised this idea concurrently with his interest in dreams. This led to his discovery of the Oedipus complex. Simply stated, he concluded that neurosis was a result of the castration complex in men and of penis envy in women. Consequently, the process of psychoanalytic treatment lengthened as theories of pathogenesis became more complex.

It is known that Freud orchestrated a number of short-term therapies. In his autobiography, the conductor Bruno Walter (1940) describes a successful six-session therapy with Freud in 1906. Ernest Jones (1957) reports that Freud successfully treated Gustav Mahler's psychogenic impotence in a single four-hour session! However, as psychoanalysis developed a more complex theoretical superstructure, treatments grew to such a length that they became interminable. Freud wrote *Analysis, Terminable and Interminable* to express these concerns in 1937.

The Pioneers

Around 1918, Sandor Ferenczi began to systematically experiment with new techniques. He called his work "active therapy." He used techniques to overcome stalemates, introduced desensitization for phobias, and tried some of the restrictive techniques that are used today to treat compulsive symptoms. He also experimented with reparative efforts of hugging, kissing, and nonerotic fondling. So he can be considered the father of both active therapeutic approaches and boundary violations in dynamic psychotherapy. Freud wrote Ferenczi a not so friendly letter putting Ferenczi's treatment technique down with humor and irony. Predicting further, more severe boundary violations by followers, Freud (Jones 1957, Vol. 3, pp. 163–164) predicts that someday Ferenczi will lament to himself, "Maybe after all I should have halted in my technique of motherly affection *before* the kiss."

Interestingly, Otto Rank collaborated with Ferenczi. Reading their work, *The Development of Psychoanalysis*, is like reading a contemporary discussion of the issues surrounding short-term/long-term therapy. They also anticipated later concepts like Alexander's "corrective emotional experience" and Davanloo's heavy emphasis on affective experience in the here and now. They asserted that psychoanalytic treatment should not remain tied to the free associative technique out of which it evolved. They criticized the preoccupation with investigating the past and stressed the essential importance of focusing on the transference in the present treatment situation. In discussing the factors of effective therapy, they stated, like Davanloo, that the analyst should "substitute by means of the technique, affective factors of experience for intellectual processes" (1925, p. 62).

Rank (1924), known as a proponent of birth trauma, actually began to play that down later in his career and recognized that separation and individuation were core processes for the work of psychotherapy. He was the first analytic therapist to set a time limit on therapy to accentuate the separation and individuation aspects during termination phase. Rank (1947) also predated Davanloo in his focus on the concept of the patient's "will." Like Davanloo, he emphasized the importance of mobilizing the patient's "will" during the course of the therapy to facilitate the process. We now have evidence from Davanloo's and others' recorded cases that he was on the right track.

Twenty years (1946) after Rank and Ferenczi's publication, Alexander and French, at the Chicago Institute of Psychoanalysis, wrote in *Psychoanalytic Therapy* about the "baffling discrepancy" between length and intensity of psychoanalytic treatment and the degree of therapeutic success. This finding was to be confirmed in later studies by David Malan at the Tavistock Clinic and eventually by the Menninger Foundation Study in Topeka. So, nearly 70 years after the discovery of psychoanalysis, in the first systematic study of its results, the validity of the technique as a therapy was disproved. However, the theory behind the technique seemed to be shown valid. Alexander stressed three important variables in the treatment process that predicted successful outcome: (1) understanding of the patient's psychodynamics, (2) understanding the genetic development of the patient's difficulties, and (3) once 1 and 2 were established, structuring the therapist's reactions to the patient in such a way as to create a "corrective emotional experience." Alexander's work was a watershed in the history of psychotherapy. Suddenly the process of psychoanalytic psychotherapy had the potential of being helpful to large populations of people suffering from neurotic and characterologic difficulties.

The 1960s saw an upsurge in research into the process of short-term dynamic therapy, fueled in part by the Federal government's funding of mental health. Malan, Wolberg, Bellak and Small, Sifneos, Balint, Mann, and Davanloo worked on this problem and interacted scientifically with each other. Somewhat separate but extremely important is the work of Aaron Beck (1970, 1976) in the cognitive behavioral realm, where the therapist attempts to correct the patient's cognitive distortions and acts as a "coach." Under rigorous scrutiny in its application to depression, this therapy has demonstrated comparable if not superior efficacy to drug therapies for depression.

Malan (1963), a continent away, scientifically confirmed Alexander and French's counterintuitive finding that long-term therapy (psychoanalysis) shows no greater—and perhaps less—change than short-term approaches. Malan standardized the Triangle of Conflict* as well as the Triangle of People[†] and invented a short-term therapy for patients whose concerns were oedipal and who could work with interpretation. Malan's approach has been compared with that of Sifneos (1972), which also applied to a narrow spectrum of patients. Mann (1973) focused on patients whose difficulties centered on loss, separation, and differentiation and so was similarly limited. Bellak and Small (1965) kept their horizon narrowly focused on symptom alleviation. They went so far as to declare that character change was not a goal of short-term therapy.

Michael Balint and his wife Enid Balint, along with Paul Ornstein (1972), began to get impressive results with their *focal psychotherapy*, in which the therapist insisted that the patient focus on a central core conflictual disturbance. They studied 39 patients and struggled to create outcome measurements for dynamic therapies. In 1975, Malan summarized what he thought the Tavistock Clinic Study by Balint and his colleagues established as a standard for psychotherapy evaluation:

1. Clear-cut results, based on statistical methods, the essence of which has been cross-validated.
2. Strong evidence about specific factors in technique that are therapeutically effective.
3. Some degree of validation of scientific principles.
4. Some evidence on the validity of psychotherapy.

The Revolution

In March 1975, Davanloo set up the first of three International Symposia on Short-term Dynamic Psychotherapy. Around 1976 Malan began collaborating with Davanloo, which resulted in the publication of his "wish-fulfillment" chapter in 1980. By that time Davanloo had turned from full-time research to disseminating his findings and teaching his technique around the world. Eventually, in the 1980s, Malan and Davanloo parted ways. Interestingly, in recent years Davanloo has spent much of his time modifying his intensive short-term dynamic psychotherapy technique, which he calls "analysis." This

---

*This concept has its origin in Ezriel (1952).

[†]This concept has its origin in Menninger's Triangle of Insight (1958).

technique is designed to induce rapid and dramatic character change in appropriate patients. Malan (in Davanloo, 1980) writes:

> He was a true researcher in the field of psychotherapy who had become
> profoundly guilty and dissatisfied at the way in which, under the classical
> psychoanalytic technique, his patients went on year after year without sub-
> stantial improvement. In consequence he began a twenty-year series of ex-
> periments, working single-handed...during this time, like Freud in the
> 1890s, he was secure in the knowledge that what he was doing was so orig-
> inal that there was not the slightest possibility that anybody else in the
> world might anticipate him.
>
> He began to videotape every session, playing the tapes over and over
> in the evenings in order to see which ingredients of his technique seemed
> to lead to progress and which to failure. When he thought he identified
> an important factor, he would systematically employ it in his next half
> dozen cases.

Davanloo *for the first time in the history of psychotherapy* applied the scientific
method to the development of specific techniques. Out of his courageous
and painstaking efforts he developed a cascade of interventions, which he
called the *central dynamic sequence*. Davanloo did not want short-term dynamic
psychotherapy to be limited in its scope to a narrow population of patients,
like the therapies of Mann, Malan, Sifneos, and Bellak and Small. He wanted
this treatment model to have as broad applicability to patients as psychoanalysis. In fact, he viewed it as an alternative to psychoanalysis. Hence the
therapy included a heavy emphasis on character and character change.

Davanloo also did something else unique in the history of short-term therapy. He went about systematically training therapists in his technique. With
the zeal of a missionary he traveled about the world demonstrating his
method. As a direct result of these efforts, short-term dynamic psychotherapy has an international presence. Now, it is perceived as a discipline of
its own with devoted practitioners. At the present time Davanloo has functioning teaching centers in Montreal, Toronto, New York, Los Angeles,
Amsterdam, Paris, Florence, and Nuremberg.

Modern History

Davanloo had a profound influence on current practitioners of short-term
therapy. Among the authors, Alpert, McCullough, and Neborsky have studied
under Davanloo, and McCullough actually studied with Malan before
Davanloo. What is important here is that most of the authors of this book

have had their ideas on the process of psychotherapy in some way directly influenced by these researcher clinicians. Of the three, McCullough is the only one who was a trained psychotherapy researcher before exposure to short-term dynamic therapy. She, in her own right, has made major scientific contributions to the field of psychotherapy. Her research on character change confirms Rank's assertion that intensity of affect experienced is a more important variable than intellectual insight. This has led McCullough, who is also a trained behavioral therapist, to see neurosis as an "affect phobia." Applying behavioral principles to dynamic psychotherapy with substantiated results, she has created a short-term dynamic therapy, which she calls short-term anxiety-*regulating* therapy. Rather than using the techniques of Davanloo or Sifneos that undo the affect phobia through "flooding," McCullough uses a prolonged and graded exposure model to decrease anxiety while increasing depth of affect and adaptation to life.

Neborsky is a clinician, teacher, and theoretician who follows Davanloo's approach clinically and sees little reason to revise it for most patients. Davanloo is confident in Neborsky's knowledge of his technique, and Malan describes Neborsky's technical skill as the closest of Davanloo's trainees to Davanloo himself. Neborsky sees Davanloo's theory of psychopathology as a subset of attachment theory and works with the model of Ainsworth's insecure attachment as the source of psychopathology. He sees trauma on a continuum, as does Shapiro, with "little t" trauma as the source of neurosis. He uses Davanloo's technique of "unlocking the unconscious" to treat a remarkably broad spectrum of patients with symptom reduction, character change, relationship enhancement, and access to creativity from the unconscious.

Michael Alpert's contribution to short-term therapy comes from the school of empathy, which originated with the work of Heinz Kohut. In 1971 a revolution occurred in psychoanalysis with the publication of Kohut's *Analysis of the Self*, Kohut infused new life into the field of psychoanalysis with his unique thoughts on the self and the psychology of self-esteem. He described two transferences: one related to the grandiose self seen in the patient's need for responsiveness from the therapist through *reflecting*; the other related to the internalized parental imago, wherein the "weak" patient's need for *protection* was satisfied by connection to the "greatness" of the therapist. These two modes of relating are called self-objects. A self-object is "a functional relationship, whose function is to restore, maintain, hold together self-esteem" (Kohut, personal communication, 1976). Arnold Goldberg (1973) dabbled with this as a cornerstone for a technique of short-term therapy, but it seemed to never have developed much of a following. However, one of Davanloo's early trainees, Michael Alpert, has developed a system of therapy called "accelerated empathic therapy" that takes this approach to a new level of application. Alpert works in an intersubjective field (see Stern, 1985; Stolorow & Atwood, 1989), accepting the patient's distortions, overreactions, and underreactions as both valid and probably unconsciously provoked by the therapist's unconscious. He is exquisitely careful to avoid intrusion and interpretation, yet gets documented results.

Marion F. Solomon can also be considered a "student of short-term psychotherapy." More precisely, she is a student of psychotherapy in general. She is not wedded to any one theoretical model but tries to seek the truth in each approach. What she has in common with Davanloo's original students is total dedication to the pursuit of the optimum method of treating patients with psychotherapy. She has been drawn to short-term therapy by the dramatic results that she has noticed on the videotapes. She has also become intrigued with the research aspects of video analysis and begun her own research into the utilization of short-term techniques with couples. It was Solomon's idea to bring together Alpert, Malan, McCullough, and Neborsky, a collaboration that resulted in this book.

Solomon and Neborsky have begun experimenting on the effect of Davanloo's intensive short-term dynamic psychotherapy (IS-TDP) on couples, realizing that this approach had not been systematically looked at in any way. While treating one member of a couple in the relationship, both members separately, or both at once, they have noted the way the neurotic balance is affected by "unlocking the unconscious" and how dramatically the capacity for intimacy improves. Couples who have been stuck in destructive patterns begin to dramatically change. Change definitely occurs! Solomon is actively researching in this area and writes here about her preliminary findings using short-term dynamic therapy with couples.

Difference between Short-term Dynamic Psychotherapy and Other Brief Therapies

Many practitioners have designed techniques of brief psychotherapy; however, few have attempted anything more than symptom reduction. For clarity, we see the term "brief psychotherapy" as defining a school of treatment that attempts to support a weakened ego by a compassionate therapist who offers support, clarification, and ego interpretation to reestablish homeostasis. In contrast to short-term dynamic psychotherapy, none of the existing brief therapies attempts the scope of effort necessary to resolve unconscious conflict created by oedipal and pre-oedipal drives.

The Adaptive Information Processing Breakthrough

In the late 1980s a new therapy developed by Francine Shapiro burst upon the scene. By serendipity, Shapiro discovered that rapid movement of the eyes in sweeps from side to side for a brief period while maintaining attention on a traumatic memory produced a dramatic release of painful affect and a shift in negative beliefs about the self (Shapiro, 1989, 1995/2001). Like short-term dynamic psychotherapy, the initial focus of the treatment was on posttraumatic stress disorder. Over time the treatment approach has been adapted to panic disorder, obsessions, personality disorders, and pathologic grief. Shapiro initially used a cognitive behavioral model to explain the effectiveness of her technique. However, she now sees a more dynamic process at hand with respect to psychopathology. Briefly, Shapiro sees that information from experience is organized at the neurological level in "networks." These networks are complex structures encoding cognitive, sensory, and affective information. In the course of new experience, this information gets linked to older neuro-networks. When a trauma of non-overwhelming nature (a "small t" trauma) occurs, an innate process digests and detoxifies it, until linkages are formed.

These linkages, otherwise known as associations, cause integration to occur. When information is highly charged with negative emotion, as during a major trauma, the innate processing system is overwhelmed. When this occurs the trauma becomes isolated in state-specific forms from other networks and hence from new learning. When trauma has overwhelming negative affect, the normative process breaks down and a negative sense of self is developed. Despite being isolated, the traumatic neuro-network continues to influence behavior and emotional states as similar stimuli trigger activation of neuro-networks and trauma is reexperienced. EMDR meets criteria 2, 3, and 4 of Malan's wish-fulfillment fantasy. Criterion 1—the applicability to a high proportion of the psychotherapeutic population—remains under active research scrutiny by Shapiro and her followers.

Convergence with Short-term Dynamic Therapy

Shapiro's discoveries are cutting-edge confirmations of earlier findings of STDP researchers and clinicians. The technique and metapsychology of Davanloo's intensive short-term dynamic psychotherapy have their origins in work with victims of acute trauma. Davanloo (personal communication, 1981) observed early on that the "unconscious" of trauma victims was easily accessed, making working through of developmental "little t trauma" easier. The other common thread between EMDR theory and STDP lies in the observation that trauma survivors develop a negative sense of self. This is a keystone in the results in both STDP and EMDR. Self-blame is in many ways part and parcel of neurotic pathology. Davanloo sees psychopathology as the result of early malformation of the superego caused by ruptured attachment bonds. Shapiro sees psychopathology developing from cumulative "little t trauma" that has been isolated in a walled-off memory circuit. She also sees that it is reactivated by adult trauma. She postulates that character pathology may just be multiple "little t traumas" isolated from process and thereby creating maladaptation. EMDR practitioners are only now beginning to struggle with the broader spectrum of patients that STDP purports to treat, and a system will have to be developed to address the problem of resistance, which Davanloo's, McCullough's, and Alpert's therapies do at present address.

We include Shapiro's chapter because all of the other authors believe in the validity of her technique and see it as a tool to understand the unconscious and the generation of both neurotic and character pathology. In our view Shapiro's therapy is a dynamic therapy, because it is designed to help patients access feelings, thoughts, and ideas that they previously believed were too painful to experience. Their symptoms replaced the original feelings and negative self-statements became part of their psyche. This, of course, raises the question why the authors stop at EMDR and do not include Beck's cognitive therapy approach in this volume, despite its proven efficacy in the treatment of anxiety and depressive disorders. The answer is that cognitive behavior therapy has abandoned the concept of intrapsychic conflict and repressed emotion as the center of neurosis and instead focuses on the tip of the iceberg: distorted thinking. Thus, we find a natural dividing line between dynamic therapy and cognitive behavioral therapy that does not exist between dynamic therapy and EMDR. Shapiro's approach is an exploratory approach. Remarkably, she has developed a protocol in which the patient is responsible for guiding himself or herself back to health with the assistance of a neutral therapist. So Shapiro emphasizes the importance of therapeutic neutrality, as does the short-term school.

A Reader's Guided Tour to this Book

The book is organized historically. In the second chapter, Robert Neborsky summarizes Davanloo's technique from the point of view a long-standing student of Davanloo's method of short-term therapy. He includes a transcript of his comprehensive 18-hour treatment of a patient with PTSD, chronic depression, substance abuse, and character pathology. Next Leigh McCullough describes her approach to short-term dynamic psychotherapy, called anxiety-regulating therapy. McCullough explains how she sees neurosis as an "affect phobia" and describes her unique desensitization of anxiety-provoking emotion. In addition, she shares a lucid summary of the scientific basis of outcome research. The authors of this book share a common dedication to scientific evaluation of the outcome of psychotherapy, so that short-term treatments do not replicate the mistake of earlier therapies that were based upon belief rather than outcome research. McCullough discusses the challenges of this process of evaluation as only a lifelong researcher in the field can do.

In chapter 4 Michael Alpert introduces his creative approach to the psychotherapeutic situation, where he does everything possible to reduce negative affective states as they emerge in therapy. Then in chapter 5, Francine Shapiro takes the reader through her discovery of EMDR and describes research validating its efficacy. After this she discusses how she feels the technique actually works and relates it to dynamic psychotherapy, wherein patients are given the tools to access painful truths in order to free themselves of neurotic incapacitation following trauma.

Marion F. Solomon then delves into the way in which neurotic marriages present to clinicians. She describes the forces that keep couples stuck in destructive patterns and offers clinical insights into how to help these couples grow beyond their unhappy relationship. In chapter 7 Neborsky and Solomon build upon the insights shared in the previous chapters to offer a unifying theory of unconscious psychopathology gleaned from observations of patients treated in intensive short-term dynamic psychotherapy and EMDR.

The book concludes with David Malan distilling his fifty years of observations of short-term psychotherapy research and practice. This chapter is appropriately entitled, "The Way Ahead."

The Present Challenge

The world is a far different place today than when the current forms of short-term therapy were developed. Psychoanalysis loomed like a Goliath in the minds of the researchers and practitioners of the era. It was the gold standard against which they competed. Today psychoanalysis is more like a dwarf than a Goliath. Practitioners today face a colossus that overshadows whatever psychoanalysis meant to the pioneers of the techniques referred to in this chapter. That colossus is of course psychopharmacology. Symptoms are rapidly and effectively ameliorated by modern drugs therapies. The challenge—and the promise—lies in psychotherapy's ability to change the pathology of malformed character. Historically, psychoanalysis has shirked its responsibility to monitor the scientific examination of its own outcome and its own cost-effectiveness as a therapy.

We would hope that current practitioners of psychoanalysis would rededicate themselves to the efforts of the early pioneers Freud, Ferenczi, Rank, Alexander, French, and Balint to achieve both depth and results in a reasonable time. If they do not return to the lofty ideals of the pioneers, then psychoanalysis is likely to move further from the mainstream of psychotherapy. Pharmacotherapy and cognitive behavioral therapies will never replace dynamic therapies because they ignore the wealth of information that resides in the human unconscious. With this in mind, short-term dynamic psychotherapy has the potential to leap into the forefront of available therapies. Perhaps Malan's heartfelt prediction that intensive short-term dynamic psychotherapy will emerge as the dominant therapy of our time will be realized after all.

References

Alexander, F., & French, T. M. (1946). *Psychoanalytic therapy*. New York: Ronald Press.

Balint, M., Ornstein, P. H., & Balint, E. (1972). *Focal psychotherapy*. Philadelphia: Lippincott.

Beck, A. T. (1970). Cognitive therapy: Nature and relationship to behavior therapy. *Behavior Research and Therapy*, *1*, 184–200.

Beck, A. T. (1976). *Cognitive therapy and the emotional disorders*. New York: International Universities Press.

Bellak, L., & Small, L. (1965). *Emergency therapy and brief psychotherapy*. New York: Grune & Stratton.

Davanloo, H. (1978). *Basic principles and techniques in short-term dynamic psychotherapy*. New York: Spectrum.

Davanloo, H. (Apr. 1979). Techniques of short-term dynamic psychotherapy. *Psychiatric Clinics of North America*, *2*, 1. Philadelphia: Saunders.

Davanloo, H. (1980). *Short-term dynamic psychotherapy*. New York: Aronson.

Davanloo, H., & Benoit, C. (1978). Basic methodology of short-term dynamic psychotherapy. *Psychotherapy and Psychosomatics*, *29*.

Eziel, H. (1952) Notes on psychoanalytic group therapy: Interpretation and research. *Psychiatry*, *15*, 119–126.

Ferenczi, S., & Rank, O. (1925). *The development of psychoanalysis*. New York: Nervous and Mental Disease Publishing Co.

Fosha, D. (2000). *The transforming power of affect: A model for accelerated change*. New York: Basic Books.

Freud, S. (1893). Studies on hysteria. In J. Strachey (Ed. and Trans.), *The standard edition of the complete psychological works of Sigmund Freud* (Vol. 2). New York: Norton, 1955.

Freud, S. (1900). The interpretation of dreams. In J. Strachey (Ed. and Trans.), *The standard edition of the complete psychological works of Sigmund Freud* (Vol. 5). New York: Norton, 1953.

Freud, S. (1937). Analysis, terminable and interminable. In J. Strachey (Ed. and Trans.), *The standard edition of the complete psychological works of Sigmund Freud* (Vol. 23). New York: Norton, 1962.

Goldberg, A. (1973). Psychotherapy of narcissistic injuries. *Archives of General Psychiatry, 28*, 722–726.

Jones, E. (1957). *The life and work of Sigmund Freud.* (3 Vols.). New York: Basic Books.

Kohut, H. (1971). *The analysis of the self.* New York: International Universities Press.

Malan, D. H. (1963). *A study of brief psychotherapy.* Philadelphia: Lippincott.

Malan, D. H. (1975). Psychoanalytic Grief psychotherapy and scientific method In D. Bannister (Ed.), *Issues and approaches in the psychological therapies* (pp. 201–202). London: Wiley.

Malan, D. H. (1976). *The frontier of brief psychotherapy.* New York: Plenum.

Malan, D. H. (1976). *Toward the validation of dynamic psychotherapy.* New York: Plenum.

Malan, D. H. (1980). The most important development in psychotherapy since the discovery of the unconscious. In H. Davanloo (Ed.), *Short-term dynamic psychotherapy.* (pp. 13–23) New York: Aronson.

Mann, J. (1973). *Time-limited psychotherapy.* Cambridge, MA: Harvard University Press.

Menninger, K. A. (1958). *Theory of psychoanalytic technique.* New York: Basic Books.

Rank, O. (1924). *The trauma of birth.* New York: Robert Brunner.

Rank, O. (1947). *Will therapy.* New York: Knopf.

Shapiro, F. (1989). Efficacy of the eye movement desensitization procedure in the treatment of traumatic memories. *Journal of Traumatic Stress Studies, 2*, 199–223.

Shapiro, F. (1995/2001). *Eye movement desensitization and reprocessing: Basic principles, protocols and procedures.* New York: Guilford.

Sifneos, P. E. (1972). *Short-term psychotherapy and emotional crisis.* Cambridge, MA: Harvard University Press.

Stern, D. N. (1985). *The interpersonal world of the infant.* New York: Basic Books.

Stolorow, R. D., & Atwood, G. E. (1989). The unconscious and unconscious fantasy: An intersubjective-developmental perspective. *Psychoanalytic inquiry, 9*, 364–374.

Walter, B. (1940). *Theme and variation.* New York: Knopf.

2

Davanloo's Method of Intensive Short-term Dynamic Psychotherapy

Robert J. Neborsky

History

DAVANLOO'S METHOD of intensive short-term dynamic psychotherapy (IS-TDP) is difficult to learn. Only a handful of the students who study the technique eventually master it. In the hands of someone who knows the technique, it looks deceptively simple. The underlying psychopathology unfolds and presents itself in beautiful ways. The cause-and-effect relationship of the dynamic past with the stresses of the present is laid out with precision. In addition, the patient undergoes a deep emotional process where buried repressed feelings from the past are experienced in an abreaction called "the breakthrough." The breakthrough leads to increased motivation for therapy and a deeper desire for freedom from the oppression of the patient's symptoms.

The factors that lead to both failed and successful intensive short-term dynamic psychotherapy therapies will be outlined in this chapter. Davanloo's method of intensive short-term dynamic psychotherapy is indeed simple. Yet in its simplicity lies its difficulty. Davanloo described and discovered a force within the psyche, which he labeled "the unconscious therapeutic alliance." Understanding this force and the skillful mobilization of its power is the secret to successful Intensive short-term dynamic psychotherapy.

16

The birth of Davanloo's IS-TDP owes a great debt to the work of Eric Lindemann (1994) and Elvin Semrad—Lindemann for his focus on the effects of trauma on mental health, and Semrad for his focus on the technique of working with trauma patients. Davanloo studied with both of them. Many of the therapeutic aspects of intensive IS-TDP involve grief-based therapy in which the patient is taught to mourn losses. The grief work is, in the words of Semrad (personal communication, 1994), "the painful process of acknowledging, bearing, and putting into perspective loss." Davanloo, as a psychiatric resident working with acute trauma victims, noted that the unconscious was open and readily accessible. This observation led him to wonder whether he could recreate this state in patients who were locked in stable neurotic conflicts. In terms of our language of today, he wondered if he could have patients relive and thus work through the acute stress disorder of their childhood traumas by exhausting resistance in the initial contact.

Thus, nearly forty years ago Davanloo asked the research question: What would happen if he focused entirely on resistance in the interview from the moment the patient entered his care? He studied Fenichel's *Psychoanalytic Theory of Neurosis* and used it as a compass to guide him in the unconscious. To his delight, the experiment was a success. Someone gave him a VCR to support his research, and he began to systematically analyze his work. This dramatically increased the breadth and efficiency of his work. He was able to systematically study the various resistances that he encountered in his neurotic population. What's more, he found that he could fine-tune his technique so that the breakthroughs became more consistent, earlier in the interview, and more affect-laden. He ultimately confirmed the hypothesis: he could create an atmosphere where patients reexperienced their deep-seated unconscious conflicts in their first visit. He also confirmed that they were not damaged by the encounter with their unconscious. On the contrary, he found that accessing their repressed emotions relieved them. He also discovered that therapy went more quickly and the relapse rate was remarkably low.

After proving, to his satisfaction, the efficacy of his technique, Davanloo took on the challenge of teaching this technique to a broad population of therapists. In this effort he encountered more difficulty than in the application of his ideas to patient care. He initially began training therapists by showing them tapes, describing technique, and teaching psychopathology. The results of this approach were mixed. It soon became apparent that many dedicated students could not learn the technique this way, because the process itself activated resistance in the trainees who were then unable to keep up with the rapidly changing resistances of the patient, resulting in misalliances. Protracted sessions of lengthy, painful challenge of resistance would occur.

Many patients were dissatisfied with the treatment process, which seemed to promise so much and deliver so little, while many therapists became frustrated and disillusioned with the technique, which looked so simple in Davanloo's hands. To address this problem Davanloo changed his teaching focus. He now teaches what he calls "the metapsychology of the unconscious." This approach emphasizes that the process is *dynamic*; the robot-like Davanloo imitation approach will not work. The process is an accelerated blending of the unconscious of the patient with the unconscious of the therapist. There is a constant sending and receiving of information between patient and therapist, and it is the quality of this send/receive that drives the therapy to successful resolution. It has been said that Davanloo has "radar" for the unconscious, and this is true. He is highly intuitive and rapidly senses where the patient is defending against genuine feeling. He also has a highly developed theatrical sense and sees the struggle against neurosis with the clarity and vision of a Greek playwright.

Therapist Qualifications

Patients who are appropriate for IS-TDP defend against the experience of their inner rage with anxiety, panic, depression, or somatization, or they punish themselves with abusive relationships or isolate themselves from intimate contact with others. The intensive short-term dynamic therapist must be able to identify defenses rapidly and accurately. The therapist must have excellent timing and allow characterologic behavior to crystallize in the transference. The therapist must have the ability to hold the patient in his/her struggle against the process without giving in or becoming counter-aggressive. It is unavoidable—indeed essential—that therapists will become anxious using this technique, and they must be able to sustain technique and empathy in the face of their own anxiety. Once master of their own anxiety, therapists must tolerate intense affects (patient and self) and bear frightening visual images of violence and sexuality. Finally, therapists must have the listening skill to accurately link past with present and establish valid, comprehensible cause-and-effect statements about the origins of the patient's difficulties.

Once a student acquires that unique mixture of abilities, what further skills are necessary in order to master Davanloo's intensive short-term dynamic psychotherapy? The successful IS-TDP therapist has the ability to think in terms of three spheres at all times: metapsychology, phenomenology, and thematic content. In supervision, I use the analogy of playing three-dimensional chess. The therapist needs to apply the triangle of conflict along the axis of the

transference, the patient's current life, as well as his or her past. The therapist integrates this material in his preconscious and applies appropriate technique. The response of the patient is again observed through the three
spheres, and the therapist's technical response again occurs. Training is, of
course, arduous, because many previously learned behavioral responses must
be unlearned.

Metapsychology

Metapsychology in Freud's system was an attempt to create a metaphysical
psychology (Jones, 1995). In contrast, Davanloo's metapsychologic system
(Said & Schubmehl, 1999) is really a blend of phenomenology, psychopathology, and technique. The three cannot be explored independent of
each other. Davanloo's conceptualization of psychopathology comes from an
interesting blend of attachment theory, structural theory, object relations, and
direct observation. He conceives of the central problem of neurotic psychopathology as the aggression that occurs when the nurturing bond between
caregiver and child is disrupted. He calls this unconscious rage or primitive
rage. This correlates with Bowlby's protest phase following lost attachment.
Depending upon the severity of the trauma, the rage can be murderous, sadistic, torturous, butcherous, or annhilatory. Severe narcissistic disorders may
have at their root rage for which there is no satiety. (These cases do not
respond to Davanloo's intensive short-term dynamic psychotherapy.) He relies
heavily on the process of projective identification as the core of symptom
formation and sees the aforementioned anger as the force that creates an
internal hostile superego. Davanloo refers to Freud as "pessimistic" in his view
that psychoanalysis could overcome the force of the superego. Davanloo
believes it is necessary to take on the superego at the immediate onset of therapy and wrest its control from the therapy. To Davanloo, the superego is the
rotting corpse of the murdered parent or sibling, returning to seek perpetual
vengeance on the self. The process of inquiry in the therapeutic setting activates the superego. In 1999 Beeber wrote a series of articles describing
Davanloo's concept of the "perpetrator of the unconscious" that explicate this
point. In short, he links Davanloo's concept of the perpetrator with the ideas
of Klein (1932), Guntrip (1961), and Fairbairn (1952). The perpetrator is
found when four common features are present (Davanloo, 1990):

  1. Self-destructive behavior.
  2. Violent and murderous impulses toward early figures in the patient's
     life orbit.

✗ 3. Intense guilt and grief in relation to the figures.

✗ 4. Impoverished personality.

If one examines this conceptualization superficially, there is really nothing revolutionary in it. However, the way Davanloo approaches this construct is crucial. He links the existence of the perpetrator with resistance against emotional closeness. This means that these patients keep their distance from the therapist at all times. They may present a mirage of closeness, but in fact they are always detached. In my experience this detachment can go on for 20 years or longer in long-term therapies. Thus, the interviewer must be aware of the detachment in the first few minutes of the interview if one is to succeed with these patients. Within 20 minutes of Davanloo's intensive short-term dynamic psychotherapy, patients consciously visualize the perpetrator and own his existence in their intrapsychic life. This breakthrough extinguishes the detachment, and working through can progress.

Patient Suitability

Let's now turn to the issue of suitability. Individuals are evaluated dynamically and by Davanloo's own specific classification according to resistance (Table 2.1). They are interviewed using the Davanloo's intensive short-term dynamic psychotherapy techniques, and their response to a trial of the therapy defines their suitability. In other words, the breakthrough into the

TABLE 2.1
Spectrum of Psychoneurotic Disorders: Davanloo's Classification

HIGHLY RESPONSIVE	MODERATELY RESISTANT	HIGHLY RESISTANT	EXTREMELY RESISTANT
Circumscribed problem	Diffuse psychoneurotic disturbances	Diffuse symptoms	Diffuse symptoms
No character disturbance	Presence of character pathology	Character neurosis and character disturbances	Major character disturbance
Single psychotherapeutic focus	Multifoci core neurotic structure	Highly complicated core pathology	Extremely complex core pathology

Reproduced from Davanloo, 1995a; with permission.

unconscious and patients' ability to make use of the material (psychologic mindednesss) defines their suitability and also predicts favorable outcome. The assessment process, using the central dynamic sequence, is known as *the initial interview* or the *trial model of therapy*. These terms are interchangeable.

The goal of this interview is to

1. Assess the patient's psychopathology,
2. Acquaint the patient with his/her defenses, – the wall? Pushing away
3. Expose the core unconscious conflict,
4. Establish domination of the forces of the unconscious therapeutic alliance over the forces of resistance (superego).

It is important to define what is meant by the unconscious therapeutic alliance. One way to define it is to call it a state of relatedness between therapist and patient in which the pursuit of truth supersedes avoidance of painful feeling. Another way to conceive of the unconscious therapeutic alliance is a combination of Winnicott's holding environment and the unconscious longing for intimacy in an empathic field. This force drives the uncovering process and carries the treatment through to termination. In IS-TDP, the therapist carries the ball at the beginning of the therapy by confronting resistance; during the middle phase and termination, the patient carries the ball. The patient usually enters the session with a conscious therapeutic alliance, which waxes and wanes throughout the interview.

The diagnostic systems in Table 2.1 and the diagnostic scheme in Table 2.2 do not correlate. Cases anywhere on Davanloo's classification may have anxiety and other conditions. Again, it is important to stress that this is a classification that is dynamically based and can only be made during a short-term dynamic interview. Symptom checklists and psychologic testing are not germane.

TABLE 2.2
Spectrum of Appropriate Cases for Davanloo's Intensive Short-term Dynamic Psychotherapy by DSM-IV

GAF > 45–50
Anxiety disorders
Depressive disorders
Somatoform disorders
Dissociative disorders
Personality disorders—Cluster C
Marital problems (see chapter 6)

The Breakthrough

In IS-TDP, the goal of each session is to overcome the superego's resistance to dealing with genuine feeling and establishing an intimate and close relationship with the therapist. What is the breakthrough? For those readers who have not seen an IS-TDP interview, the film *Good Will Hunting* shows an excellent dramatic example. The therapist, played by Robin Williams, pushes for the patient (Matt Damon) to face repressed feelings of guilt or shame related to abuse he endured as a child. As Williams repeats, "It's not your fault, it's not your fault," Damon becomes enraged and then breaks down sobbing.

So, the breakthrough is powerful abreactive state of compressed emotion from the unconscious involving grief, guilt, sadness, and pain. This is how Davanloo sees the unconscious—as an organization of layers of defense against core feelings of rage at the offending caregiver. In the breakthrough, the patient gains direct access to these feelings and examines them in the here and now of the therapy session. The patient is able experience the murderous rage, the intense guilt, and the grief-laden unconscious feelings. As this happens, the discharge pattern of anxiety changes, the defenses dissolve, and multidimensional character change occurs. Marion F. Solomon and I have coined the acronym PASO to describe this primitive, aggressive self-organization (see Figure 2.1). The nuances of the PASO as a concept in short-term therapy are described in greater detail in chapter 8.

Initial Interview: Progression

Figure 2.2 (p. 24) introduces the overall concept of how an ideal IS-TDP interview progresses. The patient presents for care and wants to cooperate with the interview, but since the emotions causing the difficulty are in the dynamic unconscious, they cannot be accessed. The emotions and their contextual memory are suppressed by defenses and characterologic patterns of conduct. At the initiation of the interview there is a conscious therapeutic alliance but not an unconscious therapeutic alliance. With the application of a series of interventions described by Davanloo and Malan called the "central dynamic sequence," a breakthrough will occur, the forces of resistance will be overcome, and the unconscious therapeutic alliance will dominate the relationship. Table 2.3 (p. 25) shows the elements of the central dynamic sequence.

By now it should be apparent how systematic this process is. First, we have a patient somewhere along the spectrum of psychoneurosis (Table 2.1). The patient's conscious experience of the disorder is the outer ring of the PASO

FIGURE 2.1
THE PASO: DEFENSES SURROUNDING GRIEF AND SADNESS,
GUILT, SEXUAL FEELING, RAGE, PAIN OF TRAUMA, AND
ATTACHMENT (LOVE)

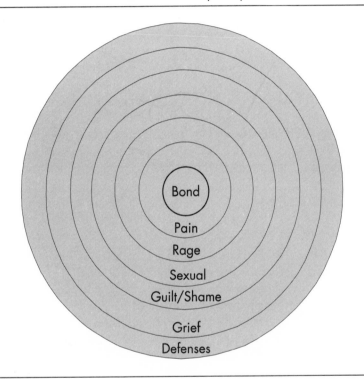

Adapted from Davanloo, 1995c; with permission.

seen in Figure 2.1. Next we have the overview of the process as illustrated in Figure 2.2, and finally we apply the central dynamic sequence in order to explore the deeper layers of the PASO (Table 2.3).

Organization of Clinical Data: Triangles of Conflict, People, Health, TCP

Before the progression of an interview can be fully understood, the student must understand how Davanloo organizes clinical phenomena. He uses a series of triangles to conceptualize the dynamic situation. These are called triangles of conflict and people, with the oedipal triangle as a subset of the latter (see Figure 2.3, p. 26).

FIGURE 2.2
THE PROGRESSION OF AN IS-TDP INTERVIEW

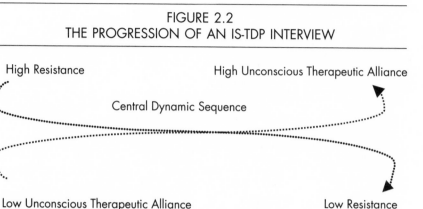

High Resistance   High Unconscious Therapeutic Alliance

Central Dynamic Sequence

Low Unconscious Therapeutic Alliance   Low Resistance

Time, 1–3 hours

Adapted from Davanloo, 1990, p. 3; with permission.

Davanloo listens to the clinical story from the point of view that patients are finding themselves in situations that recreate original traumas from the dynamic past (through the force of the superego "repetition compulsion"). So when the patient whose treatment is described later in this chapter developed chronic PTSD after accidentally killing a woman in an auto accident, it had activated dormant conflicts around guilt and aggression in her subconscious. Thereafter anger at loved figures activated anxiety, guilt, and depression.

After gathering history, the evaluator focuses on a dynamically significant area. Once this area is identified the interviewer pressures toward feeling. Low resistant patients will answer clearly and precisely. Higher resistant patients will show a series of "tactical" defenses (Table 2.4, p. 27). The interviewer gently labels these defenses and brings them to patients' attention. Soon the interviewer identifies these defenses as self-defeating, leading inevitably to patients' beginning to crystallize their character defenses, whatever they maybe. They will perhaps become passive, withholding, submissive, defiant, argumentative, or avoidant (see Table 2.5, p. 27). Some patients, whom Davanloo calls "fragile," will show projective, introjective, or dissociative phenomena at this juncture in the interview, indicative of self-fragmentation. Experienced interviewers retrace at this reaction and do a technical maneuver called "restructuring the ego," which Davanloo developed for

TABLE 2.3
Central Dynamic Sequence

PHASE	TASK
1. Inquiry	Gathering areas of disturbance; exploring the difficulties; initial ability to respond
2. Pressuring toward feeling	Leads to resistance in the form of defenses; rapid identification of the character defenses; clarification and challenge to the defenses; psychodiagnosis
3. Challenging resistances	Challenge combined with a lack of respect for resistances; crystallization of the character resistances; application of partial head-on collision to show resistance has paralyzed his functioning and to turn patient against his resistance
4. Transference resistances	Mounting challenge to transference resistance; intensify rise in transference feelings; mobilize the therapeutic alliance against the resistance; loosen the psychic system
5. Direct access to the unconscious	Intrapsychic crisis; breakthrough of complex transference feelings; direct view of the psychopathologic forces responsible for the patient's symptom and character disturbance
6. Analysis of the transference	Summarize the I/F-A-D-character system just experienced in the transference in order to resolve residual resistance
7. Dynamic exploration into the unconscious	Now the unconscious therapeutic alliance is in control of the process; patient spontaneously introduces traumatic events; repeated breakthroughs of guilt and grief-laden feelings; consolidation, recapitulation, and psychotherapeutic plan

Data from Davanloo, 1995b.

this category of patients. See Davanloo (1989c) for a more detailed description. When there are no signs or symptoms of ego fragility, the interviewer begins challenging resistances in a graded way. Davanloo has four separate protocols (1995b; Table 2.6), which determine the extent and quality of the challenge used by the interviewer.

Once the characterologic resistances crystallize, the interviewer makes the characterologic behaviors ego-dystonic. This is done by using a technique Davanloo labels "head-on collision." This is his most powerful tool in working with resistance. He tells patients in no uncertain terms that it is their

FIGURE 2.3
THE TRIANGLE OF CONFLICT
AND THE TCP TRIANGLE

1. Triangle of conflict:

IMPULSE-ANXIETY-DEFENSE (I/F-A-D)

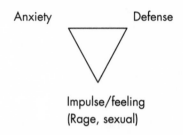

Anxiety   Defense

Impulse/feeling
(Rage, sexual)

2. The triangle of people (Menninger's Triangle of Insight) or
    THE TCP TRIANGLE

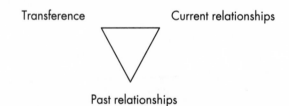

Transference   Current relationships

Past relationships

THE OEDIPAL TRIANGLE IS A SUBSET OF THE TRIANGLE OF PEOPLE*

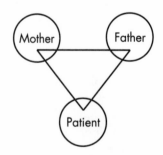

Mother   Father

Patient

*Davanloo sees the oedipal conflict as pathogenic when it disrupts the secure attachment bond with either parent. Siblings may comprise one leg of the triangle if they disrupt the security of the relationship.

TABLE 2.4
Davanloo's Tactical Defenses

Cover words	Not remembering
Blanket words	Denial
Jargon words	Externalization
Indirect speech	Obsessional indecisiveness
Rumination	Stubbornness, defiance
Vague rumination	Tangents
Rationalization	Talking to avoid the experience
Intellectualization	of feelings
Generalization	Nonverbal cues of avoidance
Diversionary tactics	Passive-compliance

Data from Davanloo, 1996a, 1996b.

choice whether or not to get down to the bottom of their difficulties. He confronts them with their crippled life and says that they must face the truth or continue to lead a crippled existence. He frequently challenges them, "Why would you want to do that?" He makes it clear that the patient is the one with the problem. He refuses to allow patients to make their problem his problem. He lets them know that failure to get to the bottom of their problem will affect him as a failure, but it will hurt them more than him because they continue to live in misery. This is then followed by one more challenge, "So, then, what are you going to do about these defenses?" He lists the defenses. This is truly an act of inspiration. Who besides Davanloo thought of turning patients against their own defenses? From the patients' viewpoint there is nothing they can do at that point. The patients are thus placed in

TABLE 2.5
Some Types of Character Resistance

Passive
Compliant
Defiant
Oppositional
Dominating
Submissive
Manipulative (seductive)
Avoidant-phobic
Dissociative
Mirage

TABLE 2.6
Davanloo's Four Ways of Accessing the Unconscious

Partial
Major
Major extended
Extended multiple major (analysis)

---

therapeutic paradox. In reality, however, what the interviewer has done is balance the forces of resistance equally against the forces of the unconscious therapeutic alliance. Physiologic anxiety, along with activation of striated muscle, then occurs (see Table 2.7). This probably correlates with limbic system activation. The cause of these symptoms of anxiety is the emergence of unconscious aggression.* It is incumbent upon the interviewer to explore patients' *experience of anxiety* and to determine if they can discriminate between the various compartments of the triangle of conflict. Highly resistant patients frequently cannot discriminate. They comingle anxiety with aggression and cannot tell them apart. Other highly resistant patients somatize the aggression in a smooth muscle pattern of discharge. This causes headaches, irritable bowel, and other psychosomatic disturbances. If this is noted, then the interviewer again defaults to the restructuring technique mentioned above.

At this point in the process, given a patient who has good clarity in the triangle of conflict, it is important to begin preliminary analysis of the transference. Here the interviewer makes anxiety an issue and explores its source. Patients will inevitably begin to describe anger and/or an inexplicable sadness.

TABLE 2.7
Physiologic Signs of Anxiety

Dry mouth
Rapid breathing (tension in intercostal muscles)
Sweating (palms, arm pits)
Papillary dilation
Twitching muscles (forearms)
Coldness
Rapid heartbeat

---

*The presence of genuine anxiety signals entree into the PASO. The aggression is NOT iatrogenic but a manifestation of repressed trauma made up of complex feelings. Jones (1995) sees the anxiety as a reflection of a traumatized state, reflecting a sense of shameful incompetence.

This is a sign that the unconscious is beginning to be accessed. It is important to note that the breakthrough can manifest itself by anger, sadness, pain, guilt, or grief; however, technique-wise it is essential that the interviewer focus the patient on the manifestation of anger in the transference. A summary statement is frequently made: "So, behind this anxiety is angry feeling." The exploration then shifts to the experience of angry emotion in the body.

Marion Solomon and I have coined the phrase "triangle of health" for this part of the process (see Figure 2.4). Here the patient is encouraged to bring the somatic manifestation of anger into consciousness and to *not* feel anxious regarding the impulses. The interviewer begins to treat anxiety itself as a wall against closeness and intimacy in the exploration of the angry impulses. Patients frequently describe the anger as heat or a boiling force inside. Once this beachhead is established, patients are asked to see in their mind's eye the way they would express the anger. I emphasize, because there is much misunderstanding on this subject: for the process to work, anxiety must be *low* at this phase of the interview. Patients enter a near-trance state where they visualize the angry impulses. Remember, these angry feelings are the unconscious feelings *brought by the patient* to the therapy session—the ones they were avoiding facing with their symptoms. Patients are then asked to fantasize expressing this anger. In the fantasy they inflict some physical harm on the person of the therapist, and so begin to experience complex feelings of guilt and grief.

part I don't like

Let us summarize. The patient enters the session in a state of unconscious resistance to awareness of frightening or painful emotions. The focus on

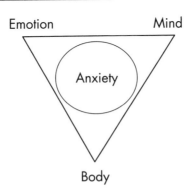

FIGURE 2.4
THE TRIANGLE OF HEALTH

Emotion   Mind

Anxiety

Body

patients' resistance brings him into a state of conflict over the resistance. There is a psychoeducational component. The patient realizes that he cannot accomplish the therapeutic goals if he holds onto the resistance. This creates a state of conflict causing the patient to experience aggression towards the interviewer. The aggression triggers anxiety and even more defense. The interviewer puts on even more pressure, pointing out the futility of this resistance, and encourages visualized discharge of the anger. Davanloo (1987b) has stated that "the royal road to the unconscious" is through analysis of the transference.

Now let's turn our attention to the triangle of people, also called the TCP triangle (see Figure 2.5). Its use is central to Davanloo's method of IS-TDP. Within each one of the triangle's vectors lie the *impulse-anxiety-defense triangle*, which has been systematically outlined for the patient in the transference. Patients quickly see that this model of their pathology applies to other intimate relationships beside the therapeutic one. At this juncture in the interview, matters can be called to a halt at a partial unlocking, or a major unlocking can be conducted wherein the patient experiences the genetic cause of his or her disturbance. Many patients will be flooded with images of their unconscious; others will need more analysis of the transference to achieve the result. Recently, a female patient imagined hitting me with the phone on the desk next to me, crushing my skull. Her associations went to her father, who died when she was 14 of a massive heart attack; his forehead was hemorrhagic from static blood when she last saw him.

Davanloo frequently asks the patient to look in the eyes of the murdered therapist. This facilitates the affective linking on the TP axis of the TCP triangle. In an unpublished paper, Malan found that the frequency of TP and TCP links correlates with mutative potency of a therapy session. The linkage derepresses affect, so that the patient experiences the core genetic

---

FIGURE 2.5
THE TCP TRIANGLE

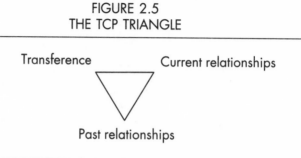

Transference   Current relationships

Past relationships

feelings. These are feelings of anger at the frustrated longings for a secure loving relationship. Because these murderous feelings toward a biologic relative are taboo, the patient experiences shame and guilt. Ironically, patients frequently incorporate the worst characteristics of the parent toward whom they are angriest. These are seen as unconsciously mediated forms of self-punishment for the very act of being angry.

Up until this point much of what has occurred has been pre-interpretive. Now the therapist introduces the ideas of resistance as *punishment* for sadism or the murder of a loved relative and of a repeated self-induced *need* for un-happiness (masochism), giving patients a sense of the motive for their un-happy state. Either implicitly or explicitly, the idea of self-directed *compassion* is expressed to the patient.

However, in order for Davanloo's approach to be successful (mutative), the patient *must experience the guilty feeling* in the session. Patients with distant parental relationships frequently sob intensely as they feel the complex feelings of love, rage, guilt, shamefulness, and longing for a close and tender relation-ship. Frequently, patients recover memories of tender experiences and the grief work of the therapy enriches their inner object tie with that parent or sibling. By the end of the first interview patients have an expanded sense of self. They are able to integrate their aggressive feelings into the tapestry of their narrative. Frequently, they are less detached from their emotions and more interested in intimate discourse. In short, motivation for health through access to true feeling has increased.

The interview ends with the therapist summarizing what has occurred. (Recently, I've experimented with the patient giving the summary, and this seems to work nicely as well.) The interviewer offers a theory of causality, recommends an approach to remedy the presenting problem, and describes a therapeutic contract regarding time and expense. Later therapy sessions follow the same format as the initial interview until the working through of uncon-scious trauma is complete. This generally takes between six and forty hours of psychotherapy, either weekly or in blocks of time at regular intervals.

Edited Clinical Transcript: The Woman Who Blamed Herself

Phase of Inquiry

The patient is a single 32-year-old model and part-time stenographer. She suffers from chronic PTSD, punctuated by periods of depression. Addition-ally, she has severe difficulties in intimate relationships with men, always choosing men who ultimately exploit her. She has tried various antidepressant medications and mood stabilizers without success. On Davanloo's scale, she represents a highly resistant character neurotic with defenses of detachment, distancing, and defiance. She was referred by her family therapist of many years, specifically for IS-TDP. The patient became motivated for psychotherapy after she became involved in a new intimate relationship. She once had a substance abuse problem, but has been sober for several years. Her boyfriend began to deal with his emotional issues in AA, and this stimulated the patient to confront the problems she had been avoiding for the past 16 years. The patient describes the essential elements of her history in the interview with me. She begins by describing a "big T Trauma" at age 16 when she was driving home and hit a patch of wet road.

P: I'm slamming on the brakes full force like this, and the car is just like going like this (*makes swinging motion with her hand*). And I'm not steering, I want to go straight (*makes steering wheel motion*). And the car is just going back and forth, and all of a sudden here comes these headlights, and I hit, I hit her.

T: Hm.

P: And I have, I have, uh, I can see her (*stops, fans herself showing signs of anxiety and distress*), blood all over her face, and the kids just not knowing what's going on, and upset. (*cries*)

T: Hm.

P: And not being able to do anything, you know, I couldn't do anything, I couldn't move. My feet were pinned in the car, so I couldn't get out of the car. Cause of the impact I guess, trapped between the floorboard and whatever the steering wheel goes down to. We didn't find out until probably 4 or 5 hours later she didn't die at the scene; she died at the hospital. And when they told me, I don't think I was getting it, y'know? And everybody that was there, because we were at my house, my parents' house, was crying and upset, and I just wasn't—

T: Processing information.

P: I guess not, cause I didn't cry, I tried to because everybody else around me was so I thought I was supposed to. And I guess, y'know, I didn't want people to think that I didn't care; of course I cared. I guess I just wasn't taking it in.

T: From the shock.

P: Until later, you know, when I was by myself, and it all kind of sunk in.

T: Remember when you were sitting here you had that hot spell where you were just fanning yourself?

P: No.

T: Yeah, it was right at the accident when you were telling me about her and seeing her and you had like a flashback right when you were here. Do you get those similar times? Do you get those flashbacks where you see her face?

P: Oh yeah. Yeah.

T: Do you have that same reaction where you flush with emotion?

P: I think I don't just burst out and cry, I have to really talk about it to cry, y'know. Or if I'm driving in a car or I hear a screeching of tires or that kind of thing, or like a noise, it's kind of like sense memory almost, it's a noise or a like the mudshot.

T: It's a startled response in the flashback.

P: Yeah, I do get a sweat, you know, and I get nervous, like anytime it's a close call in the car, I slam on the brakes, or if someone is making a bad turn or something or cuts you off, my underarms itch—I don't know what that is—there's definitely a physical reaction that happens. I think my body goes a little weird while I'm trying to focus on, you know, not getting hit or not getting into an accident.

T: Sure.

P: Um also, you know, when the date rolls around, I remember it was May 11, and when the time rolls around, it gets kinda weird.

T: Kind of like an anniversary reaction?

P: I guess, I know it, I know that was the time of the year, so I guess it makes me think about it more than normal. But usually if something doesn't trigger it's usually, I think about it a lot at night when I'm trying to go to sleep. And one of the things that I think about are these kids, cause they're adults now, and I assume, getting married.

T: So the three of them survived?

P: Yes. And I assume they're getting married and having kids, and I don't know what they were told. I don't know what they were told, and I don't know if they were told the complete truth, you know, I wonder about, do they hate me? I know it shouldn't matter, but I'm afraid—what if they're living in a life of hate because of what happened, and I was a part of it, and they think that I'm the one that killed their mother. You know, grandkids you know, their grandma's not around, and that leads me to thinking. (cries) I have my whole family and they're so wonderful, and they're so—I feel so lucky, and these three kids—

T: Survivor guilt. You feel guilty about surviving.

P: (Nods) Cause I'm gonna have my parents, and someday I assume I'm gonna have kids, and they're gonna have a grandma and a grandpa, and these kids will never have that. And I don't know if it would be easier to deal with if I was drunk or something, but it was like this accident, I wasn't even going fast or anything. If I could blame it on something besides just myself, you know, if I was drunk, you know, blame it on the alcohol, or if I was going too fast.

T: Why don't you blame it on the sprinkler?

The patient shares the history of complicated legal proceedings that followed the accident and how they worsened her guilt feelings.

T: So you're protesting the treatment from them—it's kinda misplaced. You know, you should be protesting the treatment from you against you? Do you have nightmares of the event? Do you have it in your dreams or no?

P: I don't think I relive it in my dreams, but I have tons of anxiety dreams. You know, just like worrying in my dreams, oh I have to do this or I have to do that. Or being left somewhere, or you know, not being able to get out of somewhere or running—anxiety type dreams. Or I'm stuck in a house, and I'm supposed to fix it, and I can never follow through; I can start the job or I don't know how to start the job, or I have an assignment, and I can't seem to finish it, so I get anxiety, and things keep getting in my way, preventing me from getting to the goal of fixing something.

T: I think you're going on with your guilt complex.

P: I guess.

T: The guilt that causes you not to finish your life.

P: Yeah I feel that I am not going to be successful in my career pursuits that I've been pursuing for 10 years because I feel I don't deserve to have the success that I should have.

T: What would allow you to be helped here? I mean, if this guilt problem is as bad as I think it is and as bad as you portrayed it as being, wouldn't you sabotage therapy?

P: I'm hoping not. I'm hoping—

T: I'm hoping too, but let's be forewarned as being forearmed. I'm bringing that to your attention as a—

P: No, I never thought about that. But since I've become, just in the last month, willing to talk about it after 16 years, I feel really ready, I wanna deal with this and get on with my life.

This patient's therapy represents a deviation from straightforward technique. She is showing very little resistance at the beginning of the interview. In fact, she is so detailed she initiates a flashback and concomitant anxiety in the session. I take that as a green light that the alliance is high and the unconscious is partially open. (Remember Davanloo's initial discovery that the unconscious is open in trauma cases.) So I shift the focus to the connection between her guilt and self-sabotage and alert her that this will be an issue between us and we must address it if anything good is to happen for her in the session.

T: Your motivation is great; I'm not saying you're not motivated. I'm trying to get you to think psychologically for a second as far as a roadblock, something in the road that we have to face—which would be an attempt to sabotage a therapy that's trying to make you feel better. I mean the whole purpose of you coming here is that you leave here after tomorrow, you wanna feel better, and you wanna feel freer, and you don't want to be as self-punishing as you obviously are. Isn't that correct?

P: Yes.

T: But if this is a psychological force, a guilt-laden psychological force that expresses itself by causing you to sabotage your emotional health, your mental health, your professional life, maybe even intimate relationships—we haven't talked about that—how are you going to deal with that?

P: I don't know—I'm trying to think of a specific that—

Patient now shows the vagueness resistance.

T: It's almost like a virus, like it's lurking there in the background all the time, and when you're feeling good it attacks you, or when you're on the verge of success it attacks.

P: Yeah—I—

T: And it's cruel.

P: It's not something I'm really aware of that's happening, right?

T: Right, subconscious.

P: Yeah, I don't know how you control that. I don't know.

Patient now shows the helplessness resistance.

T: But do you see what I'm saying—it's cruel?

P: Yeah, I'm just hoping to get some better answers.

T: Isn't it cruel?

P: Yeah, I think it's ridiculous, I think it's silly.

T: It's ruthless—but I saw it here. I observed it happen to you. We were moving along with this topic, and then out of nowhere you started focusing on

the children not having a mother. And then you started feeling pain, inflicting pain on yourself. I'm trying to get you to see how you're tied up with
punishing yourself.

Following the emphasis on her self-directed cruelty the next bit of history
emerges: The patient was raped at boarding school by her friend's boyfriend,
Geoff. Her friend, Linda, never believed that he raped the patient. The patient imagines mutilating Geoff and then gets in touch with her anger at
Linda. The patient explores her angry feelings at Linda for not believing her
and visualizes an attack on Linda where she beat her up. She then flashed
onto an image of the mother who was killed in the auto accident. The therapist then linked her anger at her mother for sending her away to her guilty
feelings about the accident.

Because of low resistance the therapist makes a *CPP link*. This links her anger
at Lisa in boarding school to the killed woman in the accident to her anger
at her mother for sending her to boarding school. There is no need to use the
T at this point since the patient is responding to mild head-on collisions.

P: Why? Just cause she sent me away? Well, I think that was a symptom of
something deeper in my mom, deeper problems. Well, I've come to realize
what a lot of her crap was.

T: What was that?

P: She hated her father, always said that he was a bastard, drank a lot, alcoholic, physically abused them.

T: Physically?

P: Not sexually. Physically hit, and a lot of people did back in those days,
you know. And my mom grew up that way, and so she brought me up that
way. And so she physically hit me.

T: Hit you?

P: Yeah.

T: And she thought her father was a bastard? For hitting her?

P: Right. And for drinking.

T: What do you think of your mom for hitting you?

P: Well, of course I didn't like it, and I think it was a bad thing, but as an
adult, well at the time you hate her for it, but as an adult—

T: Hate her for it?

P: Yeah, I hated her for it—

T: How deep was the hatred at the time?

P: Yeah, I guess she was gone—but she never stopped doing it until I was well into teenage years, and I told her I would hit her back if she—

T: How gone—

P: Yeah dead, or gone—there was always talk of divorce.

T: By what method?

P: Oh, uh—I don't think as a young kid—I just didn't know how people died.

The next level of resistance appears repression and denial of knowledge of aggression in childhood.

T: Come on—you're smarter than that. Did your mom have a car?

P: Yeah. I don't think it's possible.

Clinical Summary and Setting of Treatment Alliance

T: What you had was repressed murderous feelings toward your mother. When you had the accident, you got confused psychologically. Psychologically, you saw that woman's face with the blood on it, and that was the reflection back to you of your unconscious murderous feelings toward your mom, and you felt then guilty that you had killed that woman like you wanted to have your mom killed. The guilt is over the murderous feelings to your mom. That's why it's been so pathological, why it's been so excessive.

P: Do a lot of people do that?

T: Yeah. That's why you have guilt. You don't have guilt cause of what you did to George, you have guilt over what you wanted to do to your mom, cause you loved her. See you have a problem with anger. When do you think these feelings, these angry thoughts toward your mom, started?

P: Probably when my younger brother was born. She said when they brought him home from the hospital, I was only a year and a half, and they put him in a room and wouldn't let me in the room where he was, and I bit the doorknob cause I was so angry. I don't remember this of course. But later on, physically he was not a healthy child—hole in his heart—and so physically he couldn't do things. And I was very much an athlete. And a lot of the attention got focused on him and off of me and that whole sibling rivalry, and not feeling the only one. What do you call that?

T: Jealousy.

END OF FIRST PARTIAL UNLOCKING

MAJOR UNLOCKING: NEXT DAY: HOUR 4

The patient returns the next day and the therapist observes her emotional detachment.

T: Are you sensing what I'm sensing? That you're keeping your feelings kind of detached?

P: I don't know about that. I'm just trying to understand how this philosophy of twisting, that woman became my mother, y'know, if I was brought up in a different way, I would've gotten over it, like we had talked.

Therapist challenges defense of intellectualization.

T: But that's the cognition; let's go to your feelings. Because that's where the problem lies. You expressed some anger.

P: There was a sense of relief, I'm not sure if it's about the whole thing, if it was about Geoff—right. I'm just not really understanding the part about turning this woman into guilt for my mother.

T: Right. But where's the disconnect? That seems so simple.

P: I'm just not understanding it.

T: But see, you're putting it in terms of understanding, rather than in terms of you being detached. Remember how you taught me yesterday how one of your mechanisms for dealing with this problem has been to be detached from your feelings because the experience has been too painful?

Therapist challenges defenses of detachment, intellectualization, and attempt to put therapist in a teacher role (seduction).

P: Okay.

Patient crystallizes characterologic resistance and becomes compliant.

T: You told me, the accident occurred when you were 16—you said, I'm not gonna talk about it for 7 years. You detached from the emotions. See, what I'm trying to point out to you is that you're detached that way right now from your emotions. That way you make the job that you came here to have done difficult to accomplish, because the problem lies in your emotions.

P: Okay.

T: So let's explore those emotions as you feel them in the session, and come to a deeper understanding of them. Did you feel something in your body right now?

P: Yes, frustration. Because I wanna give you an answer.

With pressure to feeling patient acknowledges anger in the transference. Therapist notices that patient shows visible signs of anxiety by ringing her hands.

T: Please don't explain that away. Cause frustration is a valid feeling, isn't it? What else are you feeling besides frustration? Notice your hands right now.

P: Yeah, I do that when I'm upset.

T: You're agitated, aren't you?

P: Yeah. I guess it's from the frustration. I'm confused.

For the first time, the patient shows a possible regressive defense, "confusion." This requires exploration.

T: Three things—let's just summarize. You've got this frustrated feeling, you've got a bit of anxiety, you're jittery in your fingers, agitated in your leg, and cognitively, you're confused, see. That's pretty common for people, and particularly I can imagine for you. Anger, anxiety, and confused thinking— they go together. Is that a familiar state that you find yourself in sometime?

Therapist summarizes an I/F-A-D link and intends to note patient's ability to work psychotherapeutically.   Impulse - Anxiety - Defense

P: Probably.

Therapist ignores the defense of indefiniteness and paradoxically compliments the patient for overcoming the detachment and putting herself into a state of anxiety.

T: This is fine, this is far superior to detachment. Detachment is the defense against anger, anxiety, and jumbled thinking.

The patient realizes that she is often anxious, and that underneath her anxiety, is anger.

P: I don't know what I'm angry about.

Patient demonstrates defense of repression and denial.

T: Don't worry about that.

P: Well, I'm confused about how to get there if I don't know what the hell it is I'm angry about.

Patient demonstrates the defense of helplessness.

T: Well, can we just get in touch with it first?

Therapist pressures helplessness with appeal to alliance.

P: Okay.

Patient defends with characterologic compliance.

T: What is wrong with that suggestion?

Therapist gently challenges the compliant position.

P: Nothing, I'm just not sure I know how to do that.

Patient demonstrates the defense of helplessness once more.

T: Really?
P: Yeah.
T: So. That's what I've been pointing out to you, is that there's a wall between you and anger, and the main wall right now is anxiety. And you realize that if you remain connected to anxiety instead of connected to anger, that you're hurting yourself. That's the sabotaging thing. Agree? Not because I say so. See, I can't tell if you're people-pleasing me or if you really understand it.

This is the first of a series of head-on collisions that demonstrate to the patient the self-hurting nature of her tactical and characterologic defenses.

P: No I totally understand it, and it makes sense that there is this wall there between the anger, and the wall and me is anxiety. I'm just not—
T: Now that you've got that in the forefront of your mind, what are you gonna do about it?

Therapist cuts off patient's defense of helplessness before she can use it, and ups the ante with a challenge to be active.

P: I have to get rid of the wall.
T: That's future. What are you gonna do right now?

Therapist ignores the compliant, people-pleasing response.

P: Oh, I'm not gonna get rid of the wall right now?

Patient attempts to create confusion, passive aggressively.

T: No, I want you to get rid of the wall right now.

Therapist counters the confusion with clarity.

P: That's the part that I'm trying to figure out is how—
T: But you can't figure it out, you have to do it.

Challenge to the intellectualization.

P: Okay.
T: "Okay"—is that people-pleasing?

Pressure to the compliance.

P: Yeah. Cause I wanna do it.

T: Well good. And I want you to do it.

Reinforce positive motivation to attacking her defenses.

P: Well how do you do it?

T: See there, you become a helpless little girl. See how you immediately collapse into helplessness? Look at your foot.

*After the patient expresses her motivation she undermines it with helpless defenses, but she is
demonstrating angry impulses with her body language, which the patient attempts to ignore.
This inattention to the body—dissociation—(triangle of health)—is brought to her attention.*

P: Yeah.

T: See how you're neglecting your body?

P: Uh-huh.

T: So what are you gonna do about it? You've been doing this for a very
long time, and if you avoid the true emotions that are in your body, you
will not have gotten the treatment that I want you to have, that you want
you to have, and that will be sad, won't it? There's a lot of misery in your
life, and if you don't address this problem, the misery in your life is likely
to continue.

Therapist delivers a powerful head-on collision.

P: You know what else I feel? Like when we were talking yesterday about
my mom, I know that there are so many people that are worse off. Did I really have it bad?

T: That thought process is designed to sabotage yourself and take away your
motivation.

Therapist delivers another head-on collision.

P: I feel bad about labeling my mom as a bad mother.

The breakthrough begins with guilt.

T: You feel bad about getting help. The guilty part of you demands that you
live a crippled life, and that's the guilty part of yourself talking, that you don't
deserve to live a good life. Now is that true? Do you not deserve to live a
free life?

*Therapist reframes her response as evidence of a need for suffering (masochism) and delivers
another head-on collision.*

P: Yeah I do.

T: So what are you going to do about this wall that cripples you?

Challenge to her motivation toward health.

P: I'm gonna stop avoiding my feelings.

T: So you're avoiding them right now. I see feelings in your eyes.

Breakthrough of sadness and defense of inattention.

P: Yeah—

T: Don't pause. Tell me what is it. Tell me what the feeling is.

P: I feel bad—

T: That's just guilt. You always feel guilt. So what difference is that? But do you also see you just had a pair of fists going right then?

P: Yeah. I don't know what that was.

T: Look at your hands—

P: Yeah I was just recreating—

T: Well what is that?

P: I don't know what that is.

T: You don't know what that is?

P: Okay, that's anger?

Patient acknowledges she is feeling anger.

T: You're gonna guess. I know you're not in touch with the angry part; the anger is there in your body. Isn't it?

Challenge against indefinite defenses.

P: Yes.

T: What did you use to express your anger toward Lisa and George yesterday?

P: Violence.

T: But what part of your body did you use?

P: My hands.

T: Yeah. So you see your hands were expressing anger? It isn't what happens to you immediately; it's completely subconscious. You feel anger, you convert the anger into anxiety and then you're feeling crippled by guilt. It happens in half a second or less. I can see it, but you don't feel it, cause you've got this barrier between yourself and these emotions.

Therapist links anger with guilt and self-punishment.

The patient admits having had an impulse to smash a woman's head through a wall. The therapist asks her to examine those feelings were they to be enacted in the transference.

P: Oh, so I would be doing the same thing, right? I would wanna put your head through the wall.

T: Tell me what that would be like.

P: Uh (*makes fists*).

T: See that's right, that's the fists there. Just go with it.

P: Y'know jumping up, grabbing your hair, and the back of your coat . . .

T: Okay—

P: And, y'know, ram (*makes swinging motion*) through the wall?

T: Okay.

P: And just feeling relief.

T: Yeah, but tell me exactly what happens to me. As you picture what happens to me as my head goes through that wall?

P: Physically?

T: Yes.

P: Oh, you hurt.

T: But tell me exactly how, what you see happening.

P: I see your head through the wall, like a drywall that breaks easily, and I let go and you fall to the ground. And I pretty much go like this (*wipes hands*) and go away.

T: Is there anything you do with my corpse?

P: You know, comfort, just like an apology, like I'm sorry, I'm sorry (*makes arm-brushing motion*).

T: Kind of tender, stroking of my body. Anything else?

P: Holding your hand.

T: Uh-huh?

P: Just that tender thing, and apologizing.

T: Can you see that vividly in your mind's eye?

P: Yeah.

T: Next thing I'd like you to do is look into my lifeless eyes in your fantasy. Can you do that?

P: Yeah.

T: Can you tell me what you see when you look into those lifeless eyes?

P: Well I'm flashing on my grandma.*

T: That's terrific.

P: That's the only dead person that I've ever seen.

T: What do you see in my/her eyes?

P: She's not there. It's just a body.

T: And emotions that you feel?

P: Great sadness. (*sobs*) Cause you and her weren't supposed to die.

T: Tell me about that. It's wonderful; you're doing great. Just let it flow.

Support encouragement, and comfort during the breakthrough.

P: Well, I got angry because it wasn't fair, because she wasn't supposed to die, not yet. I knew eventually, yeah, but not yet. I mean, it's just not fair.

Rage/anger in the PASO.

T: Tell me the story.

The patient relates that her grandmother died from a fall. The therapist asks, "If you had been the cause of her death, what would it feel like to look into her eyes?"

T: Just tell me about it as a feeling as you're there with your grandmother's body. And the best way to do this is by action—what do you see yourself doing?

P: Just screaming, "Come back, come back!"

T: And what happens?

P: She doesn't.

T: And what does that produce in you, when you realize that?

P: Scared in a way.

T: Play those emotions now. What do you see yourself doing when you're scared?

P: Cry.

T: How?

P: Like a forlorn, wailing? And just denying, saying no, no, no, still I want you to come back, don't die.

---

*When Patricia Della Selva viewed this tape, she remarked on the connection with the patient's presenting symptoms when she was expressing guilt over having killed the mother whose children would never have a grandparent. She saw this as evidence of a breakthrough of genuine unconscious guilt-laden feeling toward the patient's deceased grandmother.

Pain of trauma in the PASO.

T: And does that work?

P: No.

T: So what happens when she doesn't come back? . . . Do you say anything to her spirit?

P: No, it's not like a verbalization, but in here it's just like, I love you.

T: These are deep thoughts now. I love you . . .?

Attachment bond in the eight-stage PASO.

P: I'm sorry.

T: Why are you sorry?

P: That she had to go. No.

T: No?

P: No.

T: For killing her?

P: Yeah.

T: You're sorry for having killed her.

P: Yeah. And I want her to be happy and forgive me.

T: Mm-hm. Stay with that feeling, that's like the most important feeling that you could possibly, possibly have.

P: Yeah, I just want forgiveness.

T: Mm-hm.

P: I want to feel like a good person.

T: Tell me about that. Where did that come from?

P: Cause I feel bad about killing her. By killing someone you're a bad person, and I want forgiveness so that I can know and she can know that I'm not a bad person, that I didn't want that to happen. If I'd wanted that to happen, then I'd be a bad person and I shouldn't be forgiven.

Guilty feelings in the PASO.

T: And tell me what happens when your grandma's spirit has a response?

P: She's just smiling at me lovingly.

T: And how does that feel?

P: Good.

T: What is that communicating to you?

P: That I am forgiven and it's okay and I'm not a bad person.

T: Do you accept that?

P: I don't know.

T: Why? Why is there a conflict?

P: Cause somehow I feel like I'm supposed to feel negative and bad and that I'm supposed to for some reason because I did a bad thing so I'm supposed to feel bad.

Negative identity in the unconscious from the PASO. *

T: So who says that? Whose voice?

P: My mom. I'm angry with my mom for believing that that's true and putting that on me. Does that make sense?

Negative maternal introject speaks from the unconscious. This is evidence that the unconscious therapeutic alliance is high and in control of the process.

T: Uh huh. Makes a lot of sense. Feel anger in your legs?

P: Yeah.

Patient acknowledges feeling anger toward her mother in her legs.

T: So you could work on the anger toward mom next.

P: I shouldn't have to feel bad about confronting her.

Guilt from the next PASO.

T: No? It's not her, it's your anger. This is an internal problem. You make yourself feel bad because you have anger toward your mother. And that's what makes your misery. And you're perpetuating the misery. Is that what you want to do? Haven't you suffered a lot?

P: Yeah.

T: A lot.

P: Yeah.

T: How many years have you suffered?

P: Almost all my life. Aside from the 16 years from the accident, before that as well.

T: Sure. So it's like you've almost endured a life sentence of suffering.

P: Yeah, and I have to take responsibility for that.

T: Absolutely. You have to stop inflicting this misery on yourself.

P: And I have to do that by accepting my anger.

---

*A convergence with Francine Shapiro's ideas.

Patient is starting to demonstrate signs of individuation and self-compassion.

T: Yes. Instead of defending against it.

P: Okay.

T: So how do you see the violence if it comes out of you in an explosive way?

The patient sees herself as a "wild dog" killing her mother with her teeth. The patient would like her mother's dying thought to be an apology for making the patient angry. The therapist asks, "What would your mother's dead eyes look like?"

T: What are the sad thoughts when you look at your mom's peaceful eyes?

P: That it could have been a better relationship. I am sad at the loss of the possibility of having a better relationship with her.

T: Don't defend yourself against your pain. Isn't that a painful feeling?

P: Yeah.

T: You're still defending yourself against it. Why?

P: Because I feel that there's a loss. That there's nothing I could have done.

T: See, you're sabotaging the closeness, the intimacy that you could be having if you would feel that pain, I could be more effective. That's the punishing part that sabotages intimacy. If you were to feel that pain . . .

Therapist challenges resistance against emotional closeness.

P: The sadness . . .

T: Remember what it was related to? You said it was related to the relationship that you and your mom could've had.

P: Yeah. And regrets, and not ever taking the opportunity to fix it.

T: Share those intimate thoughts with me. What comes to mind?

P: She's young and still has dark hair, and she's smiling and happy, and has a baby in her hands, and she's slightly tossing it, and the baby's laughing— that's the vision. The happy mother and child. The baby's laughing and the mother's laughing.

T: And feeling as you deserve that as you're watching?

P: I'm sad and regret that . . .

T: That's grief, isn't it?

P: I think so, because I feel like, what could I have done to change that? Could I have changed that?

T: That's the crippling part. That's interfering.

Patient's unconscious infantile omnipotence assumes responsibility for her mother's unhappiness.

P: So I couldn't have changed it?

T: No. See you're accepting that as a sad, sad, sad loss. That's grief, isn't it?

P: Yeah, yeah.

The patient says she is angry that her mother never let her express herself in any way. The therapist brings the patient's attention back to her mother's corpse.

T: Now how long can you be angry at a dead person?

P: Not long. I mean, it's pointless to hold onto all that.

T: Mm-hm. And tell me about what happens when the anger goes away?

P: Relief, freedom. Like I'm lighter, you know. And I just see myself leaving her there to walk away.

T: To rot?

Patient wants to abandon the body of her mother (like she herself was abandoned?). Therapist insists that she remain and face her feelings toward her mother's corpse.

P: Yeah, I guess.

T: It's your mom.

P: Yeah, well the logical part of me is going, she's not gonna stay there forever, we'll end up burying her.

T: Could you picture that?

P: Sure.

T: How would you like your mom to be buried?

The patient imagines "fixing up her mother's corpse," making her look "pretty," while a group of mourners comfort her. She then imagines her Dad forgiving her for the murder. The therapist asks what the patient feels at that.

P: You know, relief. Thinking he's [Dad] forgiving me. Just relief.

T: There was something that went through your face that was very complex.

P: Well, I see that when I hug him, and he's forgiving me, I get sad. (*sobs*)

T: Very sad. Don't fight it, okay? You got to feel that degree of sadness if you want this to be helpful. And show me the intimate thoughts connected to that sad and painful emotion as you're being hugged by your father, and you're being forgiven?

P: I just say I'm sorry.

T: You're flattening your feeling. You're punishing yourself, you're not accepting the forgiveness, you're pushing down your own feelings. This would be an incredible moment.

P: I don't know what I'm feeling.

T: Why are you having a problem?

P: At the hug, him forgiving me, I revert back to guilt.

Patient takes over the therapist's role and interprets the defense.

T: You're rejecting the forgiveness.

P: Yeah.

T: Why?

P: Cause it's just unbelievable to me that someone could forgive you for that.

T: So your mother has forgiven you, your father, the victim, has forgiven you, and the only person who cannot forgive herself is the perpetrator.

P: Mm-hm. Why is that?

T: I guess you're just an unforgiving person.*

Therapist challenges the patient's self-directed sadism.

P: But I forgive everybody else.

T: Then you're a hypocrite. Right?

Therapist challenges the patient's self-directed sadism again.

P: Yeah.

T: How come? Why the double standard?

P: I don't know. I guess it's unforgivable.

T: To be what?

P: To kill your mom.

T: To be a murderer.

P: Yeah. (sobs) Why can't I forgive myself?

Patient begins to long for self-directed compassion.

T: And the answer is?

P: I don't know.

T: The answer is that you were taught to be unforgiving of yourself. That's what you were taught.

The therapist gives a reconstructive statement from his unconscious in the state of unconscious therapeutic alliance.

P: Cause I wasn't allowed to make mistakes and I got punished every time I did.

---

*A convergence with Leigh McCullough's concept of self-directed compassion.

T: Let it out of your system—for every one of those punishments, because you cover every one of those pains of punishments in anger. You carried so much anger with you. If you let some of the pain out, it doesn't have to be carried as anger, does it?

P: No, I get these stupid thoughts that—

T: Of what?

P: Oh, it's not that bad, you're such a baby to cry like that.

T: That's the internal critic.

The patient demonstrates self-directed sadism.

P: Oh, big deal. You didn't have it so bad. You have no right to cry when other people have suffered much more.

T: Denial, minimization—all the defenses people who have suffered tough childhoods use. They don't want to admit how painful it was.

P: Yeah, but I went through—

T: How much skin is it off your nose to admit that your childhood was painful? I don't think you're betraying anyone.

P: Yeah, but it's just a guilty feeling of blaming mother.

T: Like you're spilling the beans to the authorities. And you're a bad girl by telling that mom was mean.

P: Yeah, because in her eyes she wasn't.

T: What did she say to you when she died?

P: That she was sorry for making me so angry.

T: And?

P: That it's okay. (*sobs*)

Deep breakthrough of pain, sadness, grief and longing for closeness with a non-blaming mother.

T: Stay with that feeling—you're doing a really good job of staying connected to your feeling. Isn't it hard sometime to stay connected to it?

Therapist delivers support and encouragement for staying with genuine feelings. This is a convergence with Alpert. When viewing this tape, Malan called it "unlike Davanloo but therapeutically effective."

P: Yeah, I want to shut it off; I don't want to feel it.

T: Anger is the biggest shut-off valve for pain. Drugs, alcohol . . .

P: So, in the fantasies, I get so violent because . . .

T: You're in so much pain.

Link between pain of trauma and the defense of anger.

P: Yeah. But why did I go to violence?

T: That was a normal place for anyone to go through as much trauma as you.

P: It just seems scary . . .

T: What's scary to me is the suffering part of you.

P: Because I would never do that?

T: No, you would hurt yourself before you would hurt someone else. And I'm trying to help you find the happy medium, where you're more self-accepting. Do you think I've made any headway?

P: Yeah, I'm a little scared about tomorrow, and what if my old habits crop up, and I get the feeling that people that I talk to that they're mad at me, that I'm goanna shut down. And scared that if I confront them or fight back, then I'm just being a bitch.

T: That's what you're afraid of—that you can't find a happy medium.

After four more hours of therapy, the patient returned for a termination session. She says that, despite all the medications other doctors had given her, no doctor had ever prescribed anything for PTSD.

P: These guys thought I was bipolar [former psychiatrists], I didn't agree.

T: No.

P: I might be a little crazy sometimes, but I don't think it's anything that's not normal.

T: What do you mean by crazy sometimes? Describe the behavior.

P: Mostly just anxieties, I mostly just have high anxiety. Like when I'm trying to go to sleep, it's like shut up already, no one cares about all this stuff.

T: Chatter.

P: Yeah.

T: That's what this medication is made to diminish. [I had prescribed a mild hypnotic for short-term use.]

P: No one told me.

T: I'm shocked.

P: Don't be. I was misdiagnosed.

T: It sounds like the PTSD is really better.

P: Definitely. It is better. I only have a few issues left.

T: Well that's what we predicted, isn't it?

P: Yeah . . . (*smiles warmly and looks genuinely happy and pleased*).

T: See, I think if you treat it for the right diagnosis with the right treatment, then things kind of fall together.

P: Yeah. I'm glad it works.

T: Me too.

After 16 hours of therapy the patient terminated. At a six-month follow-up evaluation, 100% of her PTSD symptoms were gone and 95% of her anxiety, mood, and sleep problems were resolved. Moreover, she described her relationship with her mother as improved and her jealous feelings toward her boyfriend as gone.

References

Beeber, A. R. (1999a). The perpetrator of the unconscious in Davanloo's new metapsychology. Part I: Review of classic psychoanalytic concepts. *International Journal of Short-Term Psychotherapy, 13*, 151–158.

Beeber, A. R. (1999b). The perpetrator of the unconscious in Davanloo's new metapsychology. Part II: Comparison of the perpetrator to classic psychoanalytic concepts. *International Journal of Short-Term Psychotherapy, 13*, 159–176.

Beeber, A. R. (1999c). The perpetrator of the unconscious in Davanloo's new metapsychology. Part III: Specifics of Davanloo's technique. *International Journal of Short-Term Psychotherapy, 13*, 177–190.

Davanloo, H. (1987b). Intensive short-term dynamic psychotherapy with highly resistant depressed patients. Part II. Royal road to the dynamic unconscious. *International Journal of Short-Term Psychotherapy, 2*(3), 99–132.

Davanloo, H. (1988a). Clinical manifestations of superego pathology. Part II. The resistance of the superego and the liberation of the paralyzed ego. *International Journal of Short-Term Psychotherapy, 3*(2), 1–24.

Davanloo, H. (1988b). The technique of unlocking of the unconscious. Part I. *International Journal of Short-Term Psychotherapy, 3*(2), 99–121.

Davanloo, H. (1988c). The technique of unlocking of the unconscious. Part II. Partial unlocking of the unconscious. *International Journal of Short-Term Psychotherapy, 3*(2), 123–159.

Davanloo, H. (1989a). Central dynamic sequence in the unlocking of the unconscious and comprehensive trial therapy. Part I. Major unlocking. *International Journal of Short-Term Psychotherapy, 4*(1), 1–33.

Davanloo, H. (1989b). Central dynamic sequence in the major unlocking of the unconscious and comprehensive trial therapy. Part II. The course of trial therapy after the initial breakthrough. *International Journal of Short-Term Psychotherapy, 4*(1), 35–66.

Davanloo, H. (1989c). The technique of unlocking the unconscious in patients suffering from functional disorder. Part I. Restructuring ego's defenses. *International Journal of Short-Term Psychotherapy, 4*(2), 93–116.

Davanloo, H. (1989d). The technique of unlocking the unconscious in patients suffering from functional disorders. Part II. Direct view of the dynamic unconscious. *International Journal of Short-Term Psychotherapy, 4*(2), 117–148.

Davanloo, H. (1990). *Unlocking the unconscious.* Chichester: Wiley.

Davanloo, H. (1995a). Intensive short-term dynamic psychotherapy: Spectrum of psycho-neurotic disorders. *International Journal of Short-Term Psychotherapy, 10*(3,4), 121–155.

Davanloo, H. (1995b). Intensive short-term dynamic psychotherapy: Technique of partial and major unlocking of the unconscious with a highly resistant patient. Part I. Partial unlocking of the unconscious. *International Journal of Short-Term Psychotherapy, 10*(3,4), 157–181.

Davanloo, H. (1995c). Intensive short-term dynamic psychotherapy: Major unlocking of the unconscious. Part II. The course of the trial therapy after partial unlocking. *International Journal of Short-Term Psychotherapy, 10*(3,4), 183–230.

Davanloo, H. (1996a). Management of tactical defenses in intensive short-term dynamic psychotherapy. Part I. Overview, tactical defenses of cover words and indirect speech. *International Journal of Short-Term Psychotherapy, 11*(3), 129–152.

Davanloo, H. (1996b). Management of tactical defenses in intensive short-term dynamic psychotherapy. Part II. Spectrum of tactical defenses. *International Journal of Short-Term Psychotherapy, 11*(3), 153–199.

Davanloo, H. (1999a). Intensive short-term dynamic psychotherapy—central dynamic sequence: Phase of pressure. *International Journal of Short-Term Psychotherapy, 13*(4), 211–233.

Davanloo, H. (1999b). Intensive short-term dynamic psychotherapy—central dynamic sequence: Phase of challenge. *International Journal of Short-Term Psychotherapy, 13*(4), 237–260.

Davanloo, H. (1999c). Intensive short-term dynamic psychotherapy—central dynamic sequence: Head-on collision with resistance. *International Journal of Short-Term Psychotherapy, 13*(4), 263–280.

Fairbairn, W. R. D. (1952). *Psychoanalytic studies of the personality.* London: Tavistock.

Fenichel, O. (1945). *The psychoanalytic theory of Neurosis.* New York: Norton.

Freud, S. (1923). The ego and the id. In J. Strachey (Ed. and Trans.), *The standard edition of the complete psychological works of Sigmund Freud* (Vol. 19). New York: Norton, 1961.

Freud, S. (1937). Analysis terminable and interminable. In J. Strachey (Ed. and Trans.), *The standard edition of the complete psychological works of Sigmund Freud* (Vol. 23). New York: Norton, 1961.

Freud, S. (1940). An outline of psychoanalysis. In J. Strachey (Ed. and Trans.), *The standard edition of the complete psychological works of Sigmund Freud* (Vol. 23). New York: Norton, 1961.

Guntrip, H. (1961). *Personality structure and human interaction.* New York: International Universities Press.

Jones, E. (1957). *The life and work of Sigmund Freud.* (3 Vols.) New York: Basic Books.

Jones, J. M. (1995). *Affects as process.* Hillsdale, NJ: Analytic Press.

Klein, M. (1932). *The psychoanalysis of children.* London: Hogarth Press.

Lindemann, E. (1994). Symptomatology and management of acute grief. *American Journal of Psychiatry, 151*(6 Suppl.), 155–60.

Said, T., & Schubmehl, J. (1999). Selected proceedings of audiovisual explorations of the unconscious: Parts I, II, III. Technical and metapsychological roots of Davanloo's system of intensive-short-term dynamic psychotherapy. *International Journal of Short-Term Psychotherapy, 13*(2), 83–148.

3

Desensitization of Affect Phobias in Short-term Dynamic Psychotherapy

Leigh McCullough

PART I OF THIS CHAPTER offers some basic principles for working in a short-term therapy mode that has a rapid impact on a patient's problems. Part II provides an overview of research in support of this approach.

Part I: How to do It

First and foremost this chapter describes how a simple principle from learning theory can be applied to psychodynamic theory to rapidly focus and shorten the treatment process, that is, the systematic desensitization of affect phobias. Next, a number of interventions are presented that, when applied to psychodynamic constructs, have been shown to shorten and intensify the treatment process. Following the pioneers in brief psychotherapy (Davanloo, 1980; Malan, 1979; Sifneos, 1979), therapy is made more efficient primarily through activity and focus. After reading this chapter, therapists should be able to apply some of the techniques to sharpen their therapy focus and heighten the efficacy of their interventions, with the knowledge that there is empirical support for what they are doing.

One of the main ways by which treatment is shortened is by reframing psychodynamic conflict as "affect phobias." Thus this treatment focuses on affect, and the activity brought to bear on that affect is what we have found to be the most effective for resolution of phobic behavior—systematic desensitization. Specific treatment objectives based on Malan's two triangles (1979) help to focus and streamline the process. Interventions to work through these objectives are drawn from a number of different therapy modalities: psychodynamic, cognitive, behavioral, Gestalt, and self psychology. This chapter can only provide a brief overview of the model. For more detailed discussion of how to conduct treatment, see the author's main text, *Changing Character* (1997), and workbook, *Treating Affect Phobias* (2001).

The Basic Intervention: Desensitization of Affect Phobias

AFFECT PHOBIA DEFINED

The concept of phobia is a familiar one to most therapists, and many therapists know that the most effective treatment for a phobia is exposure and response prevention leading to desensitization of the phobic stimulus. In behavior therapy, the phobic stimulus is perceived as being outside of the individual (e.g., the bridge, the spider, open spaces, heights, other people). To escape these feared objects or situations, people employ various avoidant behaviors. The bridge phobic obviously avoids going over bridges. The agoraphobic avoids open places or crowds by staying at home. The social phobic avoids people and social situations. Abundant research evidence has shown that the most effective treatment for phobias is systematic desensitization through exposure and response prevention (e.g., Barlow, 1988).

Surprisingly, similar patterns can be observed in psychodynamic therapy. After watching many hours of videotape of short-term psychodynamic therapy, I noticed that we seem to be treating phobias—but of a different sort. These phobias do not occur in the external world—outside of the person—as do bridges or snakes. These intrapsychic phobias happen in the internal world and concern feelings: sorrow/grief, anger/assertion, closeness/care, sexual desire, and joy or excitement. When people are afraid of experiencing anger or asserting themselves, they might bite their tongue and not set appropriate limits, or they might cry or feel depressed or act compliant instead. If grief is the feared feeling, they choke back the tears or chuckle to lighten up or become numb and unfeeling (various defensive maneuvers to avoid feeling sadness). When people are embarrassed or frightened to show tenderness or caring, they may avoid doing so by being tough or by devaluing others.

Looking at affect phobias within a psychodynamic framework, these maladaptive reactions can be understood as attempts to protect the self (defenses) by avoiding the experience and/or expression of some feelings (warded-off or conflicted affects) that are intolerable because of anxiety or other conflicting feelings that they arouse (e.g., superego reactions such as shame, guilt and fear of rejection). Thus, these maladaptive patterns can be thought of simultaneously as intrapsychic conflict and "affect phobias." Both can be described as defensive avoidance of one's own emotional responses because of inhibition such as anxiety, guilt, shame or pain associated with them. Both can be resolved with systematic desensitization. This represents a true integration of psychodynamic and behavioral constructs and treatment.

This therapy model is based on the hypothesis that such intrapsychic conflicts about feelings, that is, affect phobias, are the fundamental issue underlying many Axis I and Axis II disorders. Furthermore, accumulating clinical and research evidence has demonstrated that many Axis I and Axis II disorders can be resolved by using the principles in short-term dynamic psychotherapy (Svartberg & Stiles, 1999; Winston et al., 1991, 1994).

It is important to note that affect phobias are not idiosyncratic reactions in a few individuals. Indeed, conflicts or inhibitions about feelings are universal problems affecting to a greater or lesser degree most of the human race. However, when these phobias become so extreme that they impair functioning or are destructive to the self or to relationships with others, then pathology results.

Below I will go into more detail about how psychodynamic conflict can be thought of as affect phobias. Then I suggest several interventions that have been helpful in "systematically desensitizing" these "phobias" about feelings. First let's look at some examples of affect phobias.

Patient 1: "From really early on I used to be told by my mother, 'Be careful. You don't know your own strength.' I don't perceive myself, at all, as a large person or a strong person and yet the one reason why I probably never raised my voice in front of my girlfriend is because even the conception of getting angry enough at someone to hit them frightens me so badly that I would never, never, ever put myself in a situation where I'd even [think about] hitting someone."

Obviously we never consider acting out such behavior. The issue is whether the patient can bear to face angry or violent feelings (for they are universal), contain them, and respond in an appropriate manner.

Patient 2: A young woman came to treatment with social anxiety and avoidant personality disorder, with the target problem of a public speaking phobia. In working through her problem, she said, "I just panic when I have to get up and speak. I would rather die. I am always afraid I will be attacked or criticized for what I might say." The therapist asked what she would feel, and then what she would do if she were criticized. She replied, "Oh, I would want to be able to be strong and intelligent and deal with the criticism directly. But I am totally unable to do that. I just feel terror inside."

The Fundamental Change Agent: Systematic Desensitization

By conceptualizing maladaptive behaviors as affect phobias (i.e., fears of emotional responses because of conflicts associated with them), we avail ourselves of well-tested methods that have been effective in treating phobias, namely, exposure and response prevention to achieve systematic desensitization. This simplifying construct has the effect of focusing the therapist's moment-to-moment attention on deepening the patient's experience of the adaptive affect.

For example, when patients are too afraid to speak up, too guilty to get angry, too pained to bear sadness, or too ashamed to show tenderness, the therapist needs to expose them to successive approximations of the feared affect, just as the behavior therapist inches patients closer to a feared elevator or bridge. How is this done? There are a number of ways, including the two-chair technique, role-playing, or the one I use most often, guided imagery of specific problematic scenes. The patient is encouraged to find a specific incident of being, for example, too afraid to speak up or too guilty to get angry. Then this scene is imagined in vivid detail with heightened emotion while the therapist encourages the patient to enhance the bodily response of the adaptive feeling that the patient needs to acquire or free up, such as assertively speaking up, showing tenderness, or having a good cry. It is not sufficient to merely *think* about these images. Abundant clinical observation and preliminary research have demonstrated that the affect must be felt on a physiological level for change to take place.

This imaging of affective experiences constitutes an exposure. Typically, this exposure brings up anxiety, guilt, shame, or pain that needs to be dealt with or regulated. The patient is encouraged not to run away from the experience (response prevention), but to stay with it until the anxiety subsides (which would lead to desensitization). However, it is not necessary to flood a patient with intense affective experiences. Generally, it is more useful to generate images that are at an intensity level that the patient can bear and work with. Here are some examples of exposure:

- For the patient with speaking phobia: "Can you imagine standing up in front of a crowd and feeling able to handle a critical remark with assertion and confidence?"
- For a patient who cannot grieve: "Can you imagine letting go and crying here with me?" Or "Can you imagine crying in your wife's arms?

How would it be? What would be the most uncomfortable thing about doing this?"

I call these "emotional push-ups." The patient is encouraged to continue repeating the imagery until inhibition is within normal limits and the person can imagine doing what was not before possible (speaking up, grieving with a loved one, etc.). The work is then continued in many variations and in increasing intensity until new responses are carried out outside the session.

It is important to note that desensitization does not mean reducing the adaptive response. Desensitization means reducing the destructive hold of inhibition on the adaptive reaction, for example, breaking the control of anxiety on public speaking or of shame on opening up and crying.

In systematic desensitization of affect phobias, I hypothesize that defensive or avoidant behaviors occur when adaptive affects become sensitized through association with inhibitory affects (e.g., a child is made afraid of speaking up or ashamed for crying). From the perspective of respondent conditioning (e.g., Wolpe, 1958), reciprocal inhibition occurs through eliciting an adaptive affective response to compete with the anxiety response (e.g., helping a patient grieve or respond assertively in a non-shaming relationship). From the perspective of operant conditioning, repeated exposure to the phobic inner stimuli (i.e., the conflicted grief or anger) without aversive consequences results in a reduction of the anxiety or inhibition, thus ceasing to give rise to pathology and allowing the natural, adaptive affect to occur.

In this manner, the principles of exposure and response prevention are explicitly utilized for breaking the conditioned reactions of different aspects of psychodynamic conflict. The fundamental change agent is seen as the experiencing and transforming of the affective experience through desensitization (regulation of anxieties associated with affect). In my clinical experience, holding the focus on affect and using exposure techniques in moderate doses greatly shorten the process of therapy.

Treatment Modality

This short-term treatment of affect phobias is described at length in my book, *Changing Character* (McCullough Vaillant, 1997), and was initially described in McCullough, 1993 and 1994. This model grew out of the two triangle conceptual schema developed by Malan (1979), "the universal principle of psychodynamic psychotherapy," in which defenses and anxieties are seen as blocking the expression of true feelings. Put another way, people have problems (maladaptive defenses) that are due to phobic inhibitions (conflicts) about natural adaptive affective responses (feelings). These patterns of conflicted or neurotic behavior originated with past persons, are maintained with current persons, and can be observed in the relationship with the therapist. The schema of the two triangles has guided my clinical and research work for the past two decades—and with each passing year, I become more and more thankful to David Malan for his elegant simplification of an enormously complex process (see Figure 3.1).

The triangle of conflict is a conceptual schema for representing the major components of a patient's behavior pattern resulting from intrapsychic conflict

---

FIGURE 3.1
AN ADAPTATION OF MALAN'S TWO TRIANGLES FOR TREATING AFFECT PHOBIAS
The universal principle of psychodynamic psychotherapy:
Defenses and anxieties block the expression of true feeling

TRIANGLE OF CONFLICT		TRIANGLE OF PERSON	
Defense	Anxiety	Therapist	Current Persons
Maladaptive or Avoidant Thoughts, Feelings or Behaviors	Conflict/Inhibition Due to Anxiety, Guilt Shame, Pain	Where Conflict Patterns can Be Examined	Current Significant Others Where Conflict Patterns are Maintained
D	**A**	**T**	**C**

I/F

Adaptive Impulse/Feeling
Activation/Excitation

Anger, Sorrow, Fear, Tenderness,
Joy, Excitement, Sexual Desire
Care, Compassion for Self and Others

P

Past Persons

Early Life Caretakers Where
Conflict Patterns Originated

---

about feelings. In this model, the term "intrapsychic conflict" refers to the tension between emotional activation and emotional inhibition, which results in "phobic" or avoidant, defensive behavior. The bottom of the triangle represents the category of activating feelings—feelings that move us to act in some way. The upper right "anxiety" pole represents the category of inhibiting feelings—feelings that restrain or block action. (Note that "anxiety" is a basket term that includes anxiety, guilt, shame, and emotional pain.) The upper left pole of the triangle represents a wide range of responses that occur when feelings are inhibited, i.e., maladaptive defensive or avoidant behaviors.

For example, a young woman felt sadness (activation on the feeling pole of the triangle), but felt shame (inhibition on the anxiety pole) about crying or showing vulnerability. So she phobically avoided sadness by denying her feelings and becoming stoic and numb (defensive behaviors, on the defense pole of the triangle). Optimally, she would be able to express her sadness fully and openly with people whom she could trust.

Up to this point I have discussed only the triangle of conflict. The triangle of person is equally important. The conflicted behaviors and feelings schematized on the triangle of conflict do not happen in a vacuum. We all grow and develop in an interpersonal milieu, and defenses arise only from individuals' reaction to experience, which is predominantly through relationships with other people. Thus, the defensive patterns of behavior, schematized on the triangle of conflict, can almost always be associated with specific people in the patient's life, as represented by the relationships on the triangle of person, or in relationship to the self. The conflict patterns began with early caretakers and are maintained in current relationships. Furthermore, these patterns will inevitably be acted out in the relationship with the therapist, where there will be opportunities to examine and change them.

The triangle of person reminds us to examine how the triangle of conflict is played out with these three important categories of people in the patient's life. For example, if a patient has conflicts about self-worth, the therapist needs to learn how that originated with the caretakers in the past (the past persons pole of the triangle of person), how the conflicts are being maintained now with significant others (the current persons pole), and how the problem manifests itself in the therapy relationship (the therapist pole). To understand how the conflict plays out in each of these roles, the therapist needs to hear about specific incidences of the problem. For example, for the problem of self-worth, the therapist might ask, "What are some examples of times that you feel unworthy or lacking of confidence in the present time—with your spouse or with people at work?" Make sure that the examples are specific, not general, because this is where you can most clearly identify the actual defensive behaviors, the specific anxieties that arise, and the feelings that are being avoided.

When you are sitting with a patient, you can use the triangle of conflict to structure your questions. Imagine the two triangles in your mind. (Indeed, the people I teach often tell me that the two triangles are "branded on their forehead.") Next, consider how you would categorize your patient's statements in terms of defenses (think of defenses very simply at first, just as any problematic behaviors). Any problem a patient presents can be thought of as potentially "defensive" — that is, a maladaptive behavior that takes the place of or avoids a more adaptive (but conflicted) response. Of course, not all defenses are maladaptive. Some defenses, such as suppression (e.g., counting to ten when you are angry) or sublimation (e.g., writing a poem about loss when you are grieving), are highly adaptive. We need our adaptive defenses to modulate and regulate our affects. However, many defenses are maladaptive, and this is where we focus our attention. Maladaptive defenses include acting out (e.g., lashing out in anger) and projection (e.g., blaming someone else for something you construct in your mind). One objective of this treatment is to identify maladaptive versions of the defenses and help the patient become aware of and alter them.

Core Formulation

As the patient describes specific examples of problems, one by one, the therapist should listen carefully and ask the following questions, both internally and then out loud to the patient. What problematic behaviors are being described here? This will suggest responses that can be placed on the defense pole of the triangle of conflict. First the defensive behaviors need to be identified (e.g., the patient talks fast to avoid feelings: "I never realized how fast I was talking. I guess I was running away from everything."). Then the therapist can begin to wonder what underlying adaptive feelings might be being avoided (probably something painful—grief or longing for closeness). In the case of a patient with poor self-esteem, it is not hard to figure out. If a person lacks self-esteem or self-worth, the feelings he or she is "missing" are positive feelings about the self. Immediately, the goal of treatment is made clear: The patient needs help becoming comfortable and familiar with positive self regard. But then this begs the next question: Why is it that this person does not feel good about himself? This is when the therapist should consider the anxiety pole of the triangle of conflict. What inhibition blocks the natural adaptive response of healthy self-regard? Why does this person not feel confident or worthy? There are only a few choices to make. Is it anxiety, guilt, shame, or emotional pain that prevents the person from feeling worthwhile? Openly pondering these questions and exploring them with the patient is a collaborative way to generate a core formulation. This actively engages the patient in his or her own treatment from the beginning. Here are some examples.

FORMULATION OF CONSCIOUS CORE CONFLICTED AFFECTS
A young man came to treatment with symptoms of depression and passivity. He reported that he did not feel good about himself, and so he was having a hard time functioning.

T: So you feel that you are not worthwhile, is that saying it right?

P: Yes, in part, but I also feel inadequate—I think that's a better word for it.

T: OK, inadequate describes it better. We'll look at this more, but what would you like to feel instead?

This question is similar to, Who's buried in Grant's tomb? Obviously one would want to feel good about oneself. Thus, this focus is conscious and available.

P: Oh, I'd like to feel that I'm okay the way I am.

T: Sure, what do you think gets in the way of that?

P: I just feel like I'm a bad person. I hate myself.

T: Where did that come from? You didn't spring from the womb that way. Where do you think you learned it?

P: Oh, I know where I learned it. My father is the most critical person on earth.

T: That's a pretty strong statement—and it sounds painful. So you learned from him to put yourself down.

P: It sure was painful. But I never thought about it that way—that I learned to put myself down.

T: Well, think about it for a moment. Your father isn't here now. So who is the person who is making negative statements about you?

P: (Pausing thoughtfully) I guess it's me, isn't it?

Afterwards the therapist would attempt to expose the patient to the affective experience of positive feeling toward the self.

T: I wonder—have you ever felt proud of something you have done?

P: Oh, once or twice. But not very much and not fully.

T: Then can we go to one of those examples and see how you felt, and also see if we can help you amplify the experience?

The therapist would then proceed to expose the patient to feelings of healthy pride or self-confidence, using specific examples from his life. The anxieties (or more specifically in this case, shame) would be noted and worked with until the shame was reduced and less inhibiting.

T: When you completed that project and the teacher complimented you, can you begin to let yourself savor that experience in a positive way?

P: Just barely. I feel about 25% good about my work, and about 75% like I don't deserve it.

T: What gets in the way of your feeling completely deserving?

P: My father never liked anything I did. And I always felt like a failure.

T: Maybe we need to look at some feelings toward your father that may be a part of this problem.

THE UNCONSCIOUS CORE ISSUES

In this particular case the patient is acutely aware of the problem about feelings about the self. So what might be other reasons for lack of self-worth? What other underlying capacities might need to be activated? One strong possibility is the anger at his father's emotional abuse that is unexpressed and thus taken out on himself.

T: How do you feel about your father never liking anything you did?

P: I feel resignation. It would never be any other way.

T: That's how you feel inside yourself. But I want you to focus on how you feel toward your father.

P: Maybe I'm a little angry. But just barely.

T: Well that's a start. Let's focus on some of the times he has been so critical, and see if we can help you develop these feelings enough so that you can protect yourself.

Thus begins the exposure session of affect experiencing—until the anger is desensitized. There also could be unresolved grief over abandonment that had made him feel unloved or unworthy. These affect foci are often not on the surface, and thus some probing is required.

Treatment Objectives

After the core formulation has been identified, the issue becomes how to proceed through treatment. Treatment objectives follow directly from the two triangles schema of defenses, underlying feelings, and anxieties as played out with significant others. They include the restructuring of defenses, affects, and images of self and others. These are discussed from several perspectives below.

NECESSITY FOR FLEXIBILITY IN TREATMENT

It is neither wise nor even possible to rigidly structure treatment protocols. Therapists must have flexibility and free rein over their intuition in dealing with the subtleties and complexities of each patient. For this reason, I offer these few common objectives as a way to flexibly guide treatment, but I have left open the ways of intervening. Specific techniques have been useful in meeting these objectives, but they are entirely open to modification. Depending on a therapist's orientation, some of the tools I suggest may be quite familiar, while others may not. This is a partially structured treatment, with clearly defined objectives, but the therapist is free to add whatever techniques he or she feels necessary to achieve the objectives. The aim is to allow sufficient flexibility for the therapist to maintain his or her individuality and creativity.

Three Main Treatment Objectives

The three objectives focus treatment and work rapidly through the patient's problems. Each objective focuses on a different aspect of the affect phobia. Thinking of the phobias within the triangle of conflict and then working through them within these objectives can be tremendously helpful in guiding the therapist through a complex maze of material. These objectives do not follow a linear order, but are used as needed.

Each treatment objective has two sub-objectives:

- Defense restructuring (recognition and relinquishment of defenses)
- Affect restructuring (experiencing and appropriate expression of conflicted feeling or phobic affects)
- Self/other restructuring (alteration of the maladaptive inner representations of self and others)

Following is a quick walk through the six objectives, pointing out what the therapist might say and how the patient might respond. Below I will go into more detail about each objective. In order to resolve intrapsychic conflicts or affect phobias, the therapist needs to explore ways to assist the patient in achieving the following behavioral goals:

1. *Defense recognition* (recognize problem behaviors as defensive).
   T: Can you see how rapidly you talk? Do you think you might be avoiding feeling that way?

P: I never thought about it, but maybe so.

Defense Recognition is really just a repeat of the core formulation process (identifying defenses, affects, and anxieties) again and again until the patient has tremendous insight and recognition not only of the defenses, but what underlying feeling is being defended against and why.

2. *Defense relinquishing* (feel motivated to modify these defenses).

T: Do you think you could try to slow down a bit and see what might happen?

P: Yeah, I could try that.

3. *Affect experiencing* (experience the bodily arousal of the feeling in the therapy sessions)

T: What do you feel as you quiet yourself more?

P: I get this heavy feeling in my chest.

T: What feeling might that be?

P: I guess I feel like I'm going to cry. It's been so hard since my brother died.

4. *Affect expression* (learn to express those feelings interpersonally in new and adaptive ways).

T: Have you been able to share these painful feelings with your family?

P: I've just started. I was able to talk to my mother and she thanked me for bringing it up. It really helped us both to talk and cry a little about my brother.

5. & 6. *Self/other restructuring* (thus altering the sense of self in relation to others).

P: I guess I haven't been as alone as I thought I was. My mother has been much more responsive than I ever imagined possible.

In summary, in order to change maladaptive defensive behavior patterns, the person must recognize them as defensive, feel motivated to modify them, identify the avoided feelings, experience them in the therapy sessions, and learn to express them interpersonally in new and adaptive ways, thus altering the sense of self in relation to others.

These treatment objectives address potential "stuck points" in therapy that need to be worked through in order for treatment to be successful. If patients cannot see their defenses, they do not understand what needs to be changed or what the underlying feelings might be. If they do not want to change the defenses, then certainly there will be no change in the underlying affect. If affects are never experienced and desensitized in the session, it is much more difficult to express wants and needs outside the session. And finally, the sense of self and others must be strong enough or defenses and affects will not change.

In the discussion that follows, I first show how anxieties can be regulated to achieve the therapeutic goals. Then each objective is discussed in more detail. Transcripted segments from therapy cases illustrate how therapeutic techniques from various modalities can be used to achieve these treatment objectives.

INTERVENTIONS EMPLOYED TO REGULATE ANXIETIES

The restructuring of the three main objectives requires that anxieties be regulated in each. There are many potential interventions that might be useful in helping to regulate anxiety or conflict associated with the affect. One main approach is to use cognitive techniques to identify the maladaptive cognitions and dispute the logic until the anxiety can be regulated to normal limits and in a stepwise manner. As noted above, "anxiety" is a basket term for inhibition. Of course, it is not just anxiety that creates neurotic conflicts but the whole range of inhibitory affects—anxiety, guilt, shame, pain/anguish, and even contempt and disgust. Each of these must be specifically addressed.

Furthermore, in this model, anxieties are regulated, not just reduced. In the process of exposure, anxieties are initially raised to a certain degree, and then regulated to normal limits. We always need some degree of inhibition to balance activation. However, the inhibition should be flexible enough to allow for satisfying expression, not diminishing or deadening experience.

T: What is the worst thing that would happen if you were to let down your guard with your girlfriend?

P: I never show what I'm feeling because I couldn't bear it if she ever left me! I'd be devastated! So I almost don't let myself feel it.

T: Can you imagine right now how it would be to be open and loving with her?

P: That makes me feels panicky—just your words, "open and loving." (*Anxiety is initially raised.*)

T: So let's think about this and role play it until you know how to protect yourself and it doesn't feel so terrifying. (*Exposure is continued until anxiety is brought with normal limits.*)

The anxieties or inhibitory affects can act as signal anxiety or traumatic anxiety, functions that must be distinguished. Signal anxiety is the cause of defensiveness, as it inhibits the experience and expression of the activating affects (anger, grief, closeness, joy, etc.). Traumatic anxiety occurs when defenses are lacking and the anxiety itself functions defensively to block feeling, as in panic attacks. It is signal anxiety that must be "regulated" or brought within normal limits to restructure underlying affects (for a fuller discussion of this distinction, see McCullough Vaillant, 1997, pp. 25–26).

DEFENSE RECOGNITION

Defenses against feeling need to be restructured to permit the affects to be experienced. Thus, the first treatment objective is *defense recognition*, a common psychodynamic intervention to build insight in which patients are encouraged to identify how they're defending against phobic feeling.

T: You must have been so terrified when it was happening to you, but are you aware that you're smiling while you tell me this? I wonder what the smile is doing?
P: I guess I'm trying to lighten up the pain of that memory, but I hadn't realized I was doing it.

To protect patients from feeling too exposed by addressing defenses, the therapist in this treatment endeavors to engage patients as collaborators by teaching them the rationale behind the technique.

T: In this treatment sometimes I'll point out things that you may be doing to keep from experiencing certain feelings. This is not meant as a criticism, but is intended to help you see something that you may not be seeing.

Unlike in long-term psychodynamic therapy, the patient is often made aware of defenses against conflicted feelings from the very first session. However, this is done from an empathic, "experience near" therapeutic stance quite different from earlier, more confrontive and anxiety-provoking models of short-term dynamic psychotherapy (e.g., Davanloo, 1980). In addition, the patient's defenses can be put in perspective by pointing out his/her strengths. This creates a holding environment in which the patient can safely explore very painful and often shame-filled parts of the self.

DEFENSE RELINQUISHING

The next therapeutic objective is *defense relinquishing*. Insight alone, as psychodynamic therapists are well aware, does not have a good track record for causing behavior to change. Techniques useful for this objective can be drawn

in part from behavioral approaches (e.g., evaluating the consequences of behavior, both the costs and the benefits).

T: What do you think will happen if you continue to avoid people the way
you do?

P: It's inevitable. I am just going to get more isolated and miserable than I
am now.

T: I can understand that your fears of being hurt keep you alone a lot where
you feel safer — but it is sad, isn't it, to see how much the loneliness is getting to you? (*Pointing out the costs of the defenses.*)

P: I don't think I can continue on the way I've been.

Motivation to let go of defenses is heightened when the losses incurred
by the defenses are felt strongly.

AFFECT EXPERIENCING

The heart of the therapy is *affect experiencing*. As noted, in this model avoidance of adaptive affect is conceptualized as "affect phobia." Affect experiencing can be viewed as progressive exposure to the warded-off affect. Gestalt
techniques or EMDR (Shapiro, 1995/2001) are useful techniques that can has-
ten and deepen affective experiencing. Cognitive techniques are also used to
help the patient manage whatever anxieties or unpleasant feelings emerge as
defenses are addressed. Self/other restructuring is often needed to help bear
painful feelings.

T: What is the worst/most frightening/most shameful thing about experiencing these feelings?

If the therapist can provide a holding environment through active engagement with the patient, then defenses can be addressed and affects experienced
at a much more rapid pace than in traditional psychodynamic therapy.

Exposure to the physiological arousal of a specific affective experience
(anger, grief, tenderness, etc.) is crucial for desensitization (not exposure to
more general fantasies or images). Imagery is only a vehicle for the affective
arousal. The critical issue is that the feeling must create physiological arousal
in the body. Behavior change does not follow the mere intellectual imaging
of affective scenes. The body must be activated for change to occur.

On the other hand, research and clinical experience indicate that intense
levels of feeling are not necessary and can sometimes be counterproductive
to change. In earlier short-term dynamic psychotherapy models intense

experiencing of affect was viewed as necessary to produce character trans-formation; now, however, it has been found that often what patients most need is repeated exposure to slowly building mild or moderate levels of af-fect, modulated according to the patients' capacity to bear the feeling. Also, moderate affective arousal allows cognitive associations that are necessary for affect regulation and modulation. Intense levels of affect can be chaotic and disorganizing. Sometimes intense levels of feeling emerge as part of the processing. When that happens, time must be spent afterwards putting a cognitive structure around the feeling: how to make meaning of the affective experience, how to help modulate its intensity, and how to express it appro-priately to others. Interpretation can be used to provide another "cognitive cap" or "map of the territory" to help patients guide and manage strong feel-ings outside the session.

CASE EXAMPLE: THE MAN WITH EXHAUSTED ANGER
Here is a more extensive case example to demonstrate how these principles interact in therapy. The patient is a very passive man who cannot stand up for himself.

T: So let's go back to the lab manager who made you so mad. What do you feel in your body when you remember that? How do you experience the anger?

P: I don't know. It just makes me feel exhausted to think about it.

Being exhausted or fatigued by a feeling is generally a sign of inhibition. When someone is angry he or she is activated and energized, not exhausted.

T: Is that how you experience anger, or is that exhaustion something else?

P: Well, maybe I don't want to deal with those feelings.

T: What do you think makes you so exhausted by them?

P: It just seems like such a hopeless situation that I feel it's futile to try.

T: Do you notice how you've changed the anger now? You've twisted it around so you're [the one who is] sick. This guy gets protected. You get slammed. You've got a lot of power in you, but you see what you're doing? It's back on you. Why do you have to be the sick one? Where's the fight to-ward him? Let's go back to that.

P: Where's the fight?

T: Yes, where's the fight? Where's that feeling [you mentioned before], I'd like to crack him?

P: Well, for a moment I felt like grabbing him by the shirt and letting him have it.

T: Okay. Keep in mind that we're never talking about acting out such feelings, but let's at least explore your feeling. Can you let yourself imagine grabbing him and letting him have it?

P: Oh! If I let my imagination go, I just want to beat him and not stop. He made me so mad! (*pausing*) It's weird to have these feelings. Am I a psycho or something?

T: Doesn't everyone have aggressive feelings from time to time? (*Presenting reality, and thereby disputing his logic.*)

P: Sometimes it's hard to believe, and I think I'm the only weirdo out there. But I know it's true. (*His anxiety is slightly calmed.*)

T: What is important is to control these feelings and act constructively. Can you let yourself stay with that aggressive image for a while until it is not so terrifying? It is only a feeling. And we are in a safe place [the therapist's office] to explore it without hurting anyone. And, in fact, won't it help you be more assertive to do so?

P: Yeah, and it helps to be reminded.

Exposure to angry feelings would continue until the patient felt completely comfortable with the angry images, and in fact, could feel relief in sublimating them in fantasy. But that is not the end of the work, because the patient must learn how to deal effectively with such problems in the real world. Otherwise, the affect scenes that we are practicing would be useless. The problem would continue to happen, nothing would improve, and the patient would only feel more and more frustrated and hopeless.

AFFECT EXPRESSION

This therapeutic objective and the ultimate goal of this treatment model is *affect expression*. Once the affect is made bearable through exposure and desensitization in affect experiencing, patients still need to integrate these affects adaptively into their life with spouses, bosses, children, friends, etc. As in behavior or cognitive therapy, the therapist in this model collaborates with patients in finding a solution focus, provides instruction and training in areas where there are genuine deficits in knowledge or skills, and role plays difficult interactions that patients may face in their interpersonal relations. When maladaptive behavior persists, the therapist returns to defense and affect restructuring. (When the self-esteem is lacking a return to self/other restructuring is needed.)

Returning to the example of the Man with Exhausted Anger:

T: So now that you are comfortable with these feelings, how would you interact with the boss? Can we role-play an interaction?

P: Sure. I would ask for a time to see him, and would have a long talk about what had happened. This time I feel more pumped up and energized. I know I wouldn't back down.

T: What do you think you might say if your boss began to criticized you?

P: Oh, it happened the other day, after our last session. (*laughing*) He started in on me, and I just said, "Bob, that is entirely unfair. I wish you would be more supportive." It stopped him right in his tracks!

SELF/OTHER RESTRUCTURING

Self psychology approaches may be used to build the sense of self so that patients are better able to take care of themselves and are less willing to behave destructively. In very impaired patients, self/other work must precede defense and affect work. The therapist helps the patient identify destructive internalized relationships while rediscovering forgotten, more affirming relationships from the past ("recovery of lost loves").

T: Feeling entitled to stand up to the boss that way is a new part of you emerging, isn't it?

P: You bet it is! I hardly recognize myself. But it feels so good. And now that you mention it, (*tearing up*) it reminds me of my grandfather who used to say, "Fight'm back" when the school bullies picked on me. He was the only one who supported me back then. My parents just didn't seem to care.

T: So the part of you that is growing is the part your grandfather encouraged long ago.

A CRUCIAL DISTINCTION: DEFENSIVE VERSUS ADAPTIVE AFFECTS

A very important problem in eliciting affect is that defensive and adaptive affects are easily confused. Many therapists who elicit affect in session are eliciting defensive or maladaptive forms of the affect, which may only serve to reinforce maladaptive patterns. Thus, being able to identify affects that serve as defenses against feeling is a necessary skill to be able to implement in this or any other treatment in which affects are elicited.

In the case of anger, it is a strong energized feeling that is sought, not a regressive, helpless, or frustrated feeling. Road rage is not adaptive anger. With grief, crying with both positive and negative memories interwoven is the adaptive expression. Helpless weepiness that implies victimization or self-pity is typically defensive against underlying anger.

Both Therapists and Patients Fear Feelings

From extensive review of videotapes of therapy sessions, it has become evident that both patients and therapists avoid affects. Time and time again, the merciless videotape reveals therapists turning away from affect at crucial moments when patients could most benefit from a steady affect focus. Since this poses one of the major obstacles to effective treatment, it needs more study and empirical research. Just as patients need to be desensitized to feelings, so do therapists. This should be a crucial component of any psychotherapy training program.

Many times in my training workshops, I have been asked, "But aren't you afraid that the patient is going to hit you?" or "If you focus on tender feelings, aren't you afraid that—uh, gulp—sexual feelings might arise?" or "If you focus on the patient's longing for closeness, aren't you afraid she will show up on your doorstep with her suitcase and want to move in?"

The answer is the same in each situation. Help the patient experience the fullness of the feeling in fantasy—until it can be borne without anxiety or pain. Then help the patient discover what needs to be expressed or dealt with in the real world. If anger is the problem, then assertion is needed. If sexual feelings arise, then an outlet for such feelings needs to be explored, as well as the typical underlying longing for closeness. If it is closeness that is longed for, then patients need help with building social supports and trust in others and with opening themselves emotionally so that care can be given and received.

Conclusion

This short-term treatment is based on the premise that a person's maladaptive behaviors can be understood as attempts to protect the self (*defenses*) by avoiding the experience and/or expression of avoided feelings (*adaptive affects*) that are intolerable because of anxiety or other conflicting feelings that they arouse (e.g., *inhibitory affects* such as shame, guilt, fear of rejection, etc.). Although the treatment follows the fundamental structure of psychodynamic psychotherapy (i.e., analysis of defenses blocking conflicted feelings), it employs the technology of behavior change to speed up the therapy process (systematic desensitization).

The goal of treatment is to alter the avoidant defenses enough so that the person is able not only to fully experience feelings (*and contain them!*) but also to express feelings, wants and needs in appropriate ways whenever necessary. This therapy does not endorse mindless catharsis or venting of feelings. Treatment fosters deeply felt experience where emotions are consciously and maturely well-guided.

Part II: Research and Future Directions

It has been said repeatedly that research does not influence clinical practice. I am proud to say that this integrative and anxiety-regulating model of short-term dynamic psychotherapy is one of the exceptions. This treatment model has been developed and repeatedly revised in light of clinical observations and research findings. It is based on the impressive work of Malan and his colleagues, reflecting a 50-year history of careful study of "the science of psychodynamics" as applied to brief psychotherapy. This model still retains the fundamental components of Malan's model of the two triangles, as well as many of its basic principles. It has grown further by the clinical trials conducted at Beth Israel Medical Center in New York City from 1982 to1990, and just completed at the University of Trondheim, Norway (a clinical-trial comparison of this specific model with a cognitive-experiential model, 1988 to 1999), and ongoing at Harvard Medical School (intensive study of the single case). Also, Anderson and Lambert (1995) reviewed short-term psychotherapy and in an examination of 26 studies found an average effect size of .85 over controls.

This section will cite research support for short-term dynamic therapy, beginning with the most general level of analysis, i.e., psychotherapy as a whole, and moving on to research on common factors, and brief psychotherapy in general. Therefore, to the extent that other short-term treatment models in this book include similar components, the research support could also be extended to them as well. In addition, this particular model has been studied in two clinical trials on this particularly model, and finally, a number of process studies.

General Results of Psychotherapy Research

Years ago, Morris Parloff (1984) said that the effectiveness of psychotherapy had been demonstrated with "monotonous regularity." Today, after hundreds of research studies and many meta-analyses, this consistent finding of the effectiveness of psychotherapy remains the case. Psychotherapies, in general, have positive effects that are both statistically significant and clinically meaningful. Lambert and Bergin point out "Psychotherapy facilitates the remission of symptoms and often provides additional coping strategies and methods for dealing with future problems" (1994, p. 180). The average treated person is better off than 80% of the untreated sample (Lambert & Bergin, 1994, p. 144). However, the authors are careful to note that *not everyone* benefits to a satisfactory degree. The *average effect* of psychotherapy is one standard deviation unit, which is statistically large by standards developed by Cohen (1988). This amount of change exceeds the average effect sizes resulting from nine months of reading instruction in elementary school (SD .67) or from a trial of antidepressants (SD .41-.80). "Thus the effect sizes produced by the application of psychotherapies are typically as large as or larger than those produced by a variety of methods employed in medical and educational interventions" (Lambert & Bergin, 1994, p. 147).

The comparison across a wide variety of treatments reveals that differences in outcome between various forms of therapy are not as pronounced as one might expect. The reports of superior outcomes for cognitive and behavior therapy are limited. Thus, no one form of therapy is *consistently* better than another. Psychotherapy patients, however, show gains that surpass those resulting from pseudo-treatment conditions and placebos. When the effects of psychotherapy are compared to medication for many diagnoses, the effects are found to be as good or better. Thus, the effects of psychotherapy in general are solid and consistent over time; moreover, compared to the meta-analyses of 10 or 20 years ago, effects are improving from about two-thirds to one standard deviation change, on average.

Research Support for this Model from Reviews of Process Studies

The extensive review of more than 2,300 empirical findings by David Orlinsky and his colleagues (1994) highlighted certain processes that have been consistently related to outcome. "These include, among others, the overall quality of the therapeutic relationship, therapist skill, patient cooperation versus resistance, patient [affective] openness versus defensiveness, and treatment duration" (Orlinsky, Grawe, & Parks, 1994, p. 364). The process studies on STDP (discussed below) were included in this review, and our findings were in line with many others on the effects of defenses, affects, and therapist-patient relationship on psychotherapy outcome. The Orlinsky et al. review thus lends support to the effectiveness of the processes incorporated in this model.

COMMON FACTORS INCLUDED IN THIS MODEL
It has been hypothesized that different therapies embody *common factors* that are curative, even though these factors may not necessarily be explicitly stated

by the theory of change central to a treatment model. This certainly is the case with many models of STDP.

Research support is substantial that common factors across different treatments have been shown to account for much improvement in patient outcomes. Lambert and Bergin (1994) strongly recommend that therapists intentionally incorporate them. These common factors fall into three categories: (1) *support factors* (e.g., structure, reassurance, therapist skill, mitigation of isolation), (2) *learning factors* (e.g., advice, feedback, insight, changing expectations, affective experiencing, corrective emotional experiencing), (3) *action or behavioral factors* (e.g., practice, mastery, facing fears, taking risks, modeling, practice).

Each of these common factors has been intentionally incorporated into my model. For example, *support factors* in my form of short-term dynamic psychotherapy include validation of the defensive behaviors, anxiety regulation throughout the treatment, and an open, empathic, and accepting stance of the therapist in the real relationship, to name just a few. *Learning factors* include teaching patients to identify defensive patterns and label affects, to note the negative consequences of the defenses, to distinguish defensive versus adaptive functions of feelings, to express affect adaptively, and to view themselves and others in a different light. *Action factors* in this model include the repeated exposure to fearful and conflictual situations and experiences. Extensive research by Barlow (1988, 1993) and his colleagues support the value of exposure. Barlow hypothesized the following:

> ... the overwhelming evidence from emotion theory is that an essential step in the modification of emotional disorders is the direct alteration of associated action tendencies. Laughter, humor, and associated facial expressions induced during successful paradoxical intention—may be effective not because of changes in self-statements, as is often assumed. Rather, prevention of behavioral responses (including facial expressions) associated with fear and anxiety, and the substitution of action tendencies associated with alternative emotions, may account for the effectiveness of this technique. (1988, p. 312)

This strong support for emotional exposure from the cognitive vantage point demonstrates how we are moving toward a more unified model of psychotherapy. Thus, this short-term model, as well as other STDP models in this book, have incorporated many of these common factors, which have been repeatedly demonstrated to be effective.

CLINICAL TRIAL #1: THE BETH ISRAEL BRIEF PSYCHOTHERAPY RESEARCH PROGRAM

The effectiveness of short-term dynamic treatment for Axis II Cluster C personality disorders has been demonstrated in the first major clinical trial that has been completed (Winston et al., 1991, 1994). Two types of brief dynamic treatment were examined: a group that was high on confrontation of defenses, and a group that was more moderate and clarified defenses against feelings. The results showed an average of one standard deviation change in outcome measures ($X=.97$) after 40 sessions of brief, active, and focused psychotherapy. There were no significant differences between groups. This positive outcome was impressive because it was obtained in a difficult population of personality disordered patients—typically unresponsive to treatment. At one and one-half year follow-up not only had these gains been maintained, but slight improvement was noted (Winston et al., 1994).

CLINICAL TRIAL #2: UNIVERSITY OF TRONDHEIM, NORWAY
At the Department of Psychiatry, University of Trondheim, Norway, this anxiety-regulating model of short-term dynamic therapy (STDP) model has been compared to cognitive therapy (CT) in a repeated-measures comparative process-outcome design. Fifty patients meeting *DSM-III-R* criteria for Cluster C personality disorders (i.e., avoidant, dependent, obsessive, passive-aggressive, and self-defeating) were randomized to 40 sessions of either STDP or CT. Results at termination were similar to those of the Beth Israel clinical trial; there were strong improvements in both groups, but not significant differences between them. Continuing research will examine the processes and change mechanisms in both treatments. Two-year follow-up data are still being collected.

Research in Support of Defense Restructuring

In the 1980s a series of studies, which I supervised, examined the hypothesis put forth by Davanloo (1980) that confrontation would lead to decreased defensiveness, increased affective responding, and better outcomes. However, results did not support this hypothesis. In several studies, it was demonstrated that defenses were more greatly altered by *supportive, empathic,* and *clarifying* methods than by *confrontive* methods (Joseph, 1988; Makynen, 1992; Salerno, Farber, McCullough, Winston, & Trujillo, 1992).

Salerno et al. (1992) demonstrated that the higher total frequencies of therapist confrontation of defenses in the transference did not, as we had hypothesized, predict improvement at outcome. A subsequent study (Makynen, 1992) further examined the confrontations that were sustained over several minutes, hypothesizing that it was the *continued confrontation* that would "break through" the defenses. However, again counter to expectations, this did not predict improvement. The Makynen study was a strong contributor to the growing awareness of the need for a graded and empathic procedure for recognition and relinquishing of defenses. In exploratory analyses of the coding data, it was noted that when confrontations were given *along with a supportive or empathic statement by the therapist* (Foote, 1989), the combination resulted in a greater likelihood of expression of affect, a higher rating of therapist alliance, and, especially in lower functioning or more "difficult" patients, a higher probability of improvement at outcome. Patients seemed better able to take in painful information contained in a therapist's confrontation when it was paired with a statement that reflected understanding or care.

We then decided to look at patient-therapist interaction from the opposite perspective. Joseph (1988) compared the likelihood that a given therapist intervention (e.g., questions, support, clarifications, confrontations, interpretations, self-disclosure, etc.) would precede affective responding versus the likelihood that it would precede defensive responding. We had hypothesized that confrontation would elicit significantly more affective responding. But Joseph, like Makynen and Salerno et al., demonstrated that, of all the eight interventions, confrontation elicited more defensive behavior. Clarification was the only variable that significantly elicited affect. Apparently, the therapist's listening carefully and reflecting back what the patient said prepared the patient to respond in a less defensive and more open and affective manner.

These results led us to seriously question the "anxiety-provoking" techniques as the best—or only—method for altering defenses. Our inclination as clinicians, to back off and be more gentle, was supported by these studies.

Research in Support of Affect Restructuring

Two studies lend support to focusing on the experience of affect. Research by McCullough, Winston, Farber et al. (1991) demonstrated that the patient's affective response to transference interpretations significantly predicted improvement at outcome ($R=.55$). The strength of this relationship was heightened by the fact that affect following transference interpretations was a rather uncommon occurrence (a total of 61 in 64 coded sessions, i.e., less than one per session. No such responses occurred in the four poorest outcome cases). This finding suggested that affect following interpretations of the patient-therapist relationship led to improvement.

In a sample of 16 personality-disordered patients, Taurke, McCullough, Winston, Pollack, and Flegenheimer (1990) demonstrated that the ratio of affect expressed to defenses expressed was predictive of improvement. (The greater the ratio of affect to defenses in session, the greater the improvement at outcome.) Patients started with an average of one affective response per every five defensive responses at admission. At termination, the five most patients showed an average of one affective response for every two defensive responses. The five least improved patients showed no change in the 1/5 affect/defense ratio shown at admission. This study provided direct support of Malan's conceptual schema and to our hypothesis that lowering defensiveness in relation to affective expression contributes to improvement in outcome.

Observation of Videotaped Sessions

Intensive coding of hundreds of hours of videotaped sessions revealed repetitive patterns that represented obstacles to treatment progress. These repeated clinical observations, along with the studies discussed below, led to modifications in the confrontational approach (e.g., Davanloo, 1980) replacing confrontation with clarification and supportive interventions to assist the patient in the difficult assimilation of the analysis of defenses and experiencing of affect (McCullough, 1993, 1994). Both defensive and affective behaviors were rendered more manageable by regulating (i.e., bringing within normal limits) the associated anxiety, guilt, shame, or pain that plague the personality-disordered patient and typically impede therapeutic progress (McCullough et al., 1994). Techniques from many orientations have been included in the various steps of the treatment model to enhance the patient's exposure to and mastery of the specific treatment objectives.

This model intentionally attempts to standardize its approach through the focus on objectives rather than interventions, because:

1. Objectives make explicit the subgoals of treatment and provide guideposts for the therapist that help in organizing the enormous amount of complex clinical material.
2. The focus on objectives allows therapists some flexibility in how to achieve those objectives by use of their clinical skill and intuition—in addition to methods suggested. Too rigid an adherence to treatment manual interventions has been demonstrated to have a small negative relationship to outcome ($r = -10$; Hogland & Heyerdahl, 1992).
3. Standardized objectives allow the comparison to other treatments that strive to achieve similar goals (i.e., both long-term and short-term psychodynamic psychotherapies), but may do so through the use of very different interventions (i.e., free association versus high therapist activity, or the development of a transference neurosis in contrast to exposure to affective experiencing).

4. This focus is supported by research and clinical experience as detailed below.

The Achievement of Therapeutic Objectives Scale (ATOS):

Research is underway to test the objectives in this treatment model by the use of a scale developed for that purpose, the Achievement of Therapeutic Objectives Scale (ATOS; McCullough, Meyer, Cui, Andrews, & Kuhn, 2000).* The ATOS scale rates on a scale of one to one hundred the degree to which each of the treatment objectives has been met. This includes the degree of patients' recognition of defenses, the degree to which they want to give up the defenses, the degree of intensity of their experiencing of affect, and their ability to express wants and needs interpersonally, as well as the degree of their maladaptive inner representations of self or others. Identifying objectives, and then rating to what degree the therapist assists the patient in achieving those objectives, offers a new and potentially useful method for assessing therapist adherence to the model, as well as therapist competence in applying the model.

The ATOS ratings are given for each session and are correlated with various residual measures of pre-post change at termination and follow-up, e.g., severity of target complaints, ratings on the affect consciousness interviews, diagnostic criteria for Axis I and Axis II categories, ratings on the Global Assessment Form, to name only a few. Preliminary data on reliability and validity are very good and a series of studies on the ATOS-based process-outcome relationships is underway.

Future Directions

This integrative model of short-term dynamic psychotherapy is a *testable model* that has a demonstrated capacity to change long-standing and maladaptive character patterns. The next phase of the research is to experimentally examine specific change processes. We expect parts of this model will withstand the passage of time, and parts will change. The parts that we hypothesize to have the greatest staying power are the therapeutic objectives: the restructuring of defenses, affects, and relationships by the regulation of the associated anxieties or conflicted affects. These objectives follow from Freud's original principles, were simplified and operationalized by

---

*This manual may be obtained from the author by sending a self-addressed, stamped 9" × 11" envelope to the Short-Term Psychotherapy Foundation, Box 466, Dedham, MA 02026.

Malan (1979, chapter 13), and then integrated with other orientations by McCullough Vaillant (1997). We also predict that the "universal principle of psychodynamic psychotherapy" that Malan described (namely, that defenses and anxieties block true feeling with self and others) will continue to withstand the test of time. On the other hand, we expect that the interventions that assist in the achievement of those goals will evolve and change as a result of continuing process research.

Looking to the future, specific developments include the following:

Single-case experimental design. Abundant clinical trials have demonstrated that psychotherapy works, but we are only beginning to understand *how* it works. There is a great need to examine patient-specific treatment by single-case experimental designs. In the coming decades, we need a worldwide accumulation of not just hundreds, *but thousands*, of well-executed, single-case experimental designs (following a standardized format) to detail actual mechanisms of change.

Patient-specific treatment. We need research that begins to identify the *approximate minimum number of sessions* to achieve certain psychotherapeutic goals. We need to think in terms of how rapidly one can proceed in outpatient treatment versus the intensity of restructuring that might be possible with the aid of a brief hospitalization and subsequent, supportive and reconstructive treatment. We believe that there is tremendous potential for inpatient care to provide a supportive structure for character change.

Routine videotaping of sessions. All our research is based on analysis of videotaped sessions, and it is a great resource in clinical work as well. Hopefully it will become increasingly routine for patients to permit video recording of treatment—as in surgery and athletic coaching. Videotaping allows the therapist, like the football coach, to understand how important events were actually sequenced. Videotape review is a cost-efficient way of intensifying therapy for the patient and allows both the therapist and the patient to more fully assimilate emotion-laden therapy content that may be too intense to bear at first. Videotape review permits high-quality supervision by showing, not telling. Finally, videotaping offers protection for the therapist (from distorted patient allegations) as well as for the patient (in the assurance that the therapist permits his or her work to be reviewed).

Airline pilot standards for training. Before a pilot is entrusted with taking a commercial plane into the air, hundreds of hours of practice in the test cockpit are required. Unfortunately, beginning psychotherapists rarely have such practice before seeing their first patients. As well-documented single-case designs (with videotaped sessions) begin to accumulate, practice programs could be developed for trainees. Hopefully standards will evolve for "video hours logged"—not in passive watching, but in interactive coding and responding and in anticipating the "next move to be made."

Brain-imaging of psychotherapeutic outcomes. Recent advances in neurobiology and neurological technology open up great potential for psychotherapy research. An impressive example is Baxter's (1992) demonstration of caudate glucose metabolic rate changes with both drug and behavior therapy for obsessive-compulsive disordered patients. In our psychotherapy research program we are developing methods for examining brain function before and after psychotherapy and deepening our understanding of how neuronal networks might be continually altered as a result of treatment, particularly through a focus on affect. Although there is much more work to be done, these exciting developments are leading us into a new era in which psychotherapy research hopefully may be brought into "normal science" (Kuhn, 1970).

References

Anderson, E. M., & Lambert, M. J. (1995). Short-term dynamically oriented psychotherapy: A review and meta-analysis. *Clinical Psychology Review, 15*(6), 503–514.

Barlow, D. H. (1988). *Anxiety and its disorders: The nature and treatment of anxiety and panic.* New York: Guilford.

Barlow, D. H. (1993). *Clinical handbook of psychological disorders: A step-by-step treatment manual.* New York: Guilford.

Baxter, L. R. (1992). Neuroimaging studies of obsessive compulsive disorder. *Psychiatric Clinics of North America, 15,* 871–884.

Cohen, J. (1988). *Statistical power for the behavioral sciences.* Hillsdale, NJ: Erlbaum.

Davanloo, H. (Ed.). (1980). *Short-term dynamic psychotherapy.* New York: Aronson.

Foote, J. (1989). Interpersonal context and patient change episodes (Doctoral dissertation, New York University, 1989). *Dissertation Abstracts International, 51*(12B).

Hogland, P., & Heyerdahl, E. (1992). The circumscribed focus in intensive brief dynamic psychotherapy. *Psychotherapy and Psychosomatics, 61,* 163–170.

Joseph, C. (1988). Antecedents to transference interpretation in short-term psychodynamic psychotherapy (Doctoral dissertation, Rutgers University, 1988). *Dissertation Abstracts International, 50*(04B).

Kuhn, T. (1970). *The structure of scientific revolutions* (Rev. ed.). Chicago: University of Chicago Press.

Lambert, M., & Bergin, A. E. (1994). The effectiveness of psychotherapy. In A. E. Bergin & S. L. Garfield (Eds.), *Handbook of psychotherapy and behavior change* (4th ed., pp. 143–189). New York: Wiley.

Makynen, A. (1992). The effects of continued confrontation on patient affective and defensive response (Doctoral dissertation, Columbia University Teachers' College, 1992). *Dissertation Abstracts International, 54.*

Malan, D. M. (1976). *The frontier of brief psychotherapy.* New York: Plenum.

Malan, D. M. (1979). *Individual psychotherapy and the science of psychodynamics.* London: Butterworth.

Malan , D. M., & Osimo, F. (1992). *Psychodynamics, training, and outcome in brief psychotherapy.* London: Butterworth-Heinemann Ltd.

McCullough, L. (1993). An anxiety-reduction modification of short-term dynamic psychotherapy (STDP): A theoretical "melting pot" of treatment techniques. In G. Stricker & J. R. Gold (Eds.), *Comprehensive handbook of psychotherapy integration* (pp. 139–149). New York: Plenum.

McCullough, L. (1994). The next step in short-term dynamic psychotherapy: A clarification of objectives and techniques in an anxiety-regulating model. *Psychotherapy, 31*(4), 642–654.

McCullough Vaillant, L. (1997). *Changing character: Short-term anxiety-regulating psychotherapy for restructuring defenses, affects, and attachment.* New York: Basic Books.

McCullough, L., Kuhn, N., Andrews, S., Kaplan, A., Wolf, J., & Lanza, C. (2001). *Treating affect phobias: A workbook for short-term dynamic psychotherapy.* New York: Guilford.

McCullough, L., Meyer, S., Cui, X. J., Andrews, S., & Kuhn, N. (2000). *The achievement of therapeutic objectives scale manual (ATOS).* Unpublished manuscript. c/o Leigh McCullough, 943 High Street, Dedham, MA 02026.

McCullough, L., Winston A., Farber, B., Porter, F., Pollack, J., Laikin, M., Vingiano, W., & Trujillo, M. (1991). The relationship of patient-therapist interaction to outcome in brief psychotherapy. *Psychotherapy, 28*(4), 525–533.

Orlinsky, D. E., Grawe, K., & Parks, B. (1994). Process and outcome of psychotherapy—noch einmal. In A. E. Bergin & S. L. Garfield (Eds.) *Handbook of psychotherapy and behavior change* (4th ed., pp. 270–378). New York: Wiley.

Parloff, M. B. (1984). Psychotherapy research and its incredible credibility crisis. *Clinical Psychology Review, 4,* 95–109.

Salerno, M., Farber, B., McCullough, L., Winston, A., & Trujillo, M. (1992). The effects of confrontation and clarification on patient affective and defensive responding. *Psychotherapy Research, 2*(3), 181–192.

Shapiro, F. (1995/2001). *Eye movement desensitization and reprocessing: Basic principles, protocols, and procedures.* New York: Guilford.

Sifneos, P. E. (1979). *Short-term dynamic psychotherapy: Evaluation and technique.* New York: Plenum.

Svartberg, M., & Stiles, T. (1999, June). *The results of the Trondheim Psychotherapy Research Study comparing short-term dynamic and cognitive therapies.* Paper presented at the meeting of the Society for Psychotherapy Research, Braga, Portugal.

Taurke, E., McCullough, L., Winston, A., Pollack, J., & Flegenheimer, W. (1990). Change in affect-defense ratio from early to late sessions in relation to outcome. *Journal of Clinical Psychology, 46*(5), 657–668.

Winston, A., Laikin, M., Pollack, J., Samstag, L., McCullough, L., & Muran, C. (1994). Short-term psychotherapy of personality disorders. *American Journal of Psychiatry, 151,* 190–194.

Winston, A., McCullough, L., Trujillo, M., Pollack, J., Laikin, M., Flegeheimer, W., & Kestenbaum, R. (1991). Brief psychotherapy of personality disorders. *Journal of Nervous and Mental Disease, 179,* 188–193.

Wolpe, J. (1958). *Psychotherapy by reciprocal inhibition.* Stanford: Stanford University Press.

4

Accelerated Empathic Therapy

Michael Alpert

ACCELERATED EMPATHIC THERAPY (AET) is a short-term psychother-apy developed to provide efficient, effective treatment. Evolving from intensive short-term dynamic psychotherapy (IS-TDP) (Davanloo, 1978), it contains dynamic and experiential elements (Alpert, 1992). Additionally, ed-ucational, cognitive, supportive, neuropsychological, and interactive tech-niques are employed.

Education, a cornerstone of AET, begins the interview. In order to decrease patient anxiety and create a sense of safety and collaboration, the treatment is explained to the patient at the time of the first patient-therapist contact. The response of the patient to this explanation of the therapy initiates the process of assessment. Following the explanation, the therapist checks with the patient to see how well the description of AET has been understood and to find out what the patient thinks about it. The patient's reactions provide early information about the defenses to be encountered as treatment pro-gresses. Monitoring of the interaction between patient and therapist is cen-tral to the success of treatment. Besides revealing defenses, these interactions provide data on transference and areas of conflict.

In AET, unlike in IS-TDP, the therapist avoids the use of "challenge and pressure" as much as possible when interacting with the patient. Instead, the differences in the views of patient and therapist are respected. These differ-ences are labeled as valuable data that can move the therapy forward. The pa-tient is encouraged to join the therapist in exploring how they came to their different views. Next, they examine the reactions of the patient to having at-tention drawn to these differences. Although occurring at an early point in therapy, these reactions are often dramatic and linked to physical sensations.

Either their intensity or their physical manifestations can cause considerable anxiety, which can, in turn, immobilize the patient. The therapist, therefore, prepares the patient for these possible reactions during the education phase of the first session.

The first measures the therapist introduces to help in the management of anxiety involve sharing information and providing reassurance. The patient is encouraged to let the therapist know whenever he/she becomes aware of his anxiety. The therapist also watches for verbal and nonverbal signs of mounting anxiety. Should either find that anxiety is increasing, the therapist notes that it is all right to move to a less upsetting area or introduces techniques that allow the patient to process the material more comfortably.

Again, the reactions of the patient to the intervention of the therapist are explored, as are the therapist's reactions to the patient. This pattern, in which the reactions of both patient and therapist are explored, is repeated throughout the therapy. It is employed for several reasons: (1) to prevent misunderstandings, (2) to keep mounting anxiety from bringing the therapy to a standstill (McCullough Vaillant, 1997), (3) to aid assessment, (4) to build rapport, and (5) to decrease defensiveness.

Cognitive and neuropsychological approaches are used along with empathy, compassion, and reciprocal monitoring to help a patient bear and process unsettling material as it surfaces. For example, anxiety is lowered when the therapist provides cognitive explanations of how thoughts, emotions, behaviors, and physical sensations are linked. Furthermore, the patient realizes that such feelings are not abnormal. Knowing that such feelings are normal and that facing them will decrease symptoms makes it easier for a patient to begin to explore them.

Neuropsychological approaches, such as dual-brain psychology (Schiffer, 1998) and EMDR (Shapiro, 1995), decrease anxiety and speed processing. Both dual-brain psychology and EMDR gradually move patients away from ineffective coping mechanisms that have developed in response to traumatic events and help them to develop more adaptive behaviors. EMDR has additional benefits. It helps patients to incorporate relaxing and empowering imagery and emphasizes the value of the patient's thoughts as opposed to the hypotheses of the therapist. As a result, the anxiety of patients decreases, and their self-confidence increases.

Empathy, compassion, and reciprocal monitoring create an environment that promotes the sharing of feelings. When feelings are shared with others, they become more bearable. Once the unacceptable affects and memories are processed, the pathological defenses utilized to avoid them can be jettisoned. More adaptive functioning follows. These changes, coupled with greater self-esteem and a greater capacity for intimacy, lead to successful life experiences. As one success leads to the next, patient and therapist recognize that treatment is no longer necessary.

The Evolution of AET

AET has been described as one of the next generation of STDPs (Magnavita, 1993). It grew out of attempts made between 1987 and 1992 to treat the patients who did poorly when treated with IS-TDP. These were the patients who became so anxious when challenged by therapists that they ceased making progress. In fact, they often regressed. The study of these anxious patients and the search for techniques to aid them led to AET.

The identification of defenses is important in AET just as it is in IS-TDP. However, the way in which patients learn about their defenses is radically altered in AET. Additionally, the therapist/patient metaphor shifted; where in IS-TDP the therapist is portrayed as a surgeon deftly draining pathological abscesses, in AET the relationship is less hierarchical and credit for the patient's improvement is shared. In AET the therapist alternates among educating the patient, catalyzing the process, and working alongside the patient to find new solutions.

Let me describe how these technical and theoretical changes occurred. Early in the search for ways of better treating anxious patients who became flooded with feelings or confused when challenged or pressured in IS-TDP, I reviewed the notes I had taken while observing Davanloo's IS-TDP tapes. (In the parlance of IS-TDP, these patients were using regressive defenses that had to be restructured to permit the successful application of "challenge and pressure.") While studying "breakthroughs," instants when patients open up, I discovered that these did not occur immediately after defenses were challenged and the patients pressured to give them up, but when the therapist relented, stopped pressuring the patient, and became compassionate. The sudden change in the attitude of the therapist seemed to catch patients off guard. This observation led to the idea that these patients' experience of receiving their therapists' caring and concern (compassion) might have led to the recovery of buried memories and feelings. Perhaps regression could be avoided if the challenge of defenses was replaced with compassion.

I decided to try out the idea with patients by expressing my compassion for their suffering and my appreciation of their hard work. Initially these interventions had little effect on patients. Either they did not hear what I told them or they did not believe me. They had a remarkable ability to ignore my comments or minimize them as "just therapist talk."

My first thoughts were, "Did the caring and compassion have to come from a confronting and seemingly critical source if patients were to be touched deeply enough to experience their buried feelings? Did they have a corrective emotional experience because they were now getting what they had failed to get from critical parents in the past?" Pursuing this line of thought, I asked, "Why else might expressions of caring and compassion from non-critical therapists fail to move patients while compassion from seemingly critical therapists deeply moved patients?

Eventually I came up with the following set of hypotheses: When patients did not receive compassionate care and validation as children, they blamed themselves rather than their parents. To blame their caregivers would be too threatening. First, they might be attacked if they blamed their caregivers. Second, they would feel vulnerable if they recognized that they had defective parents. Thus, children blame themselves rather than their parents to maintain the fiction that they are safe. They begin to expect and accept criticism. They may even seek out critical people. In this way, their unsatisfying relationships become repetitive. Using this formulation, I could see why my expression of compassion made no sense to these patients. They neither expected compassion nor believed me.

Thinking about these ideas brought to mind patients who, despite looking for a therapist who would be different from their critical parents, always ended up feeling their therapist was criticizing them. I wondered, "What would happen if they got what they said they wanted and found an appreciative, non-critical therapist?" To find out I needed to find ways to get patients to experience caring and appreciation. One opportunity came while I was working with a passive-aggressive patient who had already failed in treatment with multiple prior therapists. He called seeking IS-TDP and told me that I was his last hope, but soon we fell into the same pattern of failure that had marked his previous treatments: After describing his failure to please his critical stepfather, he behaved in a passive-aggressive manner with me. When I labeled his defensive behaviors, he became resistant. Eventually, after I repeatedly pointed out his passive-aggressive defenses, he began to recognize them. At this point, however, he became self-condemning and felt hopeless. Challenge of his self-condemnation and hopelessness caused him to become confused. Attempts at restructuring were unsuccessful and only increased his self-condemning, hopeless stance. When he announced he was about to give up, I decided to change gears and try a gentler approach.

My initial attempts to be either compassionate or to show appreciation for his hard work fell on deaf ears. When I pointed out his lack of response, he said he had not found me convincing. In fact, he thought I was being sarcastic. He said that since I was a therapist and he was a patient, I did not really care about him, I was just doing my job. Only when I began to focus on "our" interaction and shared my thoughts and feelings instead of focusing solely on his, did he begin to believe me. He now realized that I was touched by his pain. This had a powerful effect on him.

The key to reaching this and other patients appears to be helping them to recognize that their therapists care about them. Focusing on the patient-therapist interaction, specifically the therapist's reaction to the patient and then the patient's, response to the therapist, increases the chance that patients will see the concern of their therapists. When therapists focus on their feelings for their patients, it is more likely that these feelings will be visible to their patients. When therapists share their thoughts and feelings, patients see what is actually occurring rather than what they assume is happening. Consequently, it is harder for patients to deny that their therapists really care about them. Examining the interaction in this way also shifts the clinical frame. Therapists stop talking about only the inner workings of their patients and begin also (1) to talk about their own inner workings and (2) to answer the questions of their patients concerning their own thoughts and behaviors. As a result, patients feel validated.

Some patients will be unable to accept a therapist's observations no matter how they are presented. For such patients the review of session videotapes can be useful. When I find that patients and I do not see our interaction the same way, I ask if they would like to review the tape with me. I explain that an "instant replay" might help us to find how we came to have such different views. Both views may be due to defensiveness or they may be legitimate because they are based on different assumptions. I have discovered that the review can be as informative for the therapist as for the patient and, much to my chagrin, that I am as likely to misperceive events as my patients are!

It can be upsetting as well as embarrassing for patients to find they have misunderstood their therapist. This can lead to a new set of defenses. In other words, once they see that they have misperceived the therapist, and that he/she cares about them, they may still be defensive. I think this is because the initial pleasure they feel upon recognizing the therapist's concern for them is quickly replaced with pain. Receiving the caring for which they have yearned connects them with painful repressed memories. It often turns out that avoidance of this pain has caused them to misunderstand the therapist.

When the pleasure of being cared about or appreciated reawakens buried memories of traumatic childhood years, it is not hard to understand patients' defensiveness. They are avoiding the pain, emptiness, and heaviness that will flood them. Techniques that help them tolerate and work through these upsetting feelings include support, reframing, EMDR, sharing feelings with an empathic therapist, and clarifying the difference between coping with these feelings as a child and as an adult.

Before describing these techniques, let me present portions of an annotated case transcript so that you will have a sense of the application of AET in an actual session. A review of techniques used in the session follows the transcript.

A Case Demonstrating the Application of AET

I have chosen this case because it nicely demonstrates the importance of choosing the right approach for each patient rather than trying to force all patients to fit a favorite model. This depressed 40-year-old lawyer sought me out after several previous failed therapies. Reading an article on IS-TDP made him think this could be the treatment for him. Unfortunately, his first IS-TDP therapist had not been able to break through his defenses. He decided to give it one more try with me.

I had described the ground rules over the telephone to him before our first meeting, i.e., my fee, videotaping sessions, the use of the tape for teaching and research, and the role of the trial therapy evaluation. However, at the beginning of the evaluation session he said he did not want the tapes to be used for teaching, because he needed to be comfortable to talk about difficult things and knowing the tapes would be seen by others made him uncomfortable. He had decided to come to the session without telling me of his request not to be taped, because he felt that I was his last hope and believed that I would not treat him if he voiced his reservations. As a result, he was very anxious and anticipated a confrontation.

The following transcript material begins two minutes into the first evaluative session.

Transcript from Session 1

T: What are you feeling toward me?

P: Well, I have been feeling a lot of anger toward you. (*Since the anger is conscious, the angry impulse or the experience of the anger can be pursued.*)

T: What's the anger toward me?

P: I feel that you have kind of set me up. I feel that I am in a very vulnerable situation. (*This is the reason for the anger rather than the anger itself. Therefore, it can be labeled as a defense or ignored.*)

T: But what is the anger toward me?

P: The anger is that ... feel you are taking advantage of me. (*Again, the patient defensively gives the reason for the anger.*)

T: Taking advantage of you?

P: Right.

T: That is not the anger, that is the reason for it.

P: Right.

T: Do you get angry a lot? (*His historical use of anger is explored to assess the risk of him acting out toward others or himself [suicidal behavior].*)

P: I don't get angry enough.

T: What do you mean?

P: It's very difficult for me to get angry and to show my anger.

T: Uh-huh.

P: And I ...

T: What happens when you do?

P: (*pauses*)

T: You are licking your lips now and slowing down. (*Drawing attention to defenses makes them less effective. In IS-TDP the therapist also puts pressure on the patient to stop using the defenses labeled in this way. In AET the therapist would say that the defenses are valuable as signposts pointing the way to the discovery of important material.*)

P: Right.

T: What now? This appears to be well known to you, all these things, and now sighing.

P: Yes.

T: So you are receding, sinking into the chair.

P: I guess I am, now I am laughing.

T: So this is something you know all about?

P: Yes.

T: So, what's happening now?

P: I am feeling uncomfortable now.

T: But what are you feeling toward me?

P: I am feeling increasingly angry at you.

T: And you know it's anger or you don't know that? (*If he knows he is angry, the sensations which tell him that he is angry can be pursued.*)

P: I know it.

T: So then what happens when you get angry is you become more with-drawn? (*The defensive use of withdrawal to avoid anger is clarified.*)

P: Yes.

T: And is there any reason for that? What would happen if your anger were to be experienced and/or go outwardly?

P: The problem for me with anger is that it feels as though it's going to be uncontrollable. (*Is there a risk and what would his uncontrollable anger be like?*)

T: Has it ever been that way?

P: No, not really.

T: No.

P: But I have experienced the fear, the fear of my stepfather being angry at me, where I was really terrified of it so ... essentially I think I was ...

T: He would be out of control?

P: Yes ...

Even in these early minutes of the evaluation it is easy to see that this pa-tient actually sets up the confrontation that he later says he fears. When he de-cides he wants to change our agreement he feels I have set him up. This makes him angry, as does his assumption that I will be angry with him. Apparently, he entered the session with considerable transference, expecting me to behave much as his stepfather did. I subsequently learn that his failure to keep his agree-ment with me is a reenactment of his behavior with his stepfather and that sim-ilar behavior with supervisors has cost him several jobs in the past.

These few minutes also foretold what would happen when I clarified his defenses and then challenged them. Remember, when he entered the session he was already angry and distrustful, and these feelings elicited the fear that I would retaliate. This caused him to retreat into confusion, which in turn caused him to feel helpless. Feeling that he was helpless led to self-loathing. This pattern was repeated many times in subsequent sessions. Occasionally he was able to experience some of his anger, but invariably he returned to an annoyed, confused, helpless, and self-critical position.

The pattern recurred when we explored his interactions with the signifi-cant figures in his life. He had felt manipulated by his mother, as well as by his stepfather and previous therapists. He felt weak, helpless, and guilty with his wife, friends, and siblings. When attempts to cognitively restructure his defenses only made the patient more obsessive and self-critical, I began to employ new techniques I was evaluating for use with patients who did not respond well to IS-TDP.

I had been working with three colleagues, Joe Celentano, Diana Fosha (Fosha, 1992) and Isabel Sklar, to improve our results with patients who had made little progress in IS-TDP. We first tried to find techniques to increase the experience of anger for these patients. Unfortunately, neither emphasizing the physical sensations connected with anger nor increasing vocalization or graphic imagery improved their ability to experience anger. These techniques failed to help my new patient as well.

Since his self-punishing behavior could be due to guilty feelings he had about his treatment of people in the past, I next worked with him to reactivate the grief process. Despite this work he remained mired in self-recrimination. He and I were both near giving up when I shifted my therapeutic stance. I became more open and empathic, exploring my reactions to him as well as his reactions to me. When I was able to consistently maintain this new stance in the 36th session, the patient's response was dramatic. You will next read a portion of the transcript from that session. Interestingly, it begins with the patient announcing that he is annoyed with me, much as he reported on entering the first session. Ironically, this perpetually late man is annoyed because he believes that I attempted to provoke him by being late for the session. He is still largely unaware of his role in provoking others.

Transcript from Session 36

P: I am provoked.

T: Why?

P: I was annoyed that you were late and started to fantasize that this was somehow deliberate.

T: No, I had trouble with the prior session and ended late because I was having trouble and then needed to collect my thoughts and look through your materials before I could start. But, if that makes you angry, it makes sense. (*Instead of focusing on his feeling annoyed, I tell him the reason for my lateness [to provide the information to correct his erroneous assumption]. I let him know that I too have trouble at times, and I treat his anger as a legitimate response. Sharing of views and the thoughts behind them, self-disclosure and acknowledging imperfections, and legitimizing and accepting anger are all employed here.*)

P: Well, I appreciate your explanation of it as opposed to just necessarily focusing on, you know, how I feel because then when you do that I tend to feel invalidated so, but, so that helps to ... I certainly understand your, that situation. (*The patient is no longer annoyed. In fact, he is understanding and appreciative as he explains that by responding to him with an explanation that focuses on me, rather than on his emotions, he feels validated.)*

T: You deserve to be irritated and to get an answer. The only question that you need to look at is why you would begin to think it [my lateness] is on purpose and that it's intentional to irritate you. In other words, if you believe I am doing it intentionally, you might feel angry about being manipulated, but you also put me in a powerful, manipulating stance. You prefer to think that I know what I am doing rather than think I have my problems with time, managing sessions. *(Here, in a somewhat garbled fashion, I ask him to look at how his assumptions make me powerful and manipulative rather than just another person who, like him, struggles with being on time.)*

P: Yeah, that's true. I tend to either feel victimized by other people's actions or I blame myself for whatever seems to manifest itself. The way that I function is extremely upsetting to me and creates a lot of suffering that I don't feel is necessary. That I create an environment for myself where ... I am doomed to fail, even whether the business succeeds or doesn't succeed. *(He initially acknowledges the trouble caused by his assumptions about me [a cognitive exploration of how his thoughts affect his interactions] but quickly returns to his world of victimization and failure [his defensive stance of self-criticism and suffering].)*

T: You feel every day, every day is another failure or misery for you. You are saying it's a living hell. *(I check to see if I understand him and go along with his defensive shift because I have found that labeling his defenses has only led to more self-criticism.)*

P: I live in hell ... I do ... and ...

T: Which is very upsetting to hear about ... now you look away from me. *(I tell him how it makes me feel to hear how he suffers and that I notice that he looks away when I do this.)*

P: *(Pause)* I don't know why I looked away from you.

T: I don't know, I can only guess that it has something to do with me acknowledging that you live in hell and how upsetting it is to hear. *(I note that I don't know either so that I do not appear to be all knowing or omnipotent when I suggest a possible reason for his looking away.)*

P: *(Pause)* You know, I don't know why I looked away—you tell me.

T: I don't know why. You see, this is being put into the same ball game now, the same framework, that you don't have the answer. It's more of the same hell. All you need to do is look at how you are feeling, whatever the feelings are as we talk, what you see in my face, and what you experience when I say how painful it is to hear that you live in hell. How do you feel? *(I take a chance on linking his helpless defense to living in hell and then ask him to explore his reaction to my empathic statement.)*

P: Well, (*pause*) first off, the first time you said it I felt as though you were being sarcastic, but then I felt that you were sincere. And when I felt that, I am not sure, I think on one hand I have a feeling of kind of warmth and on the other hand I feel panicked by it in some way. I don't exactly know. (*I think the repetition of my empathic statement, in conjunction with our earlier positive interaction, made him feel that I cared about him and that this caused the sensation of warmth.*)

T: Uh-huh.

P: I am thinking about why I look away. Obviously there's something I don't want to see played back or [your] concern. I think that the difficulty I have with the concern has to do with a feeling that somehow it's going to be turned against me in some way. (*He begins to explore his feelings and thoughts rather than running back to his old defenses.*)

T: Huh? (*He has caught me by surprise and has to repeat things for me.*)

P: That oftentimes I, I was seduced and then I would be particularly vulnerable ... that is the way it feels now. I used to think that if I got the concern I would be more childlike and be taken care of. So maybe there's a part of it ... (*He continues to explore his fear of my concern for him.*)

T: This point you raised, about being seduced and then hurt causing you to have to stay away, could be the explanation for why you panic when you feel warmer. There's something there. The way we are going to find out what it is will be to stay with your feeling warmer and closer. If we go back to it bit by bit, and then see what happens, we will see because it clearly cues these reactions. (*I give him credit and encourage him to continue exploring. I also suggest that we examine his feelings slowly so that his anxiety is kept in check.*)

P: (*Nods*)

T: I mean, you know, this picture of a man who longs so much to be close for the warmth, but yet is so terrified of it ... and has to suffer, be alone, torment himself ... it's a very, very upsetting picture. You see, it's like you are starving but you fear the food. If you can imagine a child who wants so much but is terrified of asking. Terrified they would be hit or something ... it would upset you very much I think. (*I restate my concern for his painful predicament and then suggest he would be concerned if he knew of a child suffering in this way. Since it is easier for most people to care for others than to accept caring from them, I hope that he will feel his concern for the child and that this will cause him to recognize my concern for him even more.*)

P: Right.

T: And that's the way you describe yourself—as in this terrible predicament.

P: *(Pause)* Yeah, right, it makes me tearful as you describe it, as I hear it played back.

T: Uh-huh.

P: *(Pause)* It's hard to place myself, place myself in that spot where I can even begin to ... *(He begins to withdraw.)*

T: Yes, I think even letting yourself feel this concern is difficult, that it frightens you. I get the sense that it's as frightening as the warm feeling and that it's a terribly painful thing that you are struggling to stay away from. Because as I think about this and how you struggle to stay away from the warmth and from the hurt and the tears and the sadness, it becomes excruciatingly painful for me. It is as if you can't even be in touch with the pain because that will lead to more agony. That is what I am feeling anyway, and every time I see it, it hurts even more. *(I try to use empathic interaction to immerse him in compassion and the pain.)*

P: That's amazing.

T: Why?

P: Well, I mean, it's amazing that you can be so much in touch with it and I can't. *(He attempts to make me bigger and himself smaller. This is an old defensive maneuver for him, one that he used earlier in the session.)*

T: But you are in touch. You were crying, you said it made you teary. Now you want to attack yourself and say you are inadequate compared to me. *(I point out his return to this old defensive stance.)*

P: Yeah, I know ...

T: You are negative and avoid your feelings toward me, because you are afraid you are going to be vulnerable if you do anything but attack yourself. *(I repeat his explanation of why he runs from closeness.)*

P: *(Pause, sigh)* I am not sure how I feel about your ... it's like it's almost hard for me to believe that you can feel these things and yet if it's played back to me, if you were to say, supposing you saw this ... *(He connects with his feelings for the terrified child.)*

T: This same child.

P: This same child.

T: Who couldn't be angry or hurt or in pain because he would be open and vulnerable, then what do you feel? *(It seems that we are in tune at this point.)*

P: That makes me feel ... I can feel pain and sad ...

T: Yes.

P: For that child.

T: It's an awful feeling.

P: I mean it feels ... that's very loving (*pause*) you would have those feelings. (*He moves back from his feelings for the child to my feelings for him and then responds to my compassion.*)

T: Yes.

P: You know, I think that if I wasn't so afraid of feeling closer, that it would make me vulnerable, that I would feel much closer to you. I feel, I feel blocked by it ...

T: Uh-huh, you look like the feeling is there, that you are letting yourself taste a little of it. (*My perception is that he is no longer so distant, but that he is again slipping away.*)

P: But ...

T: You are beginning to live [in a good place] as opposed to the hell you had restricted yourself to. As you let yourself feel, tears come to your eyes, your voice catches, and some of your affection shows. If we use that little boy, if you can see that he is touched, but feels a little better and has some feelings of appreciation, that that would make you feel very good. (*When he spoke of feeling closer, I thought his voice and eyes changed. Since I want him to be more in touch with his feelings, I return to the image of the little boy that had helped him get in touch with his feelings earlier in the session.*)

P: Yeah ...

T: Yeah ...

P: Uh, one of the feelings that I am experiencing ...

T: A feeling?

P: In a sense, I was going to say unworthy, but that's not the word exactly. I feel, somehow, that I have awful thoughts, you know. I don't know exactly how to describe it, but it's like I feel cold inside somehow and that I feel like that coldness is sort of sitting on top of this warmth.

T: What happened?

P: That I feel, you know, I can feel a warmth for somebody else, and yet as you are clearly giving to me, I feel very shut down. It sort of reminds me of times that I know that others were clearly very loving and giving to me and that I feel ...

T: Yes?

P: Panicky or cold or uncaring. They don't really care, but are manipulating me.

T: So you undo the whole thing?

P: Yes.

T: But you described a picture of this cold stuff on top of the warm stuff. (*I am trying to block his retreat, but I am failing.*)

P: What I feel and fear is that I am really a monster.

T: You fear this, you, as the monster in hell?

P: Yeah, I see the monster in me.

T: Isn't our job here to let both the monster, the cold you, as well as the warm you come to the surface, so that you can feel all of you, that you can let yourself live, and let your emotions be something that you cherish? (*I try to reframe our task in a way that accepts the cold monster in him.*)

P: (*Pause*) Well, I think I feel that this monster is so big and ugly and if I let it, if I show this side of me … why does it come out when you …? That's when I feel the monster most. Of course, there's the monster in me beating myself up and I am not describing that because I am not making a judgment on the monster now, I am just saying that …

T: It is so amazing that you see yourself as such a monster. (*I stress how my perception of him is different from his own.*)

P: Why is it so amazing?

T: What is the worst monster you can imagine? (*It is a good idea to explore the patient's worst fears.*)

P: I am talking about someone who is so selfish about giving their heart and my being … (*Unfortunately, he begins to viciously attack himself in responding to my question. I have learned that it is best to divert him to prevent the self-attack from spiraling into a helpless depression.*)

T: You don't let yourself take anything. You torture yourself. You work your-self in a terrible way. Selfishness, no, it's more that you can't let yourself open up, feel, and receive. It's just like you don't let me give to you, you don't let others, it's hardly selfishness, and you are the gentlest monster … (*Again, I note that my perception of him is very different and that I see him as very gentle.*)

P: (*Sighs, pauses*)

T: You look away again. (*His silence and avoidance indicate that he is touched by my comments.*)

P: I want to open up … (*He tries to plead helplessness.*)

T: What happens inside, what do you feel inside when I say that you are the gentlest monster? You are looking away. My sense is that [what I said] struck you.

P: It did. It felt very warm and loving.

T: And you don't see yourself that way?

P: For an instant when you said that I did.

T: And how do you feel then, when you see that I perceive you that way and you see that there's some truth to that?

P: I feel good ... I feel (*crying*). (*As he takes in my caring and appreciation, he not only feels good, but cries. Are these tears of happiness, relief, remorse, longing, or pain?*)

T: And the tears, are they so terrible or are they part of being alive? Can you let yourself have the flow of the tears? Because these currents of emotions that you fight, make you very alive. They make you a man who is much more interactive and inviting. Do you know what I am getting at? You don't seem so hidden. You seem more available. Can you let the currents be something that you pay attention to and relish?

P: I guess I can ... I am really so busy covering it up ...

T: Uh-huh.

P: I would like to try.

T: Because I have a sense it's not so terrible right now, what you are going through, that these feelings are not so unpleasant, despite the fact that these are not happy things.

P: It feels good to be in touch with them.

T: And what are the feelings you have about yourself and about me, as this happens, as you let this flow? As I see you feeling more, it gives me a lot of pleasure. It is both a happiness and a sadness to see you taking that iron mask off. There is also a sense of you caring about me which also feels very good.

P: I feel, I feel warmth, a caring ... it feels, you know, I guess it's flowing both ways.

Following this session the patient became much less defensive. He no longer saw me as manipulative, and his angry responses to me decreased. Additionally, his vicious self-criticism disappeared, and he saw others more realistically. As he reexamined his relationships with the significant figures in his past and current life, he gradually understood why he had felt so weak and manipulated. He experienced a good deal of anger toward his stepfather and mother. With his increased understanding of himself came considerable remorse over lost opportunities and wasted years. After grieving those who had died or disappeared from his life, he reexamined his behavior with his wife and son and made significant improvements in these relationships. Treatment ended at the 65th session, 29 sessions after the pivotal 36th session.

Transcript from Follow-up Session

This session took place two years after treatment had ended. In it the patient reports on how he has changed and what he has come to value in his life.

P: My stepdad and I have clearly changed, but he has changed a lot.

T: Really?

P: He is as much a different person as I am. You know what I mean? I mean I also changed through our work here. I credit it all to you really. I have made a really significant character shift. I would say that he has too.

T: Really.

P: Yes, and he and I get along pretty well. (*Has his stepfather changed, does he just see him in a different light, or does his stepfather respond differently because he has changed?*)

T: That must be nice for both of you ...

P: Yeah, yeah, it really is.

T: So, let's talk about your changes first ...

P: Really ...

T: And then we'll go to his.

P: Well, I would say it's somewhat hard to describe it. I would say I am much more toned down and mellow than I was before. I mean, I had some things that really, that really bothered me, the whole way that I dealt with things. There definitely has been a change. I am not as worried as I was about all kinds of things and I have a much more optimistic outlook. I am self-confident, and I deal with people more directly. My expectation is different, too. I think there was a big gap between an expectation I had of myself and things that, in terms of what I should be doing and how things should turn out and of other people as well.

T: Uh huh.

P: I think I am much more loving and that is why I think, you know, I think I am being much more available ... and I am much better with my son than I was.

T: Good.

P: I am really enjoying that relationship and I miss him tremendously when I don't see him but ... I enjoy playing with him much more (*pause*). One of my biggest fears with him, I mean before I had him, if you remember, had to do with, that was why I didn't want a boy, because I was concerned about that he, somehow he was going to find me deficient.

T: Uh-huh.

P: And in some way a fraud, and that I wasn't going to be able to really give him all that much. I didn't have enough self-confidence in myself to be able to say, geez, it really is wonderful to be alive. I wasn't sure I could give him what he needed. I have learned a lot from him. That was a component that I never understood would be, would be a part of child-rearing but it's more … it's not of just giving but it's also seeing what comes from him. That it's sort of more, you know, a little guidance and, you know, a strong set of values and, you know, try to be strong for him. (*He no longer feels that he is deficient, but rather that he is a good father. He takes great pleasure in his son's love and appreciates the give and take between them.*)

T: Uh-huh.

P: So, you know, realizing I don't have to be perfect for him and that's not what he is going to want and that, you know, it's all about love … love and being there, listening to him and trying to … I mean it makes me tearful— it's just a wonderful, wonderful thing.

T: I know what you mean because I certainly had the same general experience. I didn't really have the foggiest as to what it would be like [until I had a child].

P: Uh-huh.

T: It's really an eye-opener having children.

P: Uh huh. Of course, people tell you that but …

T: I just didn't know all those things I was going to feel and then how much they love you is really a wonderful thing.

P: Also, it's wonderful for my son to have a grandpa who would care so much about him, to be so involved with him.

T: Well you know it's really good to see you.

P: It's really nice to be back. I was looking forward to this.

T: I remember the last time you were here. The first follow-up after you stopped therapy.

P: The last session?

T: Yes, how you just seemed so full of yourself and really warm. I was stunned. I thought that you really had continued to change remarkably in the absence of therapy. Meeting you today, I see that it's really continued. I mean you continued to evolve and also have maintained the gains. You really have a nice quality to you. So I am …

P: You should be pleased. I am really pleased too, you know. When I came in here, you can use this as an advertisement (*laughs*), I had really kind of pretty much given up on therapy. I mean I didn't have a whole lot of hope. I felt, I had gone through the whole stream of legitimate therapy and I just felt so reluctant, so resistant to change anything. So, even, with the earlier experience, I mean I was very, very disappointed. I was very reluctant to try it again. Of course, I didn't feel I had that many choices.

T: Yes.

P: So I am just tremendously grateful and just have to tell you that.

T: That's very nice of you to say.

P: Even though I have not been in contact, I have thought about you a lot and, you know, very warm thoughts.

T: I do too. You know we went through an evolution together. We struggled in the beginning. Later I began changing the way I was doing therapy, and I think as it changed it got better for both of us.

P: Yeah, I think that is true. When I came in, I have to say this, that coming in my first impressions in the beginning was probably in some ways it felt like the worst therapy that I had. I really felt that I had sort of smacked up against a brick wall (*laughing*). I felt that I had come in to someone I could not relate to, that in some way we were not going to bond or whatever. You know, clearly there was then a change in you. It was gradual in the beginning.

T: Yes.

P: And later there was a sort of turning point.

T: I think you are right.

P: And it was one of the most helpful things. You sort of, you know, took down the wall. There was a wall between us that dropped and allowed me to be more vulnerable and sort of let go.

T: I think you are right. I think that played a big role.

P: It was what I needed, it was what I needed. I am not saying it's right for everyone, but I really needed somehow to feel as though I was being understood and not just criticized.

You may be wondering, what "wall" dropped and how the lowering of the wall was accomplished. I believe the wall perceived by the patient grew out of the combination of the pressure I initially put on his defenses and his increasingly defensive response to my pressure. This interaction is described in the first session transcript. I believe my shift to a more supportive, interactive, and validating approach was the factor that lowered the wall. This shift was described in the transcript of the 36th session. The next section describes the techniques that appear to be responsible for the lowering of the wall.

AET Techniques

There are two reasons behind my selection of the nine techniques that are included in this section—their central role in AET and their relevance to the session transcripts contained in the prior sections. The nine techniques are:

1. Examining interactions
2. Empathizing
3. Showing compassion
4. Self-disclosure
5. Reframing defenses
6. Appreciating the patient
7. Avoiding omnipotence
8. Grieving loss
9. Reviewing videotapes

Examining Interactions

Examination of the patient-therapist interaction is the centerpiece of AET. It (1) improves communications, (2) brings defenses to light, (3) promotes shared affective experiences, and (4) leads to corrective experiences. The process begins with an examination of the reaction of a patient to a thera-pist intervention. Exploring the response of the patient to the therapist often reveals idiosyncratic reactions that are connected to the patient's prob-lems. The therapist has the opportunity to wonder aloud what caused the reaction. Often the patient has made assumptions about the therapist's mo-tives that the therapist can validate or dispute by sharing his or her thoughts and motives. The more these differences in perceptions are underscored, the more the patient begins to question his or her assumptions. This examina-tion also leads to the recognition of the link between these responses to the therapist and the problems the patient encounters with others.

Analysis of the patient-therapist interaction begins with the clarification of defenses and later leads to interpretations. The interpretations explain the defensive origins of patients' symptoms. Clarifications and interpretations are employed from the time of the first patient-therapist meeting. They have a powerful impact, because the patient begins to see a pattern in what had been unexplainable.

The following case example demonstrates the value of clarifying a patient's defensive pattern: When a male patient reported that he had become de-pressed after losing his girlfriend, I attempted to explore the pain and alone-ness he was experiencing. He responded to my questions by complaining, "This won't help." When I asked why it wouldn't help, he said that he already felt too much pain. I then shifted to exploring his anger toward his girlfriend, but he again said I wasn't helping him. I then asked if he was frustrated and upset by my questions and, therefore, angry with me. After he rejected this idea as well, I began to see that his reactions to my comments were becoming predictable.

I told the patient about my observation. I reviewed what had been happening by describing how he rejected each of my suggestions. He admitted he had not found my ideas helpful. I then told him that I experienced his responses to my comments as negative and rejecting and that I wondered if others reacted to him in this way. This caught his interest and he said that this had been one of his girlfriend's complaints. He now saw there was a pattern to his behavior and that it was linked to his isolation, depression, and failed relationships.

In this case, my recognition and disclosure of my reaction to the patient's rejecting behavior helped him to recognize his destructive style of interacting. Exploring the therapist's reaction to the patient is often the key to successful treatment. As I describe the remaining eight techniques, you will see that one of the themes that links them together is exploration of the therapist's feelings in reaction to the patient.

Empathizing

Empathy is the recognition by one person of the feelings of another person. This can take the form of understanding (cognitive empathy) or experiencing the same emotions (experiential empathy). While both are important for the therapist, I have found that it is the shared experience, experiential empathy, that means the most to patients. The shared experience creates a bond between patients and therapists that enables patients to bear feelings they could not tolerate alone. This, in itself, accelerates therapy because of the importance of the experience of previously unbearable emotions.

Virtually all therapists consider themselves to be empathic. However, not all patients view their therapists as empathic. When patients do not find their therapists to be empathic, it is because either the therapists are not sending adequate empathic messages or the patients are failing to perceive them. To increase the likelihood that patients will become aware of the empathy of their therapists, AET encourages therapists to (1) be expressive when communicating their feelings verbally and nonverbally and (2) watch for the responses of their patients. Do their patients understand what was being communicated? Do they misunderstand or block out the message despite the increased expressiveness of their therapists? Review of session videotapes reveals that such failures of communication are extremely common. Therefore, when you realize you are smiling or crying, it is wise to ask your patients questions such as, "What expression do you see on my face?"

Empathic interaction refers to the back and forth exchange of empathic feelings between patients and therapists. It leads to a sharing of feelings and helps to create a sense of closeness and support. The sense of closeness and support increases the patient's capacity to bear such painful feelings and so decreases reliance on defenses that had been used to avoid unbearable feelings. Another benefit of empathic interaction is that the sense of being supported evokes feelings of being cared for, which in turn can elicit strong emotions.

Showing Compassion

By compassion, I mean feeling for and caring about another person. It is important to show compassion, although it can be very hard for patients to accept it. Receiving compassion is painful when it evokes memories of yearning for, but not receiving, caring and appreciation. Yet, as patients are helped to receive compassion and bear pain, they are simultaneously relieved of their symptoms and begin to partake of the pleasure of contact with a caring figure.

This overtly supportive, compassionate therapist stance is quite different from that of the IS-TDP therapist who pressures the patient to drop his or her defenses (Davanloo, 1980). Regardless of the therapist's intentions, such exhortations are frequently experienced as criticism. The patient feels bad, ineffective, and frustrated. Pressuring the patient to fight his defenses is like pressuring a new skier to begin by skiing down a steep trail. The beginner is likely to fall, feel inadequate, and lose confidence.

On the other hand, when the AET therapist explains to the patient how defenses are a reasonable solution to a childhood problem, the patient is helped to understand and feel better about himself. The patient's perception of the therapist's genuine concern may resonate with the patient's longings for a caring figure. This in itself can bring painful past memories to the surface.

Self-disclosure

I have found that the disclosure of my own thoughts, feelings, and reactions to my patients has invariably moved their therapy forward. I present information about self-disclosure to patients during my initial explanation of the therapeutic process. I introduce self-disclosure by saying, "It's important to compare our thoughts and feelings if we are to work together productively. We may not always agree with each other, but we will gain from knowing how we differ. Telling me your thoughts will help me to understand you. I will be able to see linkages between your thinking and your behavior. However, you must let me know when my ideas don't seem right or when I seem to misunderstand you. Likewise, I will tell you my thoughts and let you know when I think you misunderstanding me. You'll profit from my feedback and I'll gain from yours." I then ask, "What do you think of working together this way? Do you have any questions or reservations?" After they answer, I ask, "How would you describe my proposal?" This gives me an opportunity to correct any misunderstandings and reassure them as need be.

Once we get this far, I add, "Let me explain why I tell you my thoughts. I do this so you can understand my reactions, why I feel a particular way or have come to a certain conclusion. Revealing myself in this way helps you to see me more realistically." Again, the patient's responses to my comments determine whether I need to explain myself more thoroughly or not. These responses also alert me to specific areas of conflict as well as the way the patient handles such conflicts.

Next, I explain why it is important that we describe and compare the emotions that arise as thoughts and memories are recounted. "You need to tell me your feelings, particularly upsetting feelings, as you become aware of them. These feelings and how you handle them may be linked to the symptoms that led you to seek help. Does this make sense to you?" Since patients often are unwilling to admit they disagree or do not understand, it is wise to ask them to put their understanding of the idea into words.

In the course of teaching patients about emotions, therapists often have an opportunity to introduce their own reactions as examples of how people can feel in various situations. Patients are frequently surprised that their therapists have emotions. Some believe that emotions are a sign of a loss of control or weakness. Naturally, they expect therapists to be free of such defects. Such misconceptions require repeated attention because they are tied to transference distortions. Sharing your emotions not only reduces transference and corrects distortions, but also makes the emotions seem normal. Understanding how others experience emotions, and seeing their comfort with them, validates them. Additionally, a bond is created when patients see areas where they are similar to you.

Reframing Defenses

Although defenses are employed to mask or bury painful, upsetting feelings, they also provide clues to the discovery of these same buried feelings. Patients are encouraged to join you in identifying defenses as valuable signposts that point the way to buried feelings. Reframing defenses can also be helpful to the therapist, for example, in the management of a patient who defensively floods with feelings. In flooding, real affects are exaggerated and prolonged. The patient who is wracked by sobs or pours out fury can frighten the therapist. If the frightened therapist becomes defensive, the alliance can be damaged. However, when the therapist acknowledges his or her discomfort and describes why it occurred, again stressing the value of openly examining their interaction, the alliance can be repaired. Patient and therapist can proceed to examine the immediate precipitant to the flooding.

Emphasizing the contribution made by the recognition of defenses increases the willingness of the patient to be open with the therapist. Rather than labeling the defense as a weakness or barrier, which is likely to cause the patient to feel criticized and become defensive, the therapist rewards the patient for sharing thoughts and feelings.

Appreciating the Patient

AET therapists acknowledge the difficulties faced by patients in treatment. They tell their patients that they recognize how hard it can be to reveal very personal, sometimes embarrassing, details about themselves and their families. In this way they acknowledge the anxiety their patients experience. Then, as patients begin to tell their stories, they praise them for their courage and their contribution to making therapy successful.

Patients generally are not aware of how much they are contributing to their treatment. These are the factors chiefly responsible for this lack of awareness:

1. Patients are prone to self-criticism, which leads them to criticize rather than appreciate their own efforts.
2. Patients believe that progress in therapy is the result of the interventions of the therapist. They overlook their own contributions.
3. Patients assume their therapists are dissatisfied when they have trouble answering their therapists' questions, when therapists become silent, when therapists repeat their questions, and when therapists focus on defenses.
4. Therapists may not recognize the contributions of their patients, or if they do recognize them, they may not think it is important to draw attention to them.

In AET, therapists actively work to make patients aware of their contributions in three ways. First, they take pressure off their patients. For instance, when patients are uncomfortable answering a question, AET therapists say they do not need to answer until they feel ready. This reduces patients' anxiety so that, in a short time, they often report that they are ready to answer the question. As a result, patients end up feeling productive and their anxiety falls even further. Second, therapists reframe the patient's defenses. For example, if the patient defensively becomes confused, therapists explain that the confusion indicates that they are approaching a sensitive topic. The topic causes anxiety, which in turn produces confusion. Since the discovery of sensitive topics is an important step in therapy, the identification of defenses is necessary in solving their problems. Third, therapists are overt in expressing their appreciation for their patients' contributions. These expressions of appreciation can produce surprising responses that bring strong, long-hidden feelings to consciousness.

Unfortunately, it would be a mistake to assume that patients believe or absorb therapist expressions of appreciation. If you ask, "How do you feel when I tell you how much your comments have helped me?" patients often tell you that they feel nothing. When asked why they feel nothing after being told that they are doing a good job, they often say they do not understand or believe the therapist. Sometimes patients say that the therapist's praise makes them uncomfortable or sad.

Receiving appreciation or praise touches on an important and sensitive issue for many patients. It is not surprising that they defend against it. Their defense against the pleasurable feelings produced by praise is due to the link between happy and sad feelings. Many have longed for their parents' appreciation, often working hard, but unsuccessfully, for it. Receiving their therapists' appreciation makes them happy for a moment, but also reminds them of their unfulfilled longing for their parents' appreciation, hence the sadness. The movie *Shine* provides an example of this. In it, the protagonist gives his first successful concert after years of incapacity. As he listens to the applause, his smile dissolves into tears, and his expression becomes one of pain, reflecting his years of suffering. This sequence mirrors the "happy then sad" reaction of patients when they first comprehend their therapist's appreciation. It often provides the first glimpse of the painful feelings that they have been avoiding.

Avoiding Omnipotence

Therapists who attempt to be open and reveal weaknesses often face powerful patient resistances. Nevertheless, therapists must reveal their very human failings if they are not to prolong or undermine treatment. Patients are slow to leave therapy when they feel dependent on an omnipotent therapist for their well-being. In fact, giving up the search for an omnipotent parental figure may be the primary therapeutic task facing them.

Patients may become upset when therapists reveal their flaws. Some have become incensed when I admitted that I had blind spots. They wanted an all-knowing caretaker rather than a collaborator who labored along with them to find the answers.

The negative reactions of patients to therapist weaknesses can be turned into grist for the therapeutic mill. Obviously, patients want highly competent rather than incompetent therapists, and they can be expected to become angry after being disappointed by their therapists. Depending on the therapeutic goal of the session, AET therapists choose among different options for working with angry, disappointed patients:

1. This may be a good time to explore the experience (thoughts, images, and body sensations) of anger with the therapist. It also provides an opportunity to be with an authority who is open rather than defensive about personal weaknesses. The result can be a corrective experience when the therapist neither collapses nor rejects the patient.
2. The patient may not be so self-critical in the future after seeing the therapist does not need to be perfect. The therapist has modeled self-acceptance versus self-criticism. Additionally, since therapist flaws have been acknowledged, the patient no longer has to take the blame to protect the therapist (parent) as he or she did as a child.
3. Idiosyncratic reactions can provide a chance to work on previously hidden problems. Such an opportunity occurred when a patient became enraged and said she was quitting therapy when she saw me cry following her description of a traumatic event. She explained that during her childhood she only had one functioning parent. When, one day, that parent collapsed in tears she had felt totally alone. I asked her to look at me and tell me if it looked like I had collapsed. She admitted that I did not. She began to see how she had generalized from this traumatic event and come to think that crying meant collapse and abandonment of her. Subsequently, she felt more secure. She was more open with me as well as less protective of me.

Grieving Loss

There are many losses in every life. Accepting them is rarely easy. Think of the dread of losing family, job, assets, or health. People naturally want to avoid the pain, fear, guilt, anger, and emptiness attending loss. In the prior section I described how people who wish for omnipotent therapists or teachers had, as children, often denied parental flaws, because recognizing the incompetence of their parents would have meant facing the fact that they were unprotected. They did not make use of opportunities to act independently and test their self-reliance during their childhood. After leaving home they became dependent on parental substitutes. When the frailties of the substitutes could not be denied, they felt betrayed and angrily rejected those parental figures. This, in turn, would be followed by a terrible sense of aloneness. Rather than bearing the aloneness and grief, they embarked on a search for a new parental substitute. Many of the symptoms and interpersonal problems that plague them are an outgrowth of their defensive attempts to avoid facing loss. The central task of their therapy becomes giving up the search for an omnipotent parental substitute and grieving the loss.

Imagery and empathy are central to the activation of grief. In using imagery, the therapist asks the patient to describe an interaction with the lost person. The interaction can be based on a real event or on a fantasy. The detailed description of the person, place, sensations, and dialogue reconnects the patient with his or her buried feelings.

The emotions released when grief is reactivated can feel unbearable. Empathy can be employed to help patients stay in touch with these distressing feelings. The empathic sharing of the patients' pain and disclosure of the therapist's personal experience of the pain, as in empathic interaction, are two techniques that can be used in this way. When the pain is shared, it eases and becomes more bearable. Patients who lose contact with their pain, when it becomes too strong, can be reconnected with a diluted form of it when they empathize with a therapist who has been empathizing with them. Both techniques facilitate grief by prolonging contact with the painful feelings growing out of the loss.

Reviewing Videotapes

In reviewing videotapes together, patients and therapists often make surprising discoveries. They come to see themselves as others see them. They observe how they misunderstand each other (Alpert, 1996). Additionally, almost all patients given the chance to review videotapes between sessions describe this experience as very profitable (Gassman, 1992).

Patients, like therapists, are initially upset by and preoccupied with their appearance when they see themselves on videotape. Both the upset and preoccupation are markedly diminished for most patients after the first hour of viewing. At this point they begin to pay more attention to their anxiety, body language, and defensive behavior.

The review of session videotapes is particularly useful for patients who (a) project their impulses, (b) cannot remember what occurred during sessions, (c) need to be in control, and (d) are extremely anxious in the presence of the therapist. Patients who project and then angrily attack their therapists are likely to do poorly in therapy. Viewing their session videotapes can dramatically alter their behavior. Often these patients are remorseful and express concern for their therapist after witnessing their behavior on tape. Therapists become less guarded after hearing the apology and may express their appreciation in return. The therapeutic alliance is strengthened and patients' projections become more manageable.

Viewing of taped sessions by patients can be more valuable than live sessions. Patients who are forgetful or easily confused can watch sessions as often as they need to in order to remember and understand the material. Their anxiety falls when they have the time they need. Patients who fear relinquishing control sometimes make more rapid progress when they have the option of viewing their tapes alone.

Videotaped sessions give all patients the opportunity to experience particularly important sessions more than once. The review of key sessions ensures that the lessons learned in them will not be forgotten. Some patients use these tapes at times of regression during treatment as well as after termination. In this way they quickly reestablish better functioning.

Finally, patients sometimes make significant progress on their own as they review their tapes. Such independent work also enhances self-confidence and shows them that they will be able to function on their own after treatment ends.

Conclusion

In this chapter I have attempted to provide an overview of AET, from its beginning, as it evolved from IS-TDP, to its current practice. To make the chapter reader-friendly I have avoided (not always successfully) technical jargon. I have made liberal use of case material for the same reason. This approach is in keeping with the theory and practice of AET. AET encourages therapists to avoid confusing terms and to give examples to facilitate patient understanding. AET therapists also ask patients to describe what their therapists' words and facial expressions mean to them.

The exploration of the interaction between therapist and patient is the key intervention in AET. It grew out of checking on the patient's perception and understanding of the therapist. It not only uncovers defenses but also brings the patient face to face with the therapist's concern for him or her. The examination of the experience of closeness, which grows out of such interactions, often leads to decreased defensiveness, a reduction of symptoms, and the recovery of traumatic memories.

TABLE 4.1
AET Guidelines

---

1. Acknowledge the patient's strong wish for help and the hard work done to get it.
2. Validate the patient.
3. Educate/explain your therapeutic interventions.
4. Empathize.
5. Show compassion.
6. Avoid struggles.
7. Follow the patient's lead when possible.
8. Note patterns.
9. Review videotapes
10. Monitor reactions to therapist comments.
11. *Discuss the interaction* between patient and therapist—not just the patient's reactions to therapist's comments, but also the therapist's reactions to the patient.
12. Examine the feelings evoked by the therapist's expression of compassion and appreciation.
13. Explore the reaction of the patient to images such as "a child in need" to get past resistance to seeing the therapist's compassion.
14. Use neuropsychological approaches to process traumatic material when anxiety paralyzes patients.
15. Monitor the patient's use of defenses (verbal and nonverbal).
16. Explain links between defenses, anxiety, and buried memories and feelings.
17. Share your feelings when the patient is struggling due to intense pain or anxiety

---

Table 4.1 contains the key recommendations made in this chapter. I hope that you are motivated by this chapter to apply some of these recommendations in your work and that they will prove useful to you.

References

Alpert, M. (1992). Accelerated empathic therapy: A new short-term dynamic psychotherapy. *International Journal of Short-Term Psychotherapy, 7,* 133–156.

Alpert, M. (1996). Videotaping psychotherapy. *Journal of Psychotherapy Practice & Research, 5,* 93–105.

Davanloo, H. (Ed.). (1978). *Basic principles and techniques in short-term dynamic psychotherapy.* New York: Spectrum.

Davanloo, H. (Ed.). (1980). *Short-term dynamic psychotherapy.* New York: Aronson.

Fosha, D. (1992). The interrelatedness of theory, technique and therapeutic stance: A comparative look at intensive short-term dynamic psychotherapy and accelerated empathic therapy. *International Journal of Short-term Psychotherapy, 7,* 157–176.

Gassman, D. (1992). Double exposure therapy: Videotape homework as a psychotherapeutic adjunct. *American Journal of Psychotherapy, 46*, 91–101.

Magnavita, J. (1993). The evolution of short-term dynamic psychotherapy: Treatment of the future? *Professional Psychology: Research and Practice, 24*(3), 360–365.

McCullough Vaillant, L. (1997). *Changing character: Short-term anxiety-regulating psychotherapy for restructuring defenses, affects, and attachment.* New York: Basic Books.

Schiffer, F. (1998). *Of two minds: The revolutionary science of dual-brain psychology.* New York: Free Press.

Shapiro, F. (1995). *Eye movement desensitization and reprocessing: Basic principles, protocols, and procedures.* New York: Guilford.

5

Trauma and Adaptive Information-Processing: EMDR's Dynamic and Behavioral Interface*

Francine Shapiro

THE CONNECTION BETWEEN eye movements and emotional distress was noted in the 1950s by dream researchers J. S. Antrobus and colleagues (1964). In a series of experiments they found that when subjects were emotionally disturbed, their eyes moved extremely rapidly. But Antrobus and Singer didn't pursue the effect that these eye movements might be having on the subject's emotions.

Many years later, in 1987, while walking in a park, I noticed a relationship between my eye movements and my thoughts. I had been thinking about something disturbing, and I noticed my eyes were moving rapidly from lower right to upper left. The thought would move out of my consciousness, and when I brought it back, it was no longer as upsetting. That initial observation was the starting point for my developing a therapeutic procedure. Initially, because of my behavioral background, I called this technique Eye Movement Desensitization. But this turned out to be a very bad name, because the desensitization appears to be only a by-product of an overall information-processing effect. So I later added on the term "Reprocessing." But it turned out that eye movement is only one form of stimulation that can be used. Hand taps, tones, lights can also be used—there are a variety of things that work (Shapiro, 1995, 1999,

*This chapter is an edited transcript of a presentation given at the 2000 Attachment and Trauma Conference at U.C.L.A.

2000; Shapiro & Forrest, 1997). So now we simply call the approach "EMDR," much as AT&T retains the name although telegraphs are no longer used. However, let me underscore that EMDR is much more than the component of eye movement or other stimulation.

This chapter reviews some of the pertinent elements of the model we use to guide EMDR practice and a variety of its clinical applications. Since the first application of EMDR was the treatment of posttraumatic stress disorder, we'll begin there. The International Society for Traumatic Stress Studies (Chemtob, Tolin, Van der Kolk, & Pitman, 2000) has accepted EMDR as a standard and effective treatment, which has been validated in comprehensive meta-analyses of all PTSD treatments (Van Etten & Taylor, 1998).

Diagnostic Issues

In *DSM-IV* terminology, PTSD develops in response to an event that involved "actual or threatened death, or serious injury," what we call a Big-T Trauma. Research shows that 25% of those exposed to a traumatic stressor develop PTSD (Green, 1994). That, of course, is simply a mean across a variety of traumatic events; the bottom line is that millions of people are affected each year.

Now, the problem with diagnosing PTSD is the specificity of symptoms necessary to meet *DSM-IV* criteria. You need to have it all—one from Column A, two from Column B—the whole *DSM-IV* menu has to be satisfied in order for a condition to be considered full-fledged PTSD. But in the experience of most clinicians, even when clients present with some negative aftereffects of various types of trauma, they may not suffer, for instance, intrusive thoughts, a requirement for a PTSD diagnosis.

In other words, even an event that is less than catastrophic—what we call small t-trauma—can cause lasting negative effects. In fact, most dysfunctional personality development is probably based on small-t traumas, those universal events that most of us experience. For example, being humiliated in grade school is a small t-trauma. But if you remember that experience, you know that it did not feel very small at the time. Your system felt overwhelmed. Neurobiologically, you experienced that humiliation as a survival issue, the evolutionary equivalent of being cut out of the herd. That type of overwhelmed feeling—as common as it may be—may have a lasting negative effect, even if we can't officially code it as PTSD. The lasting effect would, of course, be compounded by negative relationship events in one's family.

Landmark Studies of Psychotherapy and Behavior Therapy in PTSD

PTSD was included as a DSM diagnosis in 1980, and various modalities have been used to treat it. But the actual research into what works has, until recently, been fairly sparse. By 1992 there were only eleven controlled treatment outcome studies, five of which were drug studies (Solomon, Gerrity, & Muff, 1992). Only six were clinical practice studies. One on desensitization with posttraumatic stress disorder found that, after 45 sessions of desensitization, the subjects, when compared to no-treatment control group, showed some decline of symptoms (Peniston, 1986). A 1989 study compared desensitization, hypnosis, and psychodynamic therapy (Brom, Kleber, & Defares, 1989). It found that there were small to moderate changes in 60% of all subjects.

One of the most widely studied methods of treating PTSD is prolonged exposure therapy. The research that has come out on exposure therapy with PTSD makes it clear that the method works. In the study by Foa and colleagues (1991), rape victims were treated with 24 hours of imagined exposure therapy (7 sessions plus daily homework); at the end, 55% no longer had PTSD. It is important to note, however, that 28.6% had dropped out of treatment. In a study by Richards, Lovell, and Marks (1994) with boating accident victims who had been symptomatic for two years, 50 hours of imagined exposure therapy were used. In addition, patients were taken by the therapist to the harbor, to the boat—so they had in vivo exposure. They then had to do the same type of exposure for homework for an hour a day. In the end, after all that treatment, 100% of those who completed therapy no longer had PTSD. In another study from this clinic (Marks, Lovell, Noshirvani, Livanou, & Thrasher, 1998), 75% of mixed trauma victims no longer had PTSD after approximately 100 hours of imaginal and in vivo exposure.

Empirical Research on EMDR and PTSD

Studies of EMDR for PTSD began with my published controlled study in 1989. This has been supplemented with an additional 14 controlled studies (e.g., Ironson, Freund, Strauss, & Williams, in press; Marcus, Marquis, & Sakai, 1997; Rothbaum, 1997; Scheck, Schaeffer, & Gillette, 1998; Wilson, Becker, & Tinker, 1997), which clearly indicate EMDR's effectiveness. Although PTSD has been extremely difficult to treat in veteran populations, Howard Lipke, a former director of a PTSD unit at a Veterans Administration Medical Center, has made a compelling case for the utility of EMDR. What Lipke's review (2000) makes clear is that, when head-to-head comparisons of thera-peutic methods are made with appropriate controls in place, EMDR's effec-tiveness is demonstrated. Lipke cites the study by Carlson and colleagues (1998), which treated veterans with 12 sessions of EMDR or biofeedback. The study found that patients improved significantly more with EMDR as measured by "self-report, psychometric, and standardized interview mea-sures." In fact, 75% no longer had PTSD.

A study by Marcus et al. (1997) reported that EMDR subjects "[improved] significantly from baseline, and significantly more and more rapidly than the standard care group." Silver, Brooks, and Obenchain (1995) treated chronic PTSD cases and found that, compared to relaxation and biofeedback, EMDR showed "a statistically significant advantage," so much so that they called it the treatment of choice. When Rothbaum (1997) treated 10 rape victims with three EMDR sessions, only one had a post-treatment PTSD diagnosis, compared to nearly 90% of a waitlist control group. There are other studies, too numerous to mention here, with similarly positive results. Lipke (2000, pp. 10–11) ends his review with this quote from Van Etten and Taylor (1997, p.17):

> As noted, EMDR and behavior therapy were the most effective psychother-apies, and both were generally more effective than SSRI treatments. Effect sizes were large across all PTSD symptom domains for both treatments, and treatments were statistically comparable in efficacy. EMDR tended to be more effective than behavior therapy in treating depression and anxiety, and pro-duced large effect sizes for these measures where behavior therapy produced only moderate effect sizes. Although both treatments maintained effects at follow-up, EMDR tended to increase at follow-up, whereas behavior therapy effects remained stable, but did not increase notably. Moreover, EMDR treat-ments entailed less therapy (5 vs. 15 hours) over a shorter time period (4 vs. 10 weeks) in comparisons to behavior therapy.

Differences Between EMDR and Behavior Therapies

In reporting the research, I have noted the treatment time to emphasize the importance of examining different paradigms that we use. The exposure therapies used in cognitive behavior therapy are based on exposure habit-uation paradigms. As stated by Isaac Marks et al. (1998), "Exposure gradu-ally reduces defensive responses to cues to which the subject is exposed. This habituation depends upon the dose of exposure. Continuous stimula-tion in neuronal and immune system endocrine cells tends to dampen re-sponses, and intermittent stimulation tends to increase them." Theoretically, this is why exposure therapies are done as they are. It is believed that if you interrupt the exposure, or don't prolong it, or if you distract patients in any way, they will not improve. By this definition EMDR should make people worse.

EMDR uses interrupted exposure, free association, and an alternating stimulus (the eye movement, taps, or tones), all of which are considered by major exposure researchers (e.g., Boudewyns & Hyer, 1996) to be contrary to exposure theory. In EMDR therapy the client initially holds in mind the most disturbing part of the trauma. In response to the emotional stimulation caused by the memory, the clinician introduces either a set of eye movements or auditory tones or taps, and then changes appear to occur. Connections appear to be made. After about a minute, the clinician says, "Stop. What do you get now?" The client tells what came to mind and then, depending upon what the client says, the clinician asks him to attend to something new and does it again. These rounds continue, following the client's chains of association and going in and out of the experience. While this approach is directly contradictory to techniques that maintain that prolonged exposure is critical to effective treatment, it resembles in some ways a dynamic approach that utilizes free association. EMDR also departs from those theories that seek to hold the subject within the disturbance in order to achieve a release—a catharsis. Instead, we allow the patient's free associative process to take over. In an individual session, a patient may not be in touch with the disturbing memory for more than few moments.

Something remarkable happens with EMDR therapy for PTSD. Instead of 25, 50, or 100 hours of exposure, only three hours of treatment are needed to banish PTSD symptoms in more than three-quarters of subjects in some studies (e.g., Scheck et al., 1998). After four hours, diagnoses in 85% to 90% were eliminated (Rothbaum, 1997; Wilson et al., 1997), and after five hours of EMDR, 100% of single-trauma victims no longer suffered from PTSD (Marcus et al., 1997). How can we explain this?

Adaptive Information-Processing Model

The *accelerated or adaptive information-processing model* (Shapiro, 1991, 1994, 1995, 1999, 2001, in press) I have proposed is twofold:

1. What we perceive, what we retrieve, and how we react to the world are based upon associations.
2. Our physical (inherent) information-processing system is geared to transform mental disturbance to mental health. EMDR postulates

> "humans have an internal physiological mechanism that activates emotional healing when it is appropriately accessed and directed" (Shapiro & Forrest, 1997).

Our neurobiological processing system takes any perception we have and integrates it into a memory network. When something happens in the present, we link it up to past experiences and act accordingly. For instance, if something happens to us at work that bothers us—a disagreement with a coworker, let's say—we go home, we think about it, we talk about it, we dream about it, and the next morning it doesn't bother us the same way. We have figured out what to do about it. The initial negative physical sensations, the initial negative self-talk, and the negative emotional arousal—all are gone. The experience has been taken in and assimilated by the memory network and an adaptive solution has been found.

With most experiences, what is useful is learned. It is stored with appropriate emotion and can be retrieved to guide us appropriately in the future. What is useless can be let go. When a trauma occurs, this system becomes unbalanced and the perceptions that were there at the time of the event become locked in the brain in the form they were perceived, stored separately in their own neural network, if you will. No learning takes place, as the event cannot be linked up to other appropriate information. The trauma stays that way in neurobiological stasis, and the flashbacks, the nightmares, the intrusions of posttraumatic stress disorder are the perceptions that were there at the time of the event, sparked into mind/body consciousness by external or internal stimuli. The trauma can stay that way for years. The rape victim sees the rapist's face, feels his hands, the smell, the terror, all of it, because her perceptions are locked in the nervous system, because her information-processing system has become overloaded and unbalanced. We know that an experience has not been processed when we help someone bring it back to consciousness and they not only see an image or talk about the event, but also have the physical sensations and emotions that were there at the time.

EMDR accesses this information in a certain way. We stimulate the intrinsic information processing system and the targeted information package. What was seen, thought, heard, felt, all the physical and emotional sensations—and the beliefs the person has—start moving through the information-processing system until it is able to arrive at an adaptive resolution. We go in and out of the memory as the client brings it to mind; we add a set of stimulation, and enable connections to begin to get made. The clinician says, "blank it out" or "take a deep breath." Then new information comes to mind. Each set of eye movements or other stimulation can be seen as taking this targeted experience down a train track. Each set of eye movements is like one stop along the way. At each stop, some negative information gets off, some positive information gets on.

What is occurring during this ride is movement through the associated memory network. Although you begin with the most disturbing part of the memory, that is only a starting point. In the stimulation of the processing system clients will go where they need to go in order to arrive at an adaptive resolution. The clinician is primarily the facilitator of a process that allows clients to arrive at their own unique insights, solutions, and personal growth experiences. The therapeutic goal in EMDR is to allow a complete processing of the dysfunctional material and an enhancement of positive affects, insights, and behaviors. When it is properly administered, clients will most often engage in spontaneous processing; if the processing gets stuck, the clinician's job is to try to stimulate the memory mechanism and access the appropriate information in order to mimic spontaneous processing. In other words, how do you keep that information going down that track until it arrives where it needs to go?

Interface With the Psychodynamic Approach

Now, as I have said, if I had the chance to do it over again, I would not use the words "eye movement," because other forms of stimulation can be used. I wouldn't use the word "desensitization," since I now know that the procedure is more than simply taking away anxiety. It is the processing of information, the connections that are being made, that allows new insights to emerge and personal growth to occur. When one arrives at a state of integration, of assimilation, of connection, when those earlier experiences are no longer alone in biological stasis but connect to other adaptive associations— that is when learning takes place.

Let me give you an example. An earthquake victim came into therapy as a research subject. She was stuck with the image of hiding in the doorway during the earthquake. But it turned out that she actually had another earthquake experience as well. She had been in college, during a class in hypnosis. Her professor had just put her under hypnosis when the second earthquake struck. So, here she was, as an adult, with two Big-T Traumas.

After preparing her appropriately, she identified the image where she saw herself hiding in a doorway. She identified a negative belief she had about herself as being helpless. On a zero to ten scale, where zero was neutral and ten was the worst feeling she could think of, she was fearful at about an eight level. She felt it within her body and identified the location of the physical sensation. The therapist asked her to bring the fragments of memory together during a set of eye movements. She followed a set of eye movements, and was asked what came up for her. She remembered an experience with her brother that she was laughing about. So, although she started with a present-day experience, immediately she went back to a childhood experience. Next, she had another memory, one of betrayal by her brother. She had made a connection between the earth literally shaking and an earlier scene with her brother, where her reality had been shaken. Then she had another memory, hiding under her bed to escape the family chaos, which was reminiscent of hiding in the doorway during the chaos of the earthquake.

So we begin to see how networks of memories are associated. Networks are connected in all different directions. Remember, all this client came in for was her posttraumatic stress disorder because of the last earthquake experience that she had. But all of the other experiences are clearly contributing to her symptoms.

It is critical to understanding EMDR to note that memory connections are driven by the patient, not the therapist. In fact, if I were to try to make a psychodynamic interpretation of what was going on, I wouldn't have enough information. Instead, I simply tell patients to notice what's coming up. I do this in a fully supportive way, doing everything I would be doing in any therapy, holding the space to allow the client to go in and come out with the next connection that comes to mind. EMDR, as I've written elsewhere, "focuses on personal experience, it downplays what the therapist thinks of the event and, instead, deals directly with how the experience has affected the client" (Shapiro & Forrest, 1997).

If we think of EMDR as just another short-term talking therapy, the rapidity of the multifaceted change we observe doesn't make sense. In order to understand EMDR, we need to recognize that it deals directly with physiological aspects of storage. In addition, it integrates aspects of all the major psychological orientations (Shapiro, 2001, in press). EMDR doesn't simply deal with surface issues or simple problem-solving or desensitization. It's rapid, yes, but we are not offering patients band-aids. EMDR offers comprehensive, profound, and lasting change on emotional, cognitive, physiological, and spiritual levels. It is far beyond the simple alleviation of overt suffering—it is an enhancement of comprehensive growth.

At the same time, EMDR does have some affinity with psychodynamic thought, in that it postulates that an earlier event is inappropriately stored. The adaptive information-processing model suggests that this information is stored in neurobiological stasis and is generally the basis of most pathologies—not simply PTSD. The stored information involves not only the image, thoughts, and sounds of the earlier childhood events, but also the emotions and physical sensations, as well as the perspective and beliefs that the child had at the time. When somebody enters into a situation in the present that is at all reminiscent of the past, it is linked up in the same memory network—that is how the brain makes sense of the world. When the process is stuck, the present stimulus brings up emotions and physical sensations associated with the past event—unprocessed and unchanged—in the body and mind.

This is not a simple conditioning model. In a conditioning model one would say that anxiety has become associated with something over time. For instance, if you were hit a number of times with a belt, then seeing a belt draped over a chair might elicit anxiety in the present—a simple association of conditioned anxiety. In fact, through thousands of EMDR sessions it has become clear that for most dysfunctionally stored memories, such as those that induce fear or helplessness, it is not anxiety but earlier complex stored perceptual information in the brain that is elicited. When an earlier unprocessed childhood event comes up, the *child's perspective* emerges. That's why patients often talk about an early childhood trauma in the intonation of childhood. Their tone of voice changes, their facial expression changes, their body posture changes. They are feeling what they felt then. Although it is years since the event, the perceptions are stored in state-dependent form and are reexperienced in the present. This is possible because the experience is literally stored in the brain and it is reexperienced through the afferent/efferent nervous system.

It is important to understand that the *entire childhood perspective is stored.* Coming from a cognitive behavioral perspective, one would say the person *learned* that she was worthless or helpless and is reacting that way in the present because an association has been triggered. With the EMDR processing model, we are saying that in the moment the person is reexperiencing previously stored affects. It is not that I learned that I was helpless—at the moment when this comes up, *I am helpless.* In that moment, it's not that I am remembering feeling worthless or shameful—*I am worthless.* That earlier experience is coming up, and that's what I am feeling, and that's my personal identity at the moment.

Think of the implications in cases of chronic depression and deepening depression that continues or worsens despite medication. Isn't it possible that what's actually happening is that earlier experiences of helplessness and hopelessness from childhood are stored and then similar experiences that link up to that memory network automatically elicit that earlier response? So you have the helpless and hopeless feelings from the earlier experience arising, and in addition a reaction to a new experience, where one is equally helpless and hopeless, gets stored in that network. So the patient accumulates a heavier and heavier load of old experiences and old reactions. That's why the depression continues to worsen.

EMDR processing allows the therapist to go into any of these associated experiences, those earlier stored perceptions, and by processing them, move through different channels of association. This allows the patient to "metabolize" the experience, to integrate it in the appropriate networks. When events move from implicit to explicit memory storage, the associated physical sensations and emotions dissipate. According to the medical model, the body goes toward health and healing. If we cut our hand, the body is geared to close and heal, unless there is a block. If we remove the block, the body will go back to healing. The physiological system of the brain does the same. It moves toward adaptation and resolution. That's simply what our information-processing system is geared to do.

What is useful is learned. The experience becomes stored with appropriate emotion. What is useless is discarded. The physical sensations that were there at the time are no longer useful. The emotions that were there at the time of the arousal are no longer useful. The patient introduced earlier can remember, "I was in an earthquake, and when I'm in an earthquake, I learned that the best thing to do is to hide in a doorway, but I don't have to be feeling those feelings in order to react appropriately in the present. All of that can be discarded."

This is why, after successful therapy of whatever form, when you ask clients to go back and think about a childhood molestation, they can talk about what happened, they can forgive or not forgive, they can see responsibility or lack thereof. They no longer speak to you in the language of the child or from a position of powerlessness; they no longer show that experience in their body and mind, because the physical sensations, emotions, and child perspective are not there anymore. The child's perspective—that it is *my* fault, my responsibility, I did bad, I am shameful—all of those childhood feelings, which were encapsulated in neurobiological stasis and held that way for the last however many years, are no longer there. Other life experiences have been linked to the memory. Learning has taken place.

Think of Vietnam combat veterans, some of whom have been experiencing flashbacks, intrusions, and nightmares for over 25 years. They have had therapy, they have read self-help books, they have been able to forgive comrades for what they did, but they can't forgive themselves. They feel those feelings still. The network of Vietnam experiences has been shut off from the alternative positive network. Their information-processing has been blocked.

With EMDR processing of the information, we access those earlier experiences from Vietnam and stimulate the processing mechanism, and then those positive alternative networks are able to link in sequentially.

Isn't that what we mean by "insight," two neural networks linking up? The earlier information from childhood links up with mature understanding; that's when we see change on a facial level, a full body level, an emotional level, and an insight level. It is simply two networks linking up. And if that's the case, how long does therapy have to take? Perhaps the same profound insight that we are looking for in psychodynamic therapy or the belief changes that we are looking for in cognitive therapy can take place rapidly. If the notion of time can be shifted, what is the function of time in therapy? Ironically, the idea of rapid change is acceptable to us if the intervention comes in a pill. We can say, take "X" number of pills and 40 years of obsessive compulsive behavior will disappear, because the medication will change the brain state. The same thing can happen with EMDR, but the difference is that, when you take away the pill, the obsessive compulsive behavior may recur, while with EMDR the effects are lasting. Controlled studies that have looked at follow-ups of nine months, fifteen months, or longer show that EMDR therapeutic successes are permanent. I keep in contact with combat veterans who were treated eight years ago, and they are still fine. The therapy is like a digestion process. Once you have digested lunch, you can't go back to a reconstructed sandwich. It has already been digested. The change has been integrated.

The EMDR Treatment Process

There are eight phases to effective EMDR treatment:

Phase 1: Treatment plan	Phase 5: Installation
Phase 2: Preparation	Phase 6: Body scan
Phase 3: Assessment	Phase 7: Closure
Phase 4: Desensitization	Phase 8: Reevaluation

1. Treatment Plan

The EMDR treatment plan starts with taking the client's history and looking at a full map of the clinical territory. For instance, we find with PTSD that people generally have greater susceptibility because of early childhood events; therefore, we take an early childhood history to uncover any traumatic events. When clinicians in the EMDR Humanitarian Assistance Program went to work with Hurricane Andrew victims a number of years ago, they found that within the first session 30% of the victims were no longer talking about the hurricane; instead, they were talking about early childhood events that gave them a feeling of helplessness and lack of control. We go back to that concept of the memory network. The brain links whatever occurs in the present to the past to make sense of it. And anything that happens in the present can access and trigger early experiences. So taking the client's history involves identifying traumatic events, problematic issues in the present, and skills and learning that need to be incorporated for the client to make up for the possible developmental deficits.

Clearly, if you have single-trauma PTSD and the patient's life has been safe, sane, and satisfying otherwise, then it is a very straightforward process. But what do we do with molestation victims, neglected children, the ones who throughout childhood have had one assault after another? Abilities to bond, experience joy, achieve object constancy, trust one's own perceptions, and make social connections might be missing because of severe early trauma. With EMDR we ask what will be needed to build those infrastructures and then incorporate that in our plan. When we talk about information-processing, what we are actually talking about is learning. We are orchestrating learning.

If you start from a negative platform, in EMDR the negative experiences, beliefs, images, and emotions become more diffuse and less valid. However, development also goes in a positive direction. Positive experiences, images, beliefs, and emotions are targeted and enhanced. When clients have little positive in their life, we use the transference in the therapeutic relationship to start introducing positive experiences that they did not have in childhood. We orchestrate these experiences in the relationship and then use EMDR to enhance the positive aspects and allow the individual to access them. Identifying both positive and negative experiences and attributes are all part of the initial clinical history-taking. We want to identify not only what needs to be processed *out* of the system but also what needs to be processed *into* it.

2. Preparation

The preparation phase ensures that clients have sufficient stability within the therapeutic relationship, within their own skin in terms of affect tolerance, and within their environment to be able to concentrate on the necessary processing. With someone with a dissociative disorder, it could take a year or more to build those infrastructures and the relationship necessary to do the work. Then processing can move down the track. If the person was insufficiently stabilized and just wanted to avoid key events or if she easily became afraid of her own emotions, then with EMDR the therapist might not only access the earlier events, but also elicit present terror.

During the preparation phase, we refine the work and help the stabilization of the client. If the problem is single-trauma PTSD, it is very straightforward. We teach clients a safe place technique, so that when they are disturbed, they know they can bring themselves back to it. We teach them metaphors that allow them to have an easier relationship with material as arises internally. We set up the truth-telling relationship with the clinician. Then we are set to go. Within a couple of sessions we can focus on the early trauma. But if we are dealing with serial molestation, a history of neglect, or repeated childhood physical assault, then obviously the preparation phase is going to take longer.

3. Assessment

The assessment phase is a time to target the memory that we want to process and to identify the image that is most disturbing to the client. We identify the negative belief that goes along with it—I'm worthless, I'm dirty, I'm powerless, I'm going to be abandoned, I'm not loveable, etc. It is the negative belief the client presently has. And then we identify what belief he would prefer to have along that same lines. For example, an alternative positive belief to "I'm going to be abandoned" is "I'm secure in my relationship." The alternative to "I'm helpless" is "I am now in control." Starting with the negative allows the client to begin to develop an understanding of the irrationality of his feelings, and identifying a positive alternative begins to light up the positive network that can be connected.

We then bring together the image and the negative belief and identify the client's emotion. This is significant because the emotion can be anything—guilt, shame, sadness, or anger. Commonly during an EMDR session, we see movement through these different emotions. We want to make sure where you are starting because that tells you what type of support is needed, and it also tells you literally where we are beginning. Is the person experiencing a shame-based response, or terror, or anger? This is going tell us what type of processing is needed. Then we identify the emotional level, from zero as neutral and ten as the worst they can think of. Is it minor at a two? Is it high at an eight or a ten? And then, most importantly, we ask where they feel it in their body. The body gives the physical resonance to the cognitive process, and the body reactivity will let us know whether or not the information has been processed.

We can try a little experiment to demonstrate the importance of feeling in the body. Close your eyes and just notice how your body feels. Just bring up a memory of having been humiliated in childhood and notice what happens in your body. Notice what thoughts come up about it. Now bring a curtain down over it, shake your body, bring in white light, do whatever you need to do to just get rid of it. Perhaps when you brought up that early memory you felt your body shift somewhat, you felt you had the same thoughts you had at that time. We would say that physical reactivity indicates that information has not been processed. And if you look at the characteristics of that earlier event, you might see that some of its tentacles are wrapped around things that are happening for you in the present. Maybe there is a connection between that and difficulty you have learning in public or speaking in public, or with authorities or with groups, or with new people—whatever. When something similar happens, it links up to a previous memory network, and if there are dysfunctionally stored earlier events, then those emotions and physical reactions emerge.

People who have PTSD are, we might say, the relatively lucky ones, because to diagnose PTSD you have to have an image, so you know the source of the disturbance. For other problems or diagnoses, reactions occur in the present but we don't know why. However, if we go back deep enough, we often find that these types of earlier small t-traumas are at the root of the symptomatology. The physical reactivity lets us know about the need for processing. We don't know why it is that for some people these events remain unprocessed and stuck in that manner and for others they are processed. But we do know that when we search for these earlier experiences with EMDR, sometimes we find that by identifying the earliest events that the client reports around that theme, we can go into even earlier events that had not previously been remembered. We follow the associative network. Everything that occurs with free association occurs with EMDR, but more rapidly and apparently it happens directly at the psychophysiological level.

4. Desensitization

During the desensitization phase we use the zero-to-ten scale to check whether or not the emotional aspect has been dealt with. It involves going down that memory network, where other associations, connections, insights, and memories are emerging. It is *not* just "follow my fingers with your eyes." There are a lot of procedural elements, including what you do when things get stuck and what you do in order to keep the processing dynamic.

5. Installation

The installation phase takes the positive belief and allows it to expand and link to the targeted network. We identify the most positive belief, concept, or insight that has emerged during the session and allow that to connect more fully to this associated memory network.

6. Body Scan

During the body scan the client thinks of the earlier target and the positive belief and then scans for any residual body tension. If tension remains that may indicate other channels of information that need to be processed.

7. Closure

Closure brings the client back to equilibrium at the end of each session, prepares him for the following week, and engages him in keeping a record of what happens during the week, so that at the next session we will know what needs to be done.

8. Reevaluation

During each session we clean out and go through as many networks and channels as possible, but then others might open and emerge during the week. At the next session we follow up to see if there are any ripples from the targeted material: Have they been having nightmares? Have other perspectives emerged? What do you want the client to deal with? This reevaluation phase allows us to reassess and retarget and directs our future work. So, this is not one-session therapy. It is going to take as long as it takes. It is simply more focused than most therapies since there seem to be certain typical patterns of memory association we can use in order to make sure that processing occurs rapidly and comprehensively. Different protocols are used for specific complaints.

EMDR and The Emergence of Self

The fundamental goal of EMDR treatment is to liberate the client from past experiences. Basically, *it is about how certain experiences are stored*, because they are defining who I am and how I feel about myself. A molestation client may be locked in time because of the momentary thought that went through her mind twenty years earlier as her father was raping her: "Do it and I'll have you for the rest of my life." That has been her sense of self since that time. It is the association with having done and caused this terrible thing that is the basis of her current negative self-image. After about fifty minutes of EMDR go back and ask, How is it stored now? She goes back to the pivotal image and says, "Well, I'm not feeling much." Not much in terms of emotional reaction. We might say that we have arrived at a behavioral desensitization. Is that all we want? No, I want to go further. And so we have her think of it again and continue the EMDR work, because the desensitization, the removal of the anxiety around it, is only a part of the work. Now we ask her, "When you think the words, 'I was an abused child,' how do you feel?" We are bringing in elements of cognitive therapy, because her goal was to not feel "like a whore." She wanted to believe that she was an "abused child." But how powerful is the identity of an abused child? Is that where we want our clients to be?

Clearly, we have the equivalent at this point of cognitive restructuring. She says, "I no longer feel I am a whore. I can feel, yes, I was an abused child." You can see it on her face, you can hear it. As she says, "It feels like a matter of fact." But that, again, is only part of the work, because we know that for any abused child beneath the surface, there is generally still the tendency to blame oneself, still the irrational sense of responsibility. We want to make sure to check for this. Bringing attention to that aspect of responsibility, we continue the processing, because the therapeutic work is not about taking away—it is about transmutation of the information. It's about changing the texture and the emotional and physical meaning. It's about positive identity growth. We know that the negative experience will always be in her background, but how does it reside in her? Fully expunging the negative effects on self and transmuting the memory into a positive growth experience is the ultimate work.

During the EMDR session, the client attains a redefinition of self. At the end of the session, after additional processing, she says, "I did live through this and I'm a strong resilient woman now." The same experience resides in her memory network, but it has a different sense of self connected with it, because it has been connected to other associations and other life experiences. This is a natural outgrowth of the processing experience. When it does not happen spontaneously, the clinician can assist in engendering it. EMDR is a catalyst to a natural growth process. The rapidity of EMDR work allows you to see the therapeutic process being telescoped. Consequently, what EMDR also has to offer us is an opportunity to examine what experiences we need to orchestrate to encourage comprehensive growth processes. Since results can be seen almost immediately with EMDR, it can help us to define the developmental processes necessary to move to a fully structured healthy human being, as well as to undo the earlier deficits and problematic areas.

References

Antrobus, J. S., Antrobus, J. S., & Singer, J. L. (1964). Eye movements accompanying daydreaming, visual imagery, and thought suppression. *Journal of Abnormal and Social Psychology, 69,* 244–252.

Boudewyns, P. A., & Hyer, L. A. (1996). Eye movement desensitization and reprocessing (EMDR) as treatment for post-traumatic stress disorder (PTSD). *Clinical Psychology and Psychiatry, 3,* 185–195.

Brom, D., Kleber, R. J., & Defares, P. B. (1989). Brief psychotherapy for posttraumatic stress disorder. *Journal of Consulting and Clinical Psychology, 57,* 607–612.

Carlson, J. G., Chemtob, C. M., Rusnak, K., Hedlund, N. L., & Muraoka, M. Y. (1998). Eye movement desensitization and reprocessing for combat-related posttraumatic stress disorder. *Journal of Traumatic Stress, 11,* 3–24.

Chemtob, C. M., Tolin, D. F., van der Kolk, B. A., & Pitman, R. K. (2000). Eye movement desensitization and reprocessing. In E. A. Foa, T. M. Keane, & M. J. Friedman (Eds.), *Effective treatments for PTSD: Practice guidelines from the International Society for Traumatic Stress Studies.* New York: Guilford.

Foa, E. B., Rothbaum, B., Riggs, D. S., & Murdock, T. B. (1991). Treatment of posttraumatic stress disorder in rape victims: A comparison between cognitive behavioral procedures and counseling. *Journal of Consulting and Clinical Psychology, 59,* 715–723.

Green, B. L. (1994). Psychological research in traumatic stress: An update. *Journal of Traumatic Stress,* 341–362.

Ironson, G. I., Freund, B., Strauss, J. L., & Williams, J. (in press). A comparison of two treatments for traumatic stress: A community-based study of EMDR and prolonged exposure. *Journal of Clinical Psychology.*

Lipke, H. (2000). *EMDR and psychotherapy integration: Theoretical and clinical suggestions with a focus on traumatic stress.* Boca Raton, FL: CRC.

Marcus, S., Marquis, P., & Sakai, C. (1997). Controlled study of treatment of PTSD using EMDR in an HMO setting. *Psychotherapy, 34,* 307–315.

Marks, I., Lovell, K., Noshirvani, H., Livanou, M., & Thrasher, S. (1998). Treatment of posttraumatic stress disorder by exposure and/or cognitive restructuring: A controlled study. *Archives of General Psychiatry, 55,* 317–325.

Peniston, E. G. (1986). EMG biofeedback-assisted desensitization treatment for Vietnam combat veterans post-traumatic stress disorder. *Clinical Biofeedback Health, 9,* 35–41.

Richards, D. A., Lovell, K., & Marks, I. M. (1994). Post-traumatic stress disorder: Evaluation of a behavioral treatment program. *Journal of Traumatic Stress, 7,* 669–680.

Rothbaum, B. O. (1997). A controlled study of eye movement desensitization and reprocessing for posttraumatic stress disordered sexual assault victims. *Bulletin of the Menninger Clinic, 61,* 317–334.

Scheck, M. M., Schaeffer, J. A., & Gillette, C. S. (1998). Brief psychological intervention with traumatized young women: The efficacy of eye movement desensitization and reprocessing. *Journal of Traumatic Stress, 11,* 5–44.

Shapiro, F. (1989). Efficacy of the eye movement desensitization procedure in the treatment of traumatic memories. *Journal of Traumatic Stress Studies, 2,* 199–223.

Shapiro, F. (1991). Eye movement desensitization and reprocessing procedure: From EMD to EMD/R—a new treatment model for anxiety and related traumata. *Behavior Therapist, 14*, 133–135.

Shapiro, F. (1994). EMDR: In the eye of a paradigm shift. *Behavior Therapist, 17*, 153–158.

Shapiro, F. (1995). *Eye movement desensitization and reprocessing: Basic principles, protocols and procedures.* New York: Guilford.

Shapiro, F. (1999). Eye movement desensitization and reprocessing (EMDR): Clinical and research implications of an integrated psychotherapy treatment. *Journal of Anxiety Disorders, 13*, 35–67.

Shapiro, F. (2001). *Eye movement desensitization and reprocessing: Basic principles, protocols, and procedures (2nd ed.).* New York: Guilford.

Shapiro, F. (in press). *EMDR and the paradigm prism: Experts of diverse orientations explore an integrated treatment.* Washington, DC: American Psychological Association Press.

Shapiro, F., & Forrest, M. (1997). *EMDR: The breakthrough therapy for overcoming anxiety, stress and trauma.* New York: Basic Books.

Silver, S. M., Brooks, A., & Obenchain, J. (1995). Eye movement desensitization and reprocessing treatment of Vietnam war veterans with PTSD: Comparative effects with biofeedback and relaxation training. *Journal of Traumatic Stress, 8*, 337–342.

Solomon, S. D., Gerrity, E. T., & Muff, A. M. (1992). Efficacy of treatments for post-traumatic stress disorder. *JAMA, 268*, 633–638.

Van Etten, M., & Taylor, S. (1997). *Comparative efficacy of treatments for posttraumatic stress disorder: A meta-analysis.* Paper presented in the symposium "Basic and Applied Trauma Research: New Findings" at the 27th Congress of the European Association for Cognitive and Behavioural Therapies.

Van Etten, M. L., & Taylor, S. (1998). Comparative efficacy of treatments for post-traumatic stress disorder: A meta-analysis. *Clinical Psychology & Psychotherapy, 5*, 126–144.

Wilson, S. A., Becker, L. A., & Tinker, R. H. (1997). Fifteen-month follow-up of eye movement desensitization and reprocessing (EMDR) treatment for PTSD and psychological trauma. *Journal of Consulting and Clinical Psychology, 65*, 1047–1056.

6

Breaking the Deadlock
of Marital Collusion

Marion F. Solomon

COUPLES ON A WIDE SPECTRUM seek marital therapy. Some have situational problems involving how to get along with each other on a day-to-day basis. Other couples appear to have problems getting along with each other, but on closer inspection we find that the intrapsychic role each member of the couple plays for the other has become seriously disordered. These relationships are painfully stalemated because the problems of each member of the couple satisfy unconscious neurotic needs in the partner. The partners have established a pattern of interlocking difficulties that prevents them from solving either their own problems or the problems in their relationship. Therefore, the partners feel tormented and trapped, usually blaming each other for causing the continual discomfort they both experience. This chapter clarifies the differences in the kinds of couples who seek treatment and focuses on treatment techniques for a range of negative relationship patterns, with particular emphasis on dealing with the stalemated couple.

Many intimate relationships succeed or fail because emotional interactions between the partners recreate the emotional experiences of early life. Marriage, Dicks (1953) has noted, is the nearest adult equivalent of the bond between infant and mother. Emotional health and personal enjoyment arise from the ability to experience "the joy of being known and accepted by another" (Beavers, 1985, p. 52). "The outstanding quality of the intimate experience is the sense of being in touch with our real selves in the presence of the other" (Malone & Malone, 1987, p. 19). This intimacy, although dependent on the presence of another person, is centered within each member of the relationship dyad. The self is seen through the eyes of "another who has an abiding interest" (Kelly, 1996, p. 60). Repeated failure in experiencing the self through the eyes of the other causes the greatest distress in intimate relationships. Kohut has noted:

> A good marriage is one in which one or the other partner rises to the challenge of providing the functions that the other's temporarily impaired self needs at a particular moment. And who can potentially respond with more accurate empathic resonance to a person's needs than his or her marital partner? And, conversely, who—as every analyst has ample opportunity to observe—can traumatize a person more than a wife or husband who . . . responds with flawed understanding or, feeling overburdened, refuses to respond at all? This is indeed the stuff of which the breakup of marriages accompanied by the underlying hatred of the marital partners for each other is made. (1984, p. 220)

Attachments, Affects, and the Making of a Pathological Relationship

People do not marry with the intention of living out their worst relationship nightmare. Unconsciously, they select a partner whose qualities remind them of a parent whose love they yearned for, but too often in vain. Having stealthily defended themselves against awareness of rage at parental failures, they are unable to identify the source of their failure to maintain a loving bond. The defenses they have formed to protect an original love object and themselves from sadistic impulses now poison their adult relationship.

Feelings that give rise to anxiety and defenses do not exist in a vacuum but arise from interactions with others. All human beings begin life with the basic need for nourishment and warmth, for emotional resonance and physical contact, for recognition and affirmation, as well as for reliable, salient boundaries.

An individual's particular way of being in the world grows as he or she traverses the pathway from infantile dependence to a more mature mutuality in relationships. When the primary affects such as joy, excitement, anger, sadness, grief, fear, shame, and disgust (Tomkins, 1963, 1980) are met with welcome acceptance by attachment figures, healthy development is enhanced. Alternatively, when a child's negatively laden affective experiences are responded to with injunctions that sharing such emotions is bad, then the working model of relationships that develops includes shame, guilt, and anxiety, along with defenses against these feelings.

Stern (1985) describes the clustering of emotional responses in early bonding experiences and notes that generalized representations of lived experience become embedded early and repeated in later interactions with important others. Thus, "memory, a central element of the inmost self, is inevitably linked with affect" (Kelly, 1996, p. 65). Affect, then, plays a significant role in the solidity or fragility of the inmost self.

Effect of Environment

In every culture there are prohibitions against certain behaviors of children. In every family, as well, cultural prescriptions, intergenerational dynamics, religious beliefs, and personal idiosyncrasies of the adults in the home determine the reaction to children's emotions. Not only will certain feelings such as anger be prohibited, but also in some families nothing is experienced as more threatening, or more heavily prohibited, than the expression of loving feelings (Della Selva, 1996; Suttie, 1937/1988). Adults usually do not know why they defend against feelings; nor do they recognize a tendency to protect against emergence of unconscious affect. Often, the "decision" to close off to feeling was made at an age when the language was not available to support active memory of the crucial events and reactions that produced the entrenched defensive reaction. For that reason, the feelings in question are not ordinarily accessible to the conscious mind.

Early attachment failures are instilled as working models of relatedness (Stern, 1985). Subsequent failure of contact creates uncontainable feelings that can remain throughout the course of life. Emergence of dangerous impulses causes intense anxiety, what Leigh McCullough (chapter 3) calls "affect phobia," and defenses are mobilized to obstruct awareness of the painful, anxiety-provoking thoughts and feelings. The inability to experience emotions, caused by early disruptions in normal affect and thwarted development of one's inmost self, can lead to lifelong difficulties with intimacy. By the time the person with such attachment dysfunction has reached adulthood, the disrupted growth often has led to disturbed and disappointing relationships, leaving the person more vulnerable to failure each time. The wall between self and others is erected early and is solidly rooted. Sadly, the problem is continually replayed until the unconscious impulses are brought into the open, made part of the self, and contained within the relationship (Della Selva, 1996).

The young child is totally dependent on those in his or her environment. If the child's experience of an affect-laden situation triggers intense emotional responses and is repeatedly met by the caregiver's negative reactions, the original emotional response will eventually transform into anxiety, shame, and guilt. Over time, any stirring of emotion will automatically elicit anxiety or shame, which are the building blocks of a defensive posture. Once learned, the defenses guarantee that what happened in the past will not be intolerably painful in the present.

MODES OF FUNCTIONING

Different relational environments evoke different modes of functioning. At one extreme is optimal safety; at the other are conditions experienced as threatening. One way of being with another is through risk-taking that is powered by a drive toward a corrective emotional experience (Alexander & French, 1946; Fosha, 1995). The other mode is dread-driven and is manifested in what Freud (1923) labeled the "repetition compulsion" (Fosha, 2000). When anxiety and defensive responding are intense, the person is likely to perceive danger and to repeat painful past patterns of interaction. In such cases, there is less likelihood of experiencing safety and the possibility of viewing things differently. Emotional resilience enhances the capacity to create environments conducive to growth and raises the threshold at which environments are experienced as threatening.

Fosha (2000) depicts a schema representing functioning that results from experiences with caretakers. The STDP triangle of conflict shown in Figure 6.1 depicts the intrapsychic structure of emotional experience. The defensive reactions become a feedback loop that arises from early, repeated emotional traumas and from the secondary affects that they generate. Continued reliance on defenses leads to trouble, as blocked affect is invariably reactivated by interpersonal situations reminiscent of the situation in which it originated (Fosha, 2000, p. 104).

The *triangle of defensive response* is seen in situations that are perceived as dangerous. This triangle represents functioning that results from experiences with caretakers, whose affective competence is compromised, leaving the child psychically alone in the face of overwhelming affects. As Fosha notes, "Feeling and dealing while relating is not possible in these circumstances" (p. 107). The *triangle of expressive response* (Figure 6.2) represents the risk-taking, hope-driven response to an emotion-facilitating environment in which trust is engaged and emotions are available to be accessed. Anxiety is still present, but is less pronounced and less entrenched.

When affects are not too frightening, shameful, or painful to tolerate, it is possible to think and feel at the same time. Feeling and dealing in

FIGURE 6.1
TRIANGLE OF DEFENSIVE RESPONSE

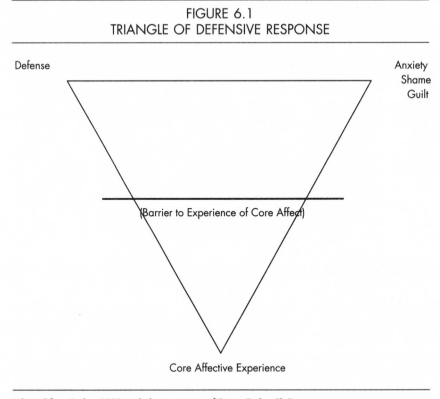

Defense   Anxiety
                                                                         Shame
                                                                         Guilt

(Barrier to Experience of Core Affect)

Core Affective Experience

Adapted from Fosha, 2000, with the permission of Diana Fosha, Ph.D.

affect-laden situations are then possible. This allows emotion along with internal dialogue about experiences in the relationship to exist without the need of defensive collusions to protect the vulnerable self of one partner or both.

When emotion is too shameful, painful, or frightening, feeling and dealing are not possible. People will do many things—preserve unhappy relationships, sink into deep depressions, or remain addicted to damaging substances or to love substitutes such as work, money, power, and sex—rather than face a change in their sense of who they are, even if they are miserable. Familiar unhappiness is safe; change involves risk and loss. Thus, a classic dilemma emerges: How can one expand one's identity, even in desirable, fulfilling ways, without losing the sense of an essential self? Moreover, how can one change one's sense of self when change invariably threatens the relational pact that has protected one from having to face the dark parts within?

FIGURE 6.2
TRIANGLE OF EXPRESSIVE RESPONSE

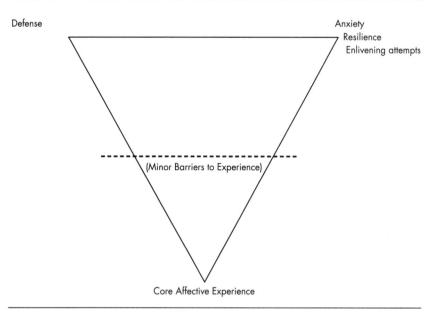

Defense   Anxiety
                                                               Resilience
                                                               Enlivening attempts

                            (Minor Barriers to Experience)

                            Core Affective Experience

Adapted from Fosha, with the permission of Diana Fosha, Ph.D.

Marriage is often the vehicle of choice to avoid changing. This is the beginning of the collusive resistance of severely disturbed couples.

The internal dialogue comes into awareness only through the affect system. When partners battle repeatedly over matters they cannot make sense
of later, it is likely that repressed or split-off affect with roots in very early
life has led to defensive enactments. If there is fear of provoking an angry response, or shame about certain fantasies, thoughts, or impulses, then one or
both use familiar, repeated dialogue to defend against frightening or dangerous affect. A relationship with such a dynamic confuses and frustrates the
partners and therapist alike.

Many couples enter therapy after a history of chronic disharmony has es-
calated to a deadlocked dyadic resistance. In almost a mirror opposite of the
bonds of new love, each partner focuses on the other's most flawed aspects
and has developed a pattern of defensive response to perceived injuries in-
flicted by the other. No longer able to sustain intimacy, the partners may experience periods of closeness alternating with repetitive clashes that keep

them enmeshed and frustrated at the same time. The question is why such a deadlocked relationship continues, with neither partner able to end it, and with both together unable to change the dynamics between them. When such couples come into therapy, each mate presents the other as the cause of their problems, but each secretly fears that the blame will be placed squarely on him or her. In such cases, both members of the couple put great energy into warding off shame, guilt, and rage. These couples require a very different kind of therapy than those who are not operating out of a solidly entrenched defensive pattern of relating.

Differential Diagnosis in Couples Therapy

Not all couples entering marital therapy display signs of psychopathology. Some problems really are caused by differences in values, beliefs, and expectations. The marital therapist needs to assess the emotional health of each of the partners, paying particular attention to how each may shape the other to fit pre-established defenses. Many couples, moreover, can make their relationship work despite individual disorders. Couples develop ways to be together that make allowance for individual difficulties. Nevertheless, many partners have severe difficulties in marriage, although they are relatively high functioning in the rest of their lives.

When the pathological disorders of both partners create a destructive deadlock in the relationship, psychological change in one partner may mean the end of the marriage if the other partner cannot or will not adapt. The fear of separation and divorce may result in an attempt to undermine the emotional growth of the partner who has changed. In extreme cases, partners find that they must choose between getting well or staying married. In other cases, the willingness of one partner to leave the relationship is the only thing that motivates the spouse to do something different. In either of these instances, change can be accomplished through a reworking of unconscious early attachment trauma.

The treatment of couples requires a differential diagnosis of the core relational issue in the interactions between the partners. Only then can the therapist select a mode of therapy that offers the possibility of change. Table 6.1 (pp. 138–140) presents a diagnostic schema for understanding relationships designed to clarify couples' dynamics. It is an overview of the kinds of imprinted patterns of relating between intimate partners that are seen in couples therapy, and includes a range of disturbances and defenses that includes most couples.

At the top of the table is a row of numbers from one to ten, which indicate the severity of pathological defenses in imprinted love patterns. The family therapy literature provides much evidence that people at the same level of pathology are drawn to each other (Gurman, 1978; Solomon, 1989). People who are in the high functional-adaptive range (9 and 10) are usually in relationships in which they are able to resolve problems when they arise. These are couples whose relationship problems are not the outgrowth of old family traumas, attachment failures, or cultural crises (war, famine, etc.). Their anxiety is fairly low and their defenses are adaptive rather than repressive, or worse, regressive. They do not erect barriers to emotional closeness and are open to the help offered by the therapist. Individuals of this type participate actively in the treatment, communicate their needs and distress, and are able to attune to the feelings communicated by a partner. They make meaningful links between their current partner and figures from the past. They do not use what they hear about a mate's earlier family experiences or current emotions against him or her. All couples encounter problems at times. Sometimes a relatively well-functioning couple needs the help of a therapist. When functional-adaptive couples seek help, they can choose from among a wide range of short-term treatments that focus on attuned communication and behavior change.

In the middle of the spectrum, the 7 and 8 clusters, are the neurotic-oedipal relationships often seen by couples therapists. These couples present a wide range of problems associated with "real life" issues, such as money, work, sex, and children. They often begin therapy with high levels of anxiety, because of their fear that unconscious emotions will break through. One member of the couple, or both, may activate repressive defenses immediately, denying that there is any problem, projecting problems onto the other, and explaining that a busy schedule precludes regular sessions with the mate. When this stratagem fails, regressive defenses, such as mood disorders, acting out, and externalization, may appear. These symptoms may cause significant personal distress, and the functioning of the relationship may be severely impaired.

Both partners may greatly desire change because the pain each experiences in the relationship is sufficiently severe that it overrides the impulse to sabotage the therapy completely. The deep pain caused by the imminent destruction of the relationship may be the basis for the therapeutic alliance and a motivation to endure the discomfort necessary to make genuine changes.

Those whose personality style falls in the borderline-narcissistic continuum, clusters 1 through 3 and 4 through 6, are likely to develop collusive relationships with others who have complementary defenses. Their presenting

TABLE 6.1
A Diagnostic Schema for Understanding Relationships

	1 BORDERLINE LOW	2 BORDERLINE MEDIUM	3 BORDERLINE HIGH
Fragility of Self	Very High	High	High
Resistance to Therapy	Very High	High	Moderate-High
Trauma	Lack of attunement by caregivers. Physical and emotional abuse. Self-abuse. Sustained failure in triangular relations.	Impaired attunement. Physical and emotional abuse common. Sustained failure in triangular relationships.	Disrupted attunement. Caregiver abuse variable. Repeated failure in triangular relationships.
Defenses	Boundary-bashing projections. Delusional fantasies. Primitive somatizaton. Hallucinatory wish fulfillment. Annihilation of the self.	Splitting and projective identification. Denial. Primitive idealization. Primitive dissociation. High somatization. Undoing. Physical mutilation of the self.	Projection. Introjection. Denial. Splitting. Primitive dissociation. Idealization. Some somatization. Compartmentalization of affect, turning aggression aginst the self.
Results on Self	No boundaries. Mood disorders. Mania. Depression. Impulsivity. Multiple personality states. Psychosomatic diseases. Suicidal behavior. Addictive behavior.	Faulty boundaries. Drug and alcohol abuse. Psychosomatic conditions. Unneeded medical procedures. Self-inflicted wounds. Dangerous self-stimulation. Stormy encounters with others.	Inconsistent boundaries. Pervasive sense of isolation. Lacking capacity to be alone. Omnipotent fantasies. Inordinate stimulation-seeking. Excessive limit-testing. Accident proneness. Substance abuse.
Effects on the Intimate Relationship	Chaos, crazy love, folie à deux. Reality always at question. Confusion over who caused what. Demand for absolute attunement. Explosive rage at disappointment.	Emotional blackmail to sustain fantasy of fusion. Identity fragments when separation occurs. Distances when intimacy too great. Expectation of mind reading by other (presumptive attunement).	Feels unrecognized and unacknowledged. Acts out aggression when disappointed in level of other's emotional availability. Children and others used as selfobjects. Turbulent relationships.

For a conference, "The Primitive Unconscious in Men and Women: Toward a Dynamic Theory of Relationships." Lifespan Learning Institute, June 5–6, 1998. Copyright © Marion Solomon, Ph.D. and Robert Neborsky, M.D.

TABLE 6.1 (continued)

	4 NARCISSISTIC/ MASOCHISTIC	5 NARCISSISTIC/ SADISTIC	6 NARCISSISTIC/ ALTERNATING
Fragility of Self	Moderate or High	Moderate or High	Moderate
Resistance to Therapy	Moderate High	Moderate	Moderate
Trauma	Disrupted attunement. Emotional disconnection by caregiver. Guilt and self-punishment common. Triangular relations blocked.	Emotionally unavailable caregiver. Inconsistent attunement. Guilt and self-punishment common. Triangular relations blocked.	Inconsistant attunement. Self-abuse common. Impaired capacity for triangular relations.
Defenses	Repression. Projective introjection. Identification with the victim. Veiled grandiosity. Avoidant distancing. Psychic destruction of the self and others.	Repression. Projective and introjective identification. Identification with the aggressor. Explosive discharge of affect. Aggressive distancing. Grandiosity. Psychic isolation of the self.	Repression. Projective and introjective identification. Psychic reciprocal mutilation and isolation of the self and other. Explosive discharge of affect (emotional or physical).
Results on Self	Martyrdom. Depression. Sense of defectiveness. Feels incomplete without powerful other person. Sets up rejection by others (concealed masochism). Loss of self boundaries under stress.	Preemptive retaliatory behavior against others for perceived injuries. Constant power plays lead to conflict with authority. Binds others to self by fear and dependency. Obsequious to strength, sadistic with weakness.	Wildly fluctuating affect. Seesaw definition of self. Massive depression when the loved one separates. Fluctuating self boundaries in stressful relationships. Proneness to substance abuse. Sense of superiority with underlying feelings of emptiness.
Effects on the Intimate Relationship	Instigates for abuse by others. Transfers power to others without accountability. Pathologic dependence on others. Compulsive caretaker to compensate for dependency.	Abuses others. Demands control over all decisions. Punishes transgressions overtly and/or covertly. Hides pathologic dependency through abuse of power.	Alternating states of abusing and being abused. Domestic violence. Marital stalemate determined by who has momentary power. Constant battle for control.

(Continued)

TABLE 6.1 (continued)

	7 NEUROTIC- OEDIPAL HYSTERICAL	8 NEUROTIC- OEDIPAL OBSESSIONAL	9 BASIC ADAPTIVE SELF- ORGANIZATION	10 MATURE ADAPTIVE SELF- ORGANIZATION
Fragility of Self	Moderate or Low	Low	Very Low	Very Low
Resistance to Therapy	Moderate or Low	Low	Very Low	Very Low
Trauma	Some impaired attunement. Needy, demanding caregiver creates parentified child. Some blocks in triangular relations.	Some impaired attunement. Extremely high expectations by caregiver. Some blocks in triangular relations.	Optimal frustration leading to resilient self. Anxiety free in triangular relationships.	Received appropriate attunement. Optimal frustration leading to resilient self. Anxiety free in triangular relationships.
Defenses	Dissociation of body sensation, selective unawareness of feelings. Conversion of emotions into physical symptoms, phobic avoidance, depersonalization, derealization, anxiousness, pseudo-affect.	Isolation of affect. Reaction formation. Distancing. Intellectualization. Rationalization. Displacement. Actual undoing. Compulsivity. Sublimation.	Tendency toward idealized love connections. Intellectual defenses. Dispenses humor. Sublimating. Creative. Expression of emotion.	Altruism. Humor. Sublimation. Appropriate self-assertion. Resolution of conflict through fantasy, artistic expression. Regression in the service of the ego.
Results on Self	Depression, false self, mirage, shallow feelings. Low libido under stress. Vulnerable to alcohol, sedative/hypnotic, marijuana abuse. Massive guilt for unconscious anger. Lack of barriers against intrusiveness of others.	Barriers between self and feelings. Wall between self and others. Excessively cognitive, avoids intimacy with others. Lives a somewhat arid emotional life, generally hidden from others. Mood disorders.	True self remains hidden. Successful facade makes self likable to others. Some moodiness.	Boundaries of self are permeable but strong. Full human potential can be actualized depending upon environmental opportunity. Opportunity to become self-actualized.
Effects on the Intimate Relationship	Manipulative lies of omission and commission. Creates images for effect. Sexual problems. Inordinate need for attention to define self. Allows abuse to atone for guilt.	Lack of intimacy. Boredom, alienation, deadened inner life. Waits for cues from others to define self.	Adaptive in relationships. Vulnerable to injury by others but recovers quickly.	Ability to love, work, play, parent, mentor. Achieves interconnectedness and interdependency. Ability to form supportive partnerships and community connections.

issues may vary but the underlying dynamics are similar. They form unconscious love bonds that help them to ward off painful or frightening emotions
and draw other members of their family into dysfunctional dynamics in order to defend a vulnerable inner core. Although they sometimes are quite
successful in other aspects of their lives, these individuals have fragile egos
and their relationships are almost invariably quite troubled.

The Functional-Adaptive Couple

A couple that offers little resistance will often present for the therapy with a
single focus of conflict. These are non-enmeshed couples with personality organization falling at level 9 or 10 in the diagnostic schema. Each member of
the couple has a mature, adaptive self-organization. These couples benefit
from an approach that emphasizes straightforward communication. Because
clarification of motives will usually help to eliminate simple misunderstandings, they will benefit from partnership education and homework assignments.
They are easily helped when they receive sexual counseling and education in
marital or parenting skills.

JULIE AND ED
Julie and Ed had been dating for two years and were engaged to marry when
Julie discovered she was pregnant. Ed was not thrilled. Their wedding was
set for June, and by that time Julie would be eight months pregnant. "I love
you and want us to marry and have children together," he said. "But we have
planned everything so carefully, our work, saving money for a house, starting a family in a couple of years. This isn't the time to have a baby."

"I know," she replied. "I was on the pill. I shouldn't have gotten pregnant.
I don't know how it happened. But I'm pregnant with your child. I can't bear
the thought of aborting our baby. I'm afraid of what it would do to us the
rest of our lives if we always had a memory of this child between us." For
some women this would not be a major issue, as it was for Julie. For some
men, having a baby with the woman they love would take precedence over
plans for a well-ordered, well-timed life.

Although Julie and Ed had strongly opposing feelings, they were able to
communicate their needs and wishes and were lovingly attuned to each other.
Therefore, they were able to resolve their conflict and did not get caught in
blame-or-shame syndrome, as couples with a collusive resistance pattern so
often do.

Ed said that to have the baby would disrupt his plans, and that they would
have to pare down their expectations about where they would live, but in

thirty years it probably wouldn't make much difference in their lifestyle. He did not want to put Julie or himself in the position of wondering whom their child might have become. "I'm still not crazy about it, but I would hate to have the big house we dreamed of filled with ghosts and an unhappy wife."

They made a decision that they both could live with. Nevertheless, when Ed said to Julie, "You owe me big," in a kidding tone, I knew it was not a joke. The *quid pro quo* of the relationship requires that, when there are differences and decisions to be made, each will hear the other out fully, and in things that are a high priority for one of them, his wishes will be considered as often as hers. The treatment for Julie and Ed was short-term, but their Christmas cards come each year with pictures of Jenny, now six, accompanied this year by a picture of twin sons. Couples like this are not stalemated, and the members of the couple do not need to expend their energy defending against the attachment trauma.

There are two necessary conditions for a healthy relationship: (a) clear boundaries and (b) emotional complementarity. There is a myth in the family therapy literature that has been long perpetuated; it is the rule of 50-50. Although it is important for the therapist working with a couple to assume that both have equal responsibility for the success or failure of a marriage, one can certainly suffer a higher degree of pathology than the other or possess a lower level of commitment to the success of the relationship. It takes two people working at it to make a relationship work but only one to destroy it.

The Neurotic-Oedipal Couple

The moderately resistant couple will typically have pathologies falling at level 7 or 8 in the diagnostic schema. Members of these couples have well integrated psyches but require some work at the unconscious level to overcome collusive patterns of relating to each other. In the moderately resistant couple, the partners have good boundaries, but one of the members of the dyad may be depressed, emotionally distant, overly demanding, or *parentifying* the other, thus sabotaging the growth of the relationship. Although the issues with which such a couple presents often at first seem to be about power and control, they more likely reflect some form of punishment to atone for guilt.

Therapy for such a couple might include education, clarification with extensive cognitive input, and gentle confrontation through light pressure on the cut-off feelings and maladaptive behavior. The purpose is to lead each of the partners through an exploration of affect, present and past, putting them in a position to make their own interpretations. Throughout the process, it is necessary for the therapist to observe feelings that influence each session and explore with the partners their experience of any similar feelings during the session or in their past relationships.

It is important to make affective links between present and past. When there are strong emotions, they are explored in terms of defenses against being hurt that were learned in the past. If resistance or defenses arise, they are reframed as normal reactions that developed in past painful relationships, and now provide an opportunity to explore what is being defended against. The examination of underlying emotions is encouraged, with the message that it is better to feel than to act the feelings out.

Use of gentle pressure on the repetitive pattern of defenses, which is almost always demonstrated as the spouses interact during sessions, mobilizes the unconscious of the partner who is using that pattern of defense. At the same time, it stimulates the reciprocal affect of the partner. Then it becomes possible to involve the partner, inviting him or her to examine, in the presence of the one who is sharing historical material, any associations or feelings that arise. In many instances, the pattern of behaving, thinking, and feeling being exposed closely resembles that developed in the presence of the parental figure.

Because we all have the capacity within our memories to "time travel," each member of the couple has the material necessary to work things through with the person closest to him or her in the present.

The Borderline-Narcissistic Couple

Highly resistant couples that constantly fight to a stalemate have a relationship dominated by disorders in the borderline-narcissistic spectrum. The hallmark of all of these types of relationships is the inability to tolerate separateness, resulting in poor boundaries between self and other. The psychic organization of each partner depends upon the presence of the other; one or both may demonstrate poor object constancy. Typically, extreme emotional abuse, physical abuse, and acting out occur when one member of the dyad attempts to move toward autonomy or takes an independent action. Although they share these important similarities, those in borderline-narcissistic relationships nevertheless divide into six distinct types, presented in Table 6.1 as types 1 through 6.

A damaged person may come to fantasize a marriage as a blissful haven, free from pain. In fairy tales, the loving kiss of a true princess transforms the frog into a real human being, and the loving kiss of a handsome prince awakens the sleeping princess to a happy world. Although the reality of a marriage cannot deliver such redemption, the wish for redemption from damage in early life remains to be assimilated into a pathological relationship. On a conscious level, each partner searches for one who will embrace him or her and be totally accepting. When this wish fails to come true and conflict ensues, reenactment of the past begins to contaminate the relationship, kindling the sadomasochistic *dance of intimacy* that so many therapists see when a couple enters the consulting room. As the "dance" unfolds, a split between conscious awareness and unconscious needs takes place. The conscious goal of each partner is to find someone who will recognize even the most terrible sins and still love the sinner, but the unconscious goal may be to retaliate, to punish and to be punished.

The force propelling both members of the couple toward the creation of a mutual hell directly reflects the collision of self-destructive forces mobilized by the aggressive feelings in the relationship. Over time, each reenacts the old scenario, testing whether *this* person can give the love, acceptance, and nurturance that the parents failed to supply. Not believing that they are worthy of being loved, one partner or both cannot fully process positive responses emitted by the other. Genuine expressions of love are therefore undermined, dismissed, ignored, or rejected, and the testing escalates until the partner fails.

Over time, each shapes the other until the partners have no way of breaking the deadlock of their collusive resistance to change. This is the toxic cycle of projective and introjective identification. By the time they seek help in couples counseling, the pattern is solidly entrenched. Rarely is there ever a way to establish who started it. Close inspection of the dynamic reveals that both partners are heavily invested in their enmeshment. Each subtly pushes the other to fulfill unconscious needs, at the same time generating conditions that make such fulfillment impossible.

The constant failure surfaces previously repressed unconscious rage. At the deepest level, this rage feels so dangerous and destructive that it must be projected out of the self into the other or it will be introjected in shame and depression. Thus, a circular attack-and-defend pattern becomes established. Commonly, one partner seems to choose the role of victim, receiving the other's sadism and feeling tortured in the relationship. Such partners may even behave in ways that seem caring and loving, but in some hidden part of themselves they are heavily defended against repressed sadistic feelings.

Each may encourage the other to act in ways that project the problem outside themselves. In that way, each one can limit access to aggressive impulses toward the other, impulses that are transferred from a parent. The behaviors of both maintain a cycle of sadomasochistic activity that stems from unconscious attachment to a parent who was not experienced as loving and nurturing.

Rage is a particularly effective—and therefore insidious—defense against the longing for the closeness and intimacy the fragile self of one or both partners cannot endure. A person who needed and loved a parent so much is naturally frightened by rage toward that parent. Consequently, he or she must live with the punishment of endless suffering in relationships for the crime implicit in this internal struggle.

As noted earlier, each partner feels trapped in a state of permanent isolation, hopeless about positive change, because unconscious forces sabotage every attempt to extricate oneself from this self-made system. The known terror of daily torture in the relationship feels less dangerous than the terror of the unknown.

Therapists working with couples who have such issues know all too well the strong emotions that define the relationship. The presenting conflict revolves around surface issues—money, work, sex, in-laws—while the underlying battle revolves around separation, autonomy, dependence and validation, or the still deeper fear of rejection and abandonment, guilt and punishment. Often there is a marital history of threats to divorce or actual separations. Reconciliation may lead to a period of peace, only to be followed by new battles, demonstrating to them that they can live neither together nor apart.

A couple with such a history will come into the early counseling sessions with specific identified problems. Upon close observation partners demonstrate a level of aggression toward each other vastly out of proportion to the problems they describe. Not only are they suffering because of deep structural divisions, but also empathy has been destroyed. They are angry at each other for the mutual lack of attunement that results.

Commonly, it is difficult to stop the "noise" and get the partners to listen to each other, to step back and understand what the other is experiencing. Each has a fixed view that includes a specific agenda for the relationship and fears opening the self to the other's perspective. The other's behavior is interpreted in terms of the reactions it produces. In extreme cases, neither partner can understand or accept that the other is a separate self with different views, feelings, or motivations.

In the most disturbed couples, urgent needs, turbulent interactions, and confusing, often chaotic responses make couples therapy seem fraught with difficulties. "These are the couples," says family therapist James Framo, "who, when they cancel appointments, the therapist is relieved."* The intensity of the interaction, fraught with power struggles, emotional manipulation, and painful drama, makes it excruciating not only for the couple but also for all around them, including children, friends, and therapist. Children of such couples often have no alternative but to act out or withdraw and disconnect. They may form their own collusive relationships among friends who have similar problems. Or they may pair off with one of the parents, adopting the position that the problems lie totally in the other.

As might be expected, the most difficult couples to treat are those in which the partners suffer borderline and narcissistic disorders. The following case describes the interaction in such disturbed relationships.

PAUL AND BETTY

The therapist's initial contact with a couple is sometimes deceptive. Betty, a striking, raven-haired woman in her early forties, charmed everyone she met. She had dozens of friends, many who wondered how she put up with Paul, her brilliant but quirky investment banker husband. They had been together for 23 years, married for 18 years, and unhappy throughout the courtship and marriage.

Paul and Betty were parents of three daughters. Betty also had a son from a short-lived prior marriage when she was 18. They came to couples therapy after three failed attempts to get help with their marriage. Each time they sought help, Paul dropped out and Betty continued. Betty, meeting regularly with the therapist, convinced herself that she was getting well, while Paul lagged behind. She had convinced Paul that their marital problems stemmed largely from his inability to accept the kind of warm, loving relationship that she had to offer.

Betty, who was physically and sexually abused as a child, had a mixed love-hate relationship with her parents. On the numerous occasions when she embarked on therapy, she idealized the therapist at first. As the idealization turned to disappointment and a sense of betrayal, she discarded the treatment and found a new therapist. She talked about past therapists who "came on" to her, who told her she was borderline, who sided with her husband, or who retired and "abandoned her." She seemed determined to make her marriage better by finding a way to improve her relationship with Paul. But according to her, Paul never did anything right for her or their children.

Because of his own history, Paul was all too ready to believe that his lively, vivacious wife, who charmed everyone, pushed him away because of his de-

*Personal communication.

ficiencies. He described a history of distant, unavailable parents. He was the youngest child of a wealthy Viennese family who immigrated to the U.S. shortly before World War II. His brother and sister, twins born in Vienna, were six years older. Because he never found a place where he fit, he felt deprived and less able than his brother, who got all the attention. He had no relationship with his sister. When his family moved to a small, insulated northwestern community, Paul felt that his parents were different, but they never talked about what they left behind or why they always seemed to be in hiding. He felt like an outsider in school and in the neighborhood. His most fervent interest was sports. Not only did he follow baseball, basketball, and football, knowing all the players, but he also played on the high school basketball team. It hurt him that his parents never came to a game. He was a sports-loving jock in a family that valued only intellectual and artistic pursuits.

Just as Paul put his energy into athletic achievements hoping to get his father to notice, he kept trying to do whatever would make Betty validate his worth. Although he was quite successful as an investment banker, Betty denigrated his work and said he was just one of those business predators who don't care about the welfare of others. She became increasingly interested in environmental causes and political reform. She belittled his constant discussions at social engagements about stocks, bonds, and other investments. He said that everyone wants to talk with him about his work because of his success. When he avoided responding to her put-downs about his business, she found other complaints. She complained that he worked too hard to be a good parent to their children. If he put any time into his sports interests, she complained that he was hurting himself physically.

When he had back surgery, rather than caring for him, Betty blamed him, saying that his long distance running had caused his injury. There was always some barrier that he had to overcome to achieve the love that he believed she was capable of giving. Paul found that all of his efforts to heal either himself or the relationship provoked some sort of negative reaction from Betty, who seemed to be fighting to maintain the status quo. Betty feared change, believing that, "The Hell I know is better than the Hell I do not know." Paul's efforts were marred by his self-effacing "Rodney Dangerfield" humor. His form of joking demonstrated a veiled sadism toward his wife, whom he viewed as a both a parental and a filial figure. On the other hand, Paul's hurtful criticisms felt abusive to Betty and reenacted her traumatic relationship with her abusive father.

Over the course of 18 years of marriage, this couple had developed a mutually frustrating interaction cycle. Both experienced themselves as victimized in their family of origin and by each other. Each split off undesirable traits within and projected them onto the other. Each at times threatened divorce, but both were terrified of separation, which would mean loss of their hated parental figures. Betty indicated that Paul must change or the marriage would not survive. Paul's perpetual complaint was, "I want a wife who loves and adores me and she doesn't." In describing the history of their relationship, Paul said that from the beginning Betty had told him that she didn't want to commit to one man. She thought that she would need different men, filling her needs by offering her different things. He pursued her ardently for over five years; they lived together and apart, never getting truly close. Eventually he convinced her to marry him.

At an unconscious level, they both knew what they were getting. She, never wanting closeness, instead sought an idealized form of love; he, never believing that there was a place where he would be accepted, wanted a family and a feeling of belonging. As it actually happened, Betty never got the love and safety that she yearned for, and Paul continued to pursue her without understanding why she had so much to give others but so little to give him. He was enraged at her, but never told her so directly. It came out in passive-aggressive, mockingly derisive remarks in front of friends. In therapy, Betty presented the problem as totally Paul's. According to her, he was emotionally distant, overly involved with his work, mean to her, and interested in her only as a sexual object. From Paul's response to her description of him as a husband, it was evident that he was not sure that she was wrong. "Sometimes I think it's hopeless. I'll never have her. Nothing I do is ever right, or enough," he said. Betty was equally pained about their relationship; "He never gives me the things that I need, no matter how much I try to tell him what they are."

Paul and Betty had shaped each other's behavior until each had turned the other into an oppressor whose behavior mimicked that of hostile figures from their families of origin. She made him into her sadistic father. He made her into his unavailable, disinterested father and mother. The marriage was a continuation of what each had learned growing up. Paul was the outsider, not deserving of the "affection, affirmation, and adoration" for which he so fervently yearned. Betty validated her deeply held belief that it is impossible for her to get what she needs from a man because men hurt and misuse women.

It was a "crazy love" marriage, one of high intensity. She offered him family, community, friends, but the price she insisted on was sexual and emotional distance. At a party she would flirt, and at home she withdrew. She got involved in sexual flings with other men, and when they were experiencing a time of sexual intimacy, she would tell him about her latest dalliance in the guise of total truthfulness as proof of love. Betty did not seem to know whether she wanted more of Paul or less of him. The harder he pushed for closeness, the more she pushed him away. When he withdrew, she pushed him to come closer. Either close or distant, Paul and Betty projected aspects of unacceptable parts of themselves into each other, and both reacted punitively to the object of their projections. At the same time they each tended to identify with the projections and proceeded to act them out by participating in a mutual cycle that become a self-fulfilling prophecy.

Changing such a relationship was like trying to capture smoke.

Rage, Shame, and Guilt

It is not sadomasochistic behavior or murderous impulses that are at the core of such painful individual patterns of interaction. Beneath the level of rage and destructive fantasies are shame and guilt for the violence *implicit* in the unconscious fantasies. Rage is an understandable, even adaptive response when the deep need for contact has been thwarted. The failure of connections results in terror of annihilation, hopelessness, rage, and despair.

Rage, shame, and guilt are important issues to explore when partners are dealing with interlocking dynamics of this type. Partners use collusive maneuvers to support entrenched defenses. Marital therapy requires the couple to become aware of how they use each other to maintain internal cohesion when the stress of life creates intense affect, anxiety, and defenses against conscious awareness of feelings. It is necessary to break apart the pathological self-organization before something new, the mature adaptive self-organization (described in the next chapter), can replace it.

Projection and Introjection

In some cases, as the therapeutic relationship progresses, one partner appears to get more emotionally unstable. The underlying lesion resides in an inability to tolerate separateness, strongly welded to a fear of closeness. Healthy couples experience increased differentiation over time, leading to an enhanced level of interdependency between two autonomous people. When anxiety about intimacy is too great, however, one partner will push away to return to a safe emotional threshold. If the pushing away leads to too much distance, the separation may generate great anxiety and fear that there will be no way to reconnect, stimulating movement toward more closeness. In that way, the couple oscillates between the point at which they are far enough away to be relatively free of anxiety, and the point at which the fear of being swallowed up by the emotions of intimacy becomes intolerable. "Don't get close, don't go away," is the constant in the relationship, the balance point at which the partners are doomed to remain stuck unless other forces intervene.

This game, played by two partners, is usually designed to defend against traumatic disruptions in each partner's past. Even if one of the partners begins the relationship less damaged than the other, living together in such circumstances soon equilibrates the distress, and both participate in the painful and seemingly eternal contest. In such intransigent relationships, any attempt by one partner to change the dynamics of their interactions is met with massive unconscious defensive maneuvers by the other. Either can put up barriers to change. Despite the pain of a dysfunctional relationship, they are used to what they have. When they come to therapy, they are not seeking true change; rather, they want to be more comfortable in their pathology. Both are frightened of exploring and understanding the primitive emotions, anxieties, and defenses that they are playing out with each other. In this series of mutually collusive interactions, each is behaviorally "shaped" to behave in ways that are demanded by powerful unconscious forces. Communication is on "auto-pilot," with each mechanically saying the expected lines. The circular dialogue is endless, which assures that they always maintain a distance. The following is typical of Paul and Betty's dialogue:

B: You never want to make love anymore.
P: You are asleep every night at 8:30.
B: Why don't we make love in the morning, when I feel like it?
P: I have to get up early and go to work. Why can't you stay up after the kids go to sleep?
B: I'm tired at night.
P: Why don't you rest during the day so you can stay awake at night?
B: I have so much to do all day.
P: Yeah, you are so busy having lunch with your friends, and shopping.
B: I have to run the house and volunteer at the children's school and work at my job, and I am tired at night.
P: Your job! You're not earning any money at that job. It's not a job.
B: You think you can pick on me and criticize the way I work and run the house, and then expect me to want to make love to you at night. Well, forget it.

Therapy with such couples requires a confrontation of their repetitive dialogue and concurrent challenge to the established pattern of self-other relationships. These patterns are often informed by strong affect and by dis-turbance in the bonds of attachment during first two years of life (Sroufe, 1995).

For Paul and Betty, to relate honestly with each other meant risking disin-tegration and loss of self-esteem. Each feared the other would feel contempt, be rejecting, or emotionally disconnect. By deadening emotions, blocking full awareness of the reality that provokes strong emotional reaction, or defend-ing against emotional closeness, each is able to protect a vulnerable self against experiences of intense affect. These measures, while useful in the short run, eventually cripple the social and emotional abilities of each partner.

With this in mind, it is possible to understand why relationships built upon this historical base are so intransigent. It is true that either partner can make the decision to opt out of the pattern, but he or she would then have to deal with the intense affect that would emerge in the absence of the relationship, the pain of which had long drowned out awareness of the deep emotional wounds received in infancy. Sometimes one partner does make the decision to change, and this can open the path for the other to change also. The other partner may, however, experience change as a threat, not only to the rela-tionship but also to the core of a very fragile self. The danger is the eruption of intense, overwhelming affect. Massive resistance, anger, and increasing barriers to change may arise in order to regain the homeostasis of the relationship. The partner who attempted to change may fall back into the old pattern, the safety of the known, to avoid the terror of the unknown. Separation and individuation are impossible within the relationship, unless the partner risks engagement in the process of the change as well.

Treatment

Couples therapy is unlikely to be successful unless the therapist establishes an alliance with each member of the relationship. Both partners must feel emotionally supported by the therapist. The purpose of therapy is, in large part, to construct a transitional relationship, not unlike a transitional object, that provides enough of a containing environment to allow both partners to tolerate frustrations and build the capacity to face their own and each other's deepest emotions. If they believe that the therapeutic relationship will help them adjust to the transformations, and that it will be better than the old col-lusive structure, then they will be able to risk change.

The treatment utilizes both verbal and nonverbal methods intended to demonstrate interest in the patients' ways of handling their most painful emo-tions. Cognitive, emotional, and interpersonal strategies are meant to keep anxiety-provoking thoughts and feelings out of conscious awareness. To counterbalance the tendency of the couple to generate interpersonal "noise" through attack and counterattack, the therapist may model *hyper-attunement* to the pain and sadness associated with the loss or anticipated loss of connection with an intimate other. When anxiety emerges, signaling a defensive reaction, the therapist can assist in refocusing on the avoided impulse or feeling. Through repeated exploration of the feelings that lie behind the defenses of anger and anxiety, the partners begin to recognize the defenses they utilize.

This approach to couples treatment utilizes discoveries of the original short-term dynamic therapy pioneers. Once they experience the therapeutic milieu as a safe environment, partners begin to acknowledge the fear of being vulnerable. A therapist who is interactive and articulates the words that neither partner can say may be in a position to confront the self-sabotaging behavior that almost inevitably results in great pain and a ruptured relationship. Refocusing the partners on what they desire from each other, while connecting how the wish in the current relationship is closely related to what they felt deprived of in the past, opens the possibility that they can stop their aggressive and defensive maneuvering. For example, it is possible to stimulate a larger awareness of what is going on by pointing out that the therapy is not effective and will fail unless each partner is willing to stop the perpetual war.

Staying focused on the mutual defense patterns in relationship, rather than singling out either one's specific pathological defense, increases the possibility of therapeutic alignment with the healthy, growth-promoting part in each of them. I invite them to consider what they might say if they did not feel shame or guilt about what the effect might be of sharing "your truth." Depending upon the degree of resistance, partners may allow feelings of sadness, anger, or fear to emerge. If they continue to avoid and resist, it may help to point out that they keep a wall up to maintain a distance in the session, just as they have had walls up between them at home. Acknowledging how difficult it is, the therapist may encourage the partners to identify their behavior in terms of normal protective defenses that worked at some point in early life but no longer are useful. The future need not be a repeat of the past, although it will be if they keep repeating the same old patterns.

With almost all clients, there is a part of the psyche that yearns for healing and growth. Effective couples therapy gives hope for a healing relationship with the partner. The therapeutic relationship simply provides the milieu in which partners can safely acknowledge deep longings, fears, and primitive affect that can suddenly flood one or both when failures of attunement, fear of abandonment, and feelings of attack are experienced in the session. When partners who during their early life learned injunctions against getting angry

allow themselves to express anger, or when partners who deny fears of abandonment by remaining distant can express needs and grieve what they never
received while the therapist makes sure they are heard and understood, something important is released, and changes in the relationship begin to occur.

Conclusion

There are many reasons why people choose to marry. To some extent, a marriage may be based on reality issues such as financial resources, beauty, or
simply availability at a time when one is ready. To some extent, as well, it
may be an unconscious search for a psychological match. "A creative successful marriage is one in which fresh discoveries are made in the to and fro
of daily contact between the partners" (Byng-Hall, 1985). A major goal of
therapy with the couple is to change the threshold of anxiety about closeness and distance, thus freeing the partners to experience both intimacy and
autonomy. The key is integrity and the patients' willingness to explore their
own projections. A mature, adaptive self-organization comes through rein-
terpreting the meaning of love. An intimate partnership is seen not as an
idealized form of a perfect need-fulfilling other, but as the union of two separate selves, each with clear but permeable boundaries that are open to each
other at times that are mutually agreeable to both. With awareness of one's
own and one's mate's early imprints, and with willingness to tolerate the
difficulties inherent in breaking old patterns, relationships can change into
partnerships that avoid the cycle of shame and blame and that more or less
unflinchingly look at underlying feelings. This will be discussed in greater
detail in the next chapter.

References

Alexander, F., & French, T. M. (1946). *Psychoanalytic therapy: Principles and application.* New
York: Ronald Press.

Beavers, W. R. (1985). *Successful marriage: A family systems approach to marital therapy.* New
York: Norton.

Byng-Hall, J. (1985). Resolving distance conflicts. In A. Gurman (Ed.), *Casebook of marital therapy* (pp. 1–19). New York: Guilford.

Della Selva, P. (1996). *Intensive short-term dynamic psychotherapy: Theory and technique.* New
York: Wiley.

Dicks, H. V. (1953). *Marital tension: Clinical studies toward a psychological theory of interaction.*
London: Routledge and Kegan Paul.

Fosha, D. (1995). Technique and taboo in three short-term dynamic psychotherapies.
Journal of Psychotherapy Practice and Research, 4, 297–318.

Fosha, D. (2000). *The transforming power of affect: A model for accelerated change.* New York: Basic Books.

Freud, S. (1923). Beyond the pleasure principle. In J. Strachey (Ed. and Trans.), *The standard edition of the complete psychological works of Sigmund Freud* (Vol. 18, pp. 7–64). New York: Norton, 1958.

Gurman, A. A. (1978). Contemporary marital therapy: A critique and comparative analysis of psychoanalytic, behavioral and systems theory approaches. In T. J. Paolino & B. S. McCrady (Eds.), *Marriage and marital therapy.* New York: Brunner/Mazel.

Kelly, V. C. (1996). Affect and the redefinition of intimacy. In D. L. Nathanson (Ed.), *Knowing feeling: Affect, script, and Psychotherapy* (pp. 55–104). New York: Norton.

Kohut, H. (1984). *How does analysis cure?* Chicago: University of Chicago Press.

Malone, T. P., & Malone, P. T. (1987). *The art of intimacy.* New York: Prentice Hall.

Siegel, D. (1999). *The developing mind: Toward a neurobiology of interpersonal experience.* New York: Guilford.

Solomon, M. (1989). *Narcissism and intimacy: Love and marriage in an age of confusion.* New York: Norton.

Sroufe, L. A. (1995). *Emotional development: The organization of emotional life in the early years.* Cambridge, UK: Cambridge University Press.

Stern, D. (1985). *The interpersonal world of the infant: A view from psychoanalysis and developmental psychology.* New York: Basic Books.

Suttie, I. (1937/1988). *The origins of love and hate.* London: Free Association Books.

Tomkins, S. S. (1963). *Affect, imagery, consciousness, Vol. 1: The negative affects.* New York: Springer.

Tomkins, S. S. (1980). Affect as amplification: Some modifications in theory. In R. Plutchik & H. Kellerman (Eds.), *Emotion: Theory, research and experience* (pp. 141–164). New York: Academic Press.

7

Attachment Bonds and Intimacy: Can the Primary Imprint of Love Change?

Robert J. Neborsky and Marion F. Solomon

ON ENTERING OUR PRACTICES, not all patients complain of problems in their intimate relationships. However, once the idealization of romantic love dissolves, many complain of their intimate partners being "insensitive" or that "the flame has gone out." We hear people describe how they feel frozen in their relationships, or how in more extreme cases they feel depressed, anxious, or worse—how they are losing themselves. Infidelity, violent acting out, and various and sundry addictive behaviors are common symptoms of unconsciously disordered attachment/affiliation systems. There are nearly as many varieties of complaints as there are people and couples. The capacity to experience maximum fulfillment in relationships requires a healthy attachment/affiliation system. The central topic of this chapter—Can the way we love be changed?—speaks to this very issue.

The chapter puts forth a new concept to understand the unconscious origin of adult psychopathology viewed through the lens of recent discoveries in short-term therapy and attachment theory. We describe the kinds of trauma (abuse, natural disasters, attachment failures) that infants and children experience, the way that trauma is organized in the unconscious, how it is transformed into adult psychopathology, how it initially manifests as resistance, and ultimately how it can be corrected in a short-term format.

The capacity to relate is hardwired into each of us. We exercise our primary ability to attach and affiliate to the other in our early relationship with mother in the first year of life (Bowlby, 1969; Schore, 1998; Siegel, 1999; Stern, 1985). The experience of self emerges within the attachment dyad, and the first "group experience" soon follows. By this we mean awareness of a third party, which occurs at around eight months of life. This is signaled by the appearance of stranger anxiety (Emde, Gaensbauer, & Harmon, 1976). At some point in time, a new attachment occurs, and this third person is usually called "father." This is the underpinning of what Freud eventually labeled as the Oedipal triangle. The way in which these competing attachments unfold defines the love imprint. The central hypothesis of this chapter is that the capacity for mature adult love is determined by how these early attachments are recorded in the memory network of each and every one of us. Sibling attachments also occur somewhere in the developmental sequence, and, depending on the core family constellation, this powerful new relationship may or may not create dormant conflict in the capacity for adult love (Neborsky, 1998).

As we have described in earlier chapters, stressful adult life situations as well as the normative experience of intimate relationships—loving and being loved—are both potential catalysts for ignition of repressed or dissociated unconscious trauma. The state of being in love is idealized by our culture; however, the reality of love and intimate relationships is a far different thing. We believe that whatever went wrong in the childhood of each of us will be tested in the relationships with our intimate partner, our children, and our in-laws. If early childhood trauma were significant, then the individual would frequently invoke defenses to cure the feelings stimulated by the relationship difficulty, and then the normative growth of intimacy, empathy, connection, understanding, and healthy dependency that ordinarily occurs over time would not unfold. Instead, stalemate, stagnation, alienation, and inability to resolve conflict would occur.

There are complex reasons why this happens. What we frequently see is that the growth-seeking part of the person, yearning to heal the early injury, seeks intimate connection with a partner whose conscious and unconscious qualities are reminiscent of significant parental figures. What then happens is a repetitive pattern (shaping of response) in which the internal working models of each trigger the underlying unconscious emotional reactions that created the original difficulty. This creates a counterreaction and eventually shapes the partners' responses such that each becomes a reenacting figure similar to the original inadequate caregiver. Other therapists, such as Henry Dicks (1953) in England and David and Jill Scharff (1990) at the Washington

School of Psychiatry, as well as Marion F. Solomon (1989, 1994), have described this process as projective and introjective identification in couples.

A Brief Review of Attachment Theory

By the middle of the twentieth century John Bowlby in England turned to animal behavior studies to enrich the traditional analytic views of child development, pointing out that parents have instinctual responses to their infants and that those responses are elicited by the infants' behaviors, such as the social smile of the two-month-old. Bowlby (1969, 1973, 1980) wrote about attachment, separation, and loss in ways that powerfully influenced such practices as the establishment of primary caregivers in orphanages and in pediatric hospital wards. His idea was simple and powerful: the nature of the infant's attachment to the parent would become internalized as a working model of attachment. If this model represented security, the baby would be able to explore the world and separate and mature in a healthy way. If the attachment relationship was problematic, the internal working model of attachment would not give the infant a sense of a secure base and the development of normal behaviors, such as play, exploration, and social interactions, would be impaired. He described the inevitable consequence of attachment loss: protest, despair, and detachment. Spitz (1945; Spitz & Wolf, 1946) went even further and described the morbidity associated with attachment failure.

Mary Ainsworth (1978, 1991), who studied and worked with Bowlby, was interested in developing a research measure, a quantifiable instrument capable of assessing the security of attachment. She studied the mother-infant bond over the first year of life. After observing the interactions of the pair in their home, Ainsworth brought them into a laboratory setting, the so-called "strange situation," and observed the infant with mother alone, with mother and a stranger, and with a stranger alone. What Ainsworth found was that the infant's behavior at reunion fell into specific styles of responding (secure, ambivalent, and avoidant). Each of these styles corresponded in a significant way to the independently performed home observation ratings for the year prior to the laboratory assessment. Mary Main later described the disorganized attachment style.

The early response patterns seen in the Ainsworth's strange situation were evoked later as the children grew into adolescents and adults. This correlation suggests that patterns of relating between parent and child have significant influences in later life. This work has been furthered through the research of Mary Main (1991, 1993, 1995), and coworkers, who found that the type of internal attachment of a parent (as measured by an Adult Attachment Interview [AAI]) correlated with the type of attachment shown by the child in a strange situation study. Further work suggests that an incoherent autobiographical life narrative in the parent predicts the appearance of specific attachment patterns in her child (Main, in press). Sroufe (e.g., Sroufe, Egeland, & Krentger, 1990) also examined the fate of early experience following developmental change with similar findings.

Daniel Stern's synthesis of many infant development studies confirmed and amplified Bowlby's and Ainsworth's work. Stern (1985) described the emergent self of the infant and then tracked the development of mental representations in the first year of life. He described RIGs (representations of interactions generalized) as the way that the infant develops imprints for relating to others right from the beginning of life. Calling upon the findings of developmental research, Stern proposed that the newborn comes into the world with an emergent self. This self demonstrates an ability to recognize mother from the first weeks of life. Once patterns begin and are reinforced by repetitions of the same interactions, they provide templates for viewing and relating to others.

Erik Erikson (1963) proposed that a person moves through various developmental phases characterized by particular conflicts and challenges; if the conflict of a phase is not resolved it will affect further growth. Stern, by contrast, saw the self developing throughout various phases, adding new self-organizations over time. Nothing is lost. The same early RIGs are present and can be evoked by a sensory stimulus in the 6-year-old, the 16-year-old, and the 60-year-old. Unless some intervening relational input causes significant change in these internal representations, interactions in adult relationships will call forth early, perhaps distorted RIGs. The clinical question that we raise is: Does early developmental trauma result in a distorted RIG?

Intensive microanalysis of videotapes of work with adults with pathogenic developmental situations shows that these "RIGs" may be more complex than originally described by Stern. Upon clinical examination, they contain unconscious, unneutralized, aggressive and shame/guilt-laden feelings toward the parent or sibling that caused the trauma. The theoretical and clinical observations of Melanie Klein (1932), Winnicott (1951), Fairbairn (1952), and Guntrip (1961) imply this conclusion as well. The systematic clinical research by Davanloo on the centrality of aggression/superego manifestations in neurosis lends further support to this conclusion. Neborsky (2001) finds manifestations of a distorted "RIG" originating even from early perinatal trauma.

A New Representational Concept: PASO—Primitive Aggressive Self-Organization

To avoid confusion with Stern's concept of a RIG, which is a normal process, we use the acronym PASO (primitive aggressive self organization) (Figure 7.1) to describe a pathologic entity. We see these self-organizations as "RIGs" that have become not only frozen in time but also unavailable for scrutiny by the conscious mind. These structures are at the center of neurotic, narcissistic, and borderline psychopathology. In our view this is the missing link in present attachment theory. What we believe we are describing is the psychic impact of the protest phase (Bowlby, 1973) of the childhood reaction to loss of security. These emotions are imprinted into a dissociated brain neural network and, as Shapiro describes, split off into consciously inaccessible areas of the mind. The consequence of this sealing-off is that the normative forces of pleasure seeking become warped, so that the supraordinate self-organization shifts into a pain-seeking, masochistic working model of relationship. So much of what we see clinically in adult disturbed relationships is ultimately caused by unconscious feelings from early attachment failures. Historically, these failures created unconscious sadistic feelings toward biological relatives that became internalized as superego. The PASO is the unconscious portion of the insecure attachment phenomenon that is in all neurotic adults. In other words, in order to have a "secure" relationship, these patients must sacrifice part of self.

In our approach to psychopathology it is important to understand that the child seeks secure attachment and connection with each parent. Triangulation of any of these relationships can threaten the security of the attachment, thus creating a PASO. Once a PASO is created, it is like a virus in the psyche and can be reactivated when exposed to the test of an adult love relationship.

Let us look at PASO as depicted in Figure 7.1. Beginning at level 1 we have schematized the state of trauma-free attachment.* This encompasses intrauterine life, perhaps including any healthy symbiotic stages of post-uterine development. In essence, this is the state of pure love and is experienced in secure attachment. Next, at level 2, we have the pain of trauma (loss, separation, self-injury, emotional disconnection). Level 3 is the sadness or grief resulting from 2. Level 4, which is more difficult to observe, is the retaliatory

---

*More precisely this represents the potential for secure attachment—the source of calmness and the reservoir of hope.

FIGURE 7.1
TOPOGRAPHICAL MAP OF THE UNCONSCIOUS ATTACHMENT SYSTEM (PASO)

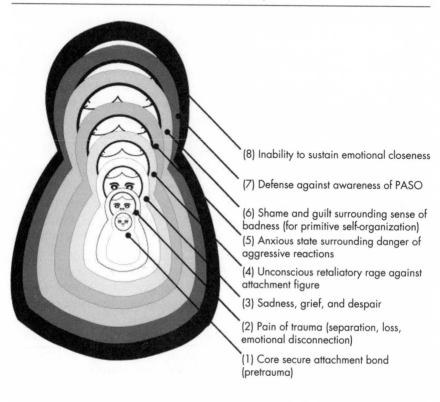

(8) Inability to sustain emotional closeness

(7) Defense against awareness of PASO

(6) Shame and guilt surrounding sense of badness (for primitive self-organization)

(5) Anxious state surrounding danger of aggressive reactions

(4) Unconscious retaliatory rage against attachment figure

(3) Sadness, grief, and despair

(2) Pain of trauma (separation, loss, emotional disconnection)

(1) Core secure attachment bond (pretrauma)

rage (protest) against the attachment figure, which rapidly enters the child's unconscious system. This retaliatory rage is critical to the development of neurotic and characterologic disturbances. Depending on the patient's age, constitutional factors, and the extent of the trauma, the retaliatory rage is annihilatory, butcherous, torturous, or simply murderous. Level 5 is the anxiety that the rage generates. The safety of the child/adult is jeopardized by the recognition of the extent of this rage because self-love (secure attachment) is jeopardized. So it is connected to the emotion of anxiety. The affect of shame and guilt is seen at level 6. These are inhibitory emotions, which create a sense of badness of the self when the impulse to damage the offending caregiver is acknowledged. Commonly associated with level 6 emotions is a need for punishment for these "bad" wishes. In level 7 are the defenses that contain the PASO, which may, over time, become ossified into character. This can be conceptualized as a secondary "secure" attachment that occurs at the cost of free access to feelings.

Frequently the PASO breaks down under the stress of an intimate relationship. In patients with severe early trauma Davanloo (Konzelmann, 1995) has described a new dynamic defense that he calls a resistance to emotional closeness (level 8). This is actually an inability to sustain emotional closeness in the face of failure of emotional resonance, whether in therapy or with an intimate partner. This is probably a cluster of many different defensive operations. What it refers to is a defective way of relating to others, where one can remain constantly detached from one's own feelings. It appears as though the patient is narcissistically preoccupied and results in relating to others as objects (objectification).

Developmental Complexity—Effect Becomes Cause

The above schema highlights another facet of the unconscious. The infant develops increasingly complex brain systems, which are influenced by his/her unique experience. Depending upon both temperament and environment, the child begins to experience his/her own emotions, and expression of affect influences environmental responses and the quality of relationships. In other words, the child's interpretation of the input he/she receives from the environment determines the child's behavior, thereby shaping the response pattern of the environment to the child. In complexity theory, which we will discuss later, this is called a "recursive pattern" (Boldrini, Placidi, & Marazzita, 1998). For example, the child who is frightened by aggressive feelings and/or responses from the parent may put on a "goody-two shoes" façade (as described in Alice Miller's *Prisoners of Childhood*). When that occurs the capacity for a genuine intimate connection with that parent is lost. The child may experience it as parental withdrawal. In a downward spiral, deepening loss of tenderness occurs, creating anger, creating more need for a rigid goody-goody child response pattern to the parent. Ultimately, the child feels shame and guilt for his or her "badness." Cause and effect become confused and the child blames himself/herself for "badness," which seems to have caused the loss of unconditional love.

Modern Attachment Theory and the Concept of Trauma

Modern attachment theory focuses on the process of attunement, which is largely nonverbal right hemispheric mode of communication between caregiver and child (Schore 1994, Siegel 1999). Affect and its regulation through psychic and somatic mechanisms are of critical importance in healthy development. When the child and environment are out of balance, and no repair occurs, small-t trauma occurs and then anger and eventually defenses result. What leads to a traumatized state of mind? The key ingredient seems to be a state of helplessness in the face actual (or perceived) danger (Freud, 1926). Anna Freud (1967), in discussing the use of the term "trauma," pointed out that it is used two ways by clinicians. One way almost trivializes the concept of trauma, but in common usage it means an event that causes emotional disruption (today we refer to this as small t trauma); the second way is what we call Big-T trauma—an overwhelmed state wherein the individual is powerless to exert control over the environment.

Attunement failures between parent and child are small-t traumas. If they are repetitive, fixed, and rigid, there is no way to process the negative emotion that the trauma creates, and the effects become cumulative (Kahn, 1963). Ideally, small and even big traumatizing experiences are processed in the parent-child dyad. However, when there is *impairment of parental empathy* these affects are not processed interpersonally; instead, they are stored. In an attempt to define trauma, Jones (1995, p. 116) explains, "a traumatized state occurs when a person is unable to respond appropriately to a situation; in turn, this inability to respond is signaled by anxiety-panic." Depending upon (1) the child's temperament, (2) the degree of the trauma, and (3) the capacity of the caregivers to respond, a PASO may form. In the optimal situation, in Shapiro's metaphor (see chapter 5), the negative affects may be "digested" and no pathology results. Table 7.1 categorizes the types of traumas that patients bring with them to therapists in clinical practices.

Historical and Contemporary Views of the PASO

Early object relation theorists referred to these emergent PASOs as the paranoid and the depressive positions (Klein, 1932). Davanloo (1995b) sees the disturbed attachment system as the central core of psychopathology. Currently, Schore (in press) has correlated loss responses with increased adrenergic discharges states (anger) and eventually hypertonic parasympathetic states (despair) in infants exposed to environmental failure. Through complex developmental and neurobiological growth processes, the normative attach-

---

TABLE 7.1
The Spectrum of Trauma: *Small-t Progressing to Big-T*

RELATING

Faulty attunement by either or both caregivers
Faulty empathy by either or both caregivers

PARENTING

Faulty application of boundaries from caregivers
Favoritism; sibling rivalry
Defective affect regulation

EXPLOITATIVE

Sexual abuse
Physical abuse
Power: children as pawns or scapegoats
Triangulation

ENVIRONMENTAL

Death of parent or sibling
Injury of person or body part
Divorce
Poverty
Natural disasters
Social discrimination: sex, race, cultural

---

ment sequence evolves into self-regulation processes in which inhibitory affects emerge. These affects appear to be mediated by the parasympathetic nervous system (Schore, in press).

Direct child observation classically supports the appearance of shame (guilt*) at about eighteen months. Operationally, shame is considered a right hemisphere affect associated with the experience of incompetence. Guilt is defined as the affect associated with destructive use of power. There is some evidence that guilt is more left hemispheric in origin (Schore, personal communication). The internal operation of this capacity inexorably alters the interpretation of experience, because the child learns to define him/herself as good or bad based upon internal affective experience in addition to outward input from caregivers. Affects develop earlier than language; nonetheless, at a certain time in development they become intertwined with thought. Thereafter, a host of affective nonrepresentational events are stored in the unconscious and affect mood and behavior.

---

*Defined as a sense of badness over destructive impulses toward the caregiving object.

❧

Attachment Blends with Affect and Cognition to Create Self-regulation

At some point in development, cognition itself can provoke affect, through symbol of self (I am good; I am bad) or representation of other (loving or hating). Thought can also produce affect through hippocampal (language-based memory of experience) activity. Nonverbal or implicit memory can also produce affect. This seems to be located in the right hemisphere. An example of this is a sympathetic panic reaction around bees in an adult stung by a bee as a child before the capacity for linguistic memory had developed. (Posttraumatic stress disorder is an example of a disorder of explicit memory processing (Siegel, 1995).) Of central importance is the finding that the body self is connected through thalamic connections to this particularly important type of memory. Pleasurable as well as painful physical experiences are recorded in implicit memory irrespective of consciousness. This part of psychic experience is not accessible through language, but only through imagery and fantasy (Tomkins, 1962, 1963).

Of further significance is the finding that fantasy develops utility as an affect regulator and/or creator. Feelings of weakness and vulnerability can be altered by superman or wonder woman fantasies. Anxiety can be created by fantasies of monsters lurking under the bed. So all of us develop the capacity to alter our affect states through a series of self-interventions. Where there has been cumulative trauma, or major trauma, this organization can break down, and under stress symptoms of anxiety or depression may develop and become fixed experiences.

The PASO, Memory, Therapeutic Action,
and Hemispheric Synchronization

Psychoanalysis activates the unconscious through a unique affiliation called a transference neurosis. It then utilizes resistance interpretation and dream analysis (use of image) to access part of the PASO within the frame of free association. On the other hand, STDP utilizes waking fantasy or "dreaming while awake" to access the PASO. Similar to psychoanalysis, the PASO is activated by the pressure of the therapist to acknowledge true transference feelings. EMDR bypasses transference and explores spontaneously occurring images and sensory experiences that were activated by acute trauma.

Exploring the PASO inevitably activates autobiographical as well as nonverbal memory, particularly when the PASO is activated in the transference. In this way, the therapy encourages the exploration of the patient's narrative and "forces" the integration of the split-off right hemisphere autobiographical memory system with the logical making sense part of the left hemisphere

(Siegel, 1999). This is a challenge, of course, to the left hemisphere, which has written a narrative based upon the incomplete information that was available to it. The two hemispheres are challenged to communicate with each other. New neural integration must occur, also between sub cortical and cortical areas of the brain. Synchronization of the hemispheres occurs as the emotions, images, and intellectual schemes are integrated. The therapeutic process of co-construction of a new narrative ends with the successful resolution of the therapy (Siegel, 1999).

Each of the therapies in this book describes techniques to probe and alter this nonverbal memory system. Shapiro first used EMDR to access this area of the brain *once big-T trauma has occurred.* The trauma itself has given access to the system. Her work demonstrates that noninterpretive techniques can be used to access implicit memory of trauma. She has confirmed the finding that big-T and little-t traumas become intertwined. In order for health to be restored, both systems must be addressed by the client. Prior to Shapiro, Davanloo (personal communication, 1979), Erikson (1963), and Freud (1917) expressed similar thoughts when exploring traumatic neurosis.

Because early painful encounters are frequently preverbal or are followed by defenses designed to protect the vulnerable self of the developing child, clear cognition of traumatic events is lost via repression or dissociation. What remains are the emotional reactions to the painful moment, the unconscious repressed emotion, and later, a faulty narrative designed to explain the surges of pain that suddenly arise in relationships. Our clinical observations have now confirmed Freud's (1911) dictum that we are destined to repeat that which we do not remember. Inevitably, the repressed trauma is reenacted in the intimate relationship. Rather than a continuous coherent narrative, we observe a precise "narrative reenactment." Faulty, rationalized narratives develop, which further confound the truth. Blaming some defect in self or others is one way to keep the memory surge in the unconscious.

Defenses as Neurobiology—Promulgating Psychopathology

Davanloo's way of looking at defense is unique, and it fits with the affect regulation theorists (Schore, 1997; Siegel, 1999). Davanloo sees the classical and tactical defenses (chapter 2, Table 2.4) as part of the superego. In other words, the defenses are organized in such a way as to produce and perpetuate suffering. Using attachment and affect theory, we see the defenses as part of the self-crippling response of the depressive position. Loss of attunement is felt; protest occurs. Protest in the unconscious sphere is experienced as retaliatory rage. The child then feels responsible for the fantasized destruction and develops parasympathetic inhibitory defenses. These can be brain centered (lowered mood) or body centered (diarrhea, asthma, migraine). So the process of cumulative (Kahn, 1963) small-t trauma may, over time, lead to an adult prone to depression, anxiety, or psychosomatic illness. If early infant interactions are particularly neglectful or abusive, retaliatory rage is intense. The adult may then be prone to explosive destructive antisocial behavior or, in more severe cases, senseless violence. There is evidence to suggest that early infant neglect may lead to structural brain pathology, particularly in the orbital frontal area (Schore, 1996). Apparently, this area contains the richest neural connections between the limbic and cortical area of the brain. In health, this area of the brain plays a major role in integrating affect, cognition, insight, and relatedness to the emotions of others. If this model is correct, then it is likely that the parasympathetically mediated "self-destroying" defenses impair neural integration in this area of the brain. Intensive therapy that accesses the autobiographical memory of emotional trauma has the potential to free the traumatized brain to grow new neural networks and there is reorganization of the internal attachment model (Siegel, 1999). This is what we mean by rewriting of the love imprint.

Cases presented in this chapter were frequently treated unsuccessfully with psychopharmacologic agents. There is significant crossover between the effect of mood-altering drugs and the attachment affiliation system we are describing. Further research should clarify the relationship between intensive psychotherapy aimed at the attachment/affiliation system and alterations of neurotransmitter balances.

Sexuality and the PASO

Freud (1898, 1905) originally conceptualized neurosis as resulting from frustrated infantile libidinal wishes towards parents or siblings. In our contemporary view, we see neurosis resulting from the frustrated wish for secure attachment. This naturally raises the question: What is the role of sexuality in neurosis and particularly within the PASO? Sexual feelings are strong and prevalent throughout childhood and seem to peak in intensity around age three to six with a recrudescence in puberty. So sexual feelings for biological relatives (incestuous feelings) are a normal developmental experience. Along with the sexual feelings come territorial feelings, creating rivalries with competitors for the sexual object. This in turn creates anxiety over the potential aggressive conflict with a loved and a more powerful rival. Normally, these intense feelings, associated with shame, guilt, and anxiety, are repressed and can only be accessed through techniques of dynamic therapy, dreams, myths, or works of art. Freud (1900) discovered this area of repressed emotion and labeled it the Oedipal Complex after Sophocles' play *Oedipus Rex*. It is important to note that in the play Oedipus' father, Laius, initiated the conflict with not one, but two, attempts to injure Oedipus (Devereux, 1964). In metaphor, Oedipus' security was being threatened by his father's aggression. Thus, it is implied that neurosis in the child is generated by the parents' unconscious process.

Frequently in small-t trauma, the normal sexual feelings of the child become contaminated or commingled with issues surrounding the area of trauma. Freud (1909) described this beautifully in the case of Little Hans, tracing the development of Hans's horse phobia back to a sexually overstimulating relationship with his mother. Hans then both wanted to castrate and feared retaliatory castration from his father. He displaced this conflict onto horses, whose large penis frightened him. The reason for the commingling of sexual and aggressive feelings in the PASO is developmentally complex, but the finding is consistently noted in neurotic patients. The results are fantasies that express aggression (power, domination-submission, sadism, violence, rape, etc.) along with sexuality. Another common leitmotif presents as acts of punishment of the self (turning against self) for the repressed aggressive impulse toward the sexual object as a requirement for sexual functioning. Uniformly, underlying the aggression is a deep unconscious longing for a tender (nonsexual) connection with the parent who was the original source of the trauma.

For example, Cindy was being treated for severe major depression and long-standing pattern of love affairs with unavailable men. (Her father was unavailable by being submissive to her mother and collaborated with her mother to undermine Cindy's autonomy and capacity to separate from her mother.) In visualization while awake, she murdered her lover in an angry rage. After the murder, to her surprise, she reported feelings of sexual arousal. She visualized placing his flaccid penis between her legs and masturbating to climax. I linked her "taking in" of her lover's soft penis with a prior visualization of her holding her "murdered" father's heart. She understood the affective linkage with the longed for tender relationship with her father and sobbed profusely. She completely recovered from her depression and also ended the affair.

The Goal of Dynamic Psychotherapy

So, what we are calling for therapy to do is to resurrect in an adult love relationship the pre-traumatized capacity to feel loved, joyful, attached, attuned, empathic, and compassionate. Therapy removes the unconscious reflex to protect other at the expense of self or to attack other through transferential misperceptions. What follows is a synopsis of the treatment of three individuals who have had their dormant unconscious conflicts activated by relationships. We trace each case from start to termination to illustrate the way the love imprint is eventually restored. In the technique of short-term therapy, the PASO is exposed in the initial contact, so that the patient can be in touch with it. Repressing the PASO is made unacceptable through short-term techniques; this accelerates working through. Thereafter, the PASO is addressed in each session; in each developmental relationship the PASO is made conscious, felt, and altered. The feelings that heretofore were experienced as intolerable, overwhelming, or deadly are held and contained in the therapeutic milieu. The result is that the patient increases his/her ability to tolerate the intolerable and develops the courage to face that which was felt to be too unbearable to experience. Miller, in describing the goal of psychotherapy, writes

> We have only one enduring weapon in our struggle against mental illness: the emotional discovery of truth about the unique history of our childhood. In order to become whole we must try, in a long process,* to discover our own personal truth, a truth which may cause pain before giving us a new sphere of freedom. (1996, p. 1)

The presence of the therapist is, of course, key. First and foremost the role of the therapist is like Diogenes eternally seeking truth. The therapist allies with the part of the patient that is courageous and truth-seeking as well. The therapist then becomes like Beatrice was to Dante, a guide through a horrible place. The patient trusts the guide and believes that the two will survive the journey into the hell of the past and exit back into the real world in a transformed state. The journey, then, rewrites the narrative, which had heretofore been incoherent. A coherent narrative of self emerges and, along with it, increased flexibility in emotionally challenging, intimate situations. Facing the feared emotion itself is curative.

> *Consciously experiencing our legitimate emotions is liberating,* not just because of long held tensions in the body but above all because it opens our eyes to reality (both past and present) and frees us of lies and illusions. It is therefore empowering without being destructive. Repressed emotion can be resolved as soon as it is felt, understood, and recognized as legitimate. (Miller, 1996, p. 115)

Also, responding in a behavioral way differently to situations in which the emotion is felt is empowering and builds self-esteem. So self-esteem is bolstered by the journey into the abyss and the courageous encounter with inner sadness,

---

*The authors propose techniques *to shorten* the process.

rage, fear, shame, or guilt. Ultimately, the relationship takes on the quality of Alexander's "corrective emotional experience," in which the therapist provides for the patient the empathic capacity that the parent could not provide for the child. The result is that the defensive system is reorganized and the patient is now free to learn and practice intimacy. The therapeutic experience of anger, sadness and pain liberates the ability to experience joyfulness.

Short-Term Psychotherapy with Three Insecure Attachment Styles

The following are three cases seen by Robert Neborsky in the past two years. They demonstrate treatment with three different insecure attachment styles.

Insecure Attachment: Avoidant Style—The Tin Man

Alan had not been in therapy in the past. He sought therapy after an outburst of anger that frightened both him and his fiancée, Janet. After two years of dating, their relationship had reached a stalemate, and neither knew how to break the cycle of dissatisfaction and despair. Describing him as the man who wasn't there, she continually pushed for a level of closeness that seemed to him overly needy and demanding. As she increasingly complained and urged him to display signs of intimacy, he became more and more agitated. One evening, they engaged in their usual dispute, but he lost control of his emotions. He began choking her and came to his senses just before she passed out. They were both shocked and frightened. He was referred by Janet's therapist to a female therapist (Dr. G.) who attempted to break through his emotional wall but failed, just as Janet had. The therapist referred him for a trial of IS-TDP.

On initial contact, I found Alan to be as Janet and his therapist described. He was fastidious, precise, and sinewy. He was a world-class mountain climber with powerful, Popeye-like forearms. He told me of the episode of domestic violence and was ashamed of himself. He felt it was out of character and could not remember ever attacking anyone else. He deeply loved Janet and felt confused and helpless as to how to meet her emotional needs.

Alan began his interview demonstrating helplessness and a sense of failure in his relationship and in his previous therapy with Dr. G. He was remote, passive, detached, isolated, and self-critical. The therapy began with a confrontation about using the same defenses with me that he used with Dr. G. and that he used with Janet. He was challenged to desist from employing his avoidant and passive defenses. After a period of time, he became angry and expressed the implicit behavioral impulse to strangle me with those power-ful Popeye arms. Encouraged to visualize his fantasy and look into the eyes of my murdered corpse, he transformed me into his older brother Eric. Eric, it seems, physically tormented Alan throughout his childhood. Alan was truly in terror of him. Moreover, he was also deeply saddened and disappointed by the fact that Eric, whom he hero-worshiped, had rejected him. He sobbed at the sight of Eric's corpse and at the grief over the lost closeness between the two of them. In a poignant fantasy, he gave his brother a Viking funeral, burning his murdered body on a boat he set out to sea. I linked the pain of lost closeness between him and Eric to the relationship between him and Janet, pointing out that he had unconsciously created a wall between him-self and Janet, recreating the painful isolation in order to punish himself for his rage at Eric. He sobbed even more deeply. The reconstruction emerged that he blamed both his mother and father for not controlling Eric and pre-serving his safety. Angry with both parents, he isolated himself and withdrew into the world of ideas and pursuit of perfection.

Each session progressively opened up a new PASO in each of Alan's core relationships: mother, father, and brother. Subsequent traumas were revealed. In one he and Eric were on a camping trip with an older male guide. Alan believed the guide was going to molest Eric so he accepted the role of vic-tim to "protect" Eric from suffering the molestation. This turned out to be a highly rationalized narrative. With deeper exploration, it turned out that Alan was hoping that the guide would violently rape Eric, so to punish himself for these bad thoughts he took Eric's place.

After forty hours of IS-TDP, Alan had multiple breakthroughs in many tri-angular situations. His relationships with both parents, as well as with Eric, improved. He and Janet became very close both emotionally and physically. She took a teaching position at an East Coast school and they briefly lived on opposite coasts. He went into a deep depression over her leaving, even though it had been mutually agreed upon. This depression was dealt with as protest rage over his loss of a secure attachment. I linked it to his sense of loss in the relationship with me. When I confronted his defenses, he linked them to his anger at his mother for her bystander role when it came to pro-tecting him from Eric. He understood the triangle of jealousy linking him-self, mother, and Eric and how his clinging, dependent attachment to his mom infuriated Eric, who then tormented him. He realized he had actually rejected his father to prolong the attachment to his mother. We interpreted the homosexual rape as unconscious punishment for his oedipal victory over father and Eric. We connected this to his sabotage of closeness and intimacy with Janet—further punishment for guilt over his incestuous attachment.

Once he gained coherence in the narrative and saw his role and responsibility in the tragedy of his lost childhood, there was a paradigm shift within his psyche. He left his final session with a new sense of security based upon truth. He faced his demon, looked it squarely in the eye, and accepted his part in the drama. With this, the damage to his capacity to love was repaired.

A six-month follow up demonstrated lasting change in the capacity for intimacy.

Insecure Attachment: Ambivalent Style—The Guilty Scientist

Elise began therapy in an eating disorders group for women during a lengthy course of individual therapy. She was an attractive, full-busted woman who was significantly overweight. When thinner she had a history of promiscuity and unhappy relationships with men. In the eating disorders group she found that she was constantly angry with Sheri, one of the more dynamic members of the group. Despite the anger, she became close friends with Sheri, who recognized that she had deeper issues that Elise was avoiding in her two therapies and told her about Davanloo's method of IS-TDP. She booked an appointment for therapy.

Both of Elise's parents were alcoholics. She became estranged from both her mother and father because of their drinking. Elise's mom stopped drinking after divorcing her husband and she and her daughter reconnected. Several years later her mother was diagnosed with a terminal brain tumor, and Elise nursed her mom through her final illness. Her father was an end-stage alcoholic living in another state. She had little contact with him.

As is the usual custom, the interview began by gathering her areas of disturbance. In addition to a quiescent eating disorder, she suffered from moderate depression along with disabling panic attacks. She suffered from these for many years. She did not want antidepressants, which she had tried in the past with mixed results. She reported low self-esteem and said she was easily angered and withdrew in a pouty way with poor conflict resolution abilities. She had made a serious suicide attempt in the past following the loss of a male relationship. Presently, she was in a committed relationship with a fellow scientist but could not tolerate sexual intimacy with him. She would accept oral sex from him but could not reciprocate. She reported that she was unable to experience tenderness and passion in the same relationship with the same person at the same time. She was a successful scientist but was terribly unhappy in her position and had difficulty asserting herself with her group leader.

The initial challenge phase of the resistances revealed ego fragility with heavy projective and introjective defenses. This required Davanloo's technique of restructuring of the ego (see chapter 2) before any meaningful work on the unconscious could begin. I was surprised how regressive her defenses were given the extent of her previous therapy. After 90 minutes the first break-through occurred with the fantasized murder of her friend Sheri, who was linked by her unconscious with her younger brother with whom she felt an intense sibling rivalry. She was flooded with grief, sadness, and pain of loss as she remembered her mother abandoning her at 18 months to two years of life. The perceived abandonment was precipitated by the birth of her brother and her mother's interaction with him. She said, "That was my mother; she could only be a mother to one of us at a time! It was like we didn't exist after the next one was born." She was the only daughter with an older brother and two younger brothers. She was flooded with anxiety as her primitive rage toward her mother bolted into consciousness. She visualized butchering her mother in a psychotic rage. We took a break to let the dust settle.

The second session focused on the exploration of the transference. When she was stronger and understood the process, we began to explore the anxi-ety that she felt in the room with me. A profound resistance against emotional closeness was discovered, and this was handled by Davanloo's method of "head-on collision." The patient encountered strong and frightening impulses to mur-der me with a knife. This was compounded by feelings of inexplicable grief and sadness. She soon realized that she murdered her father in fantasy, and it was his corpse before her eyes. The following narrative emerged.

Elise attached deeply and profoundly to her father after being dropped by her mother in favor of her brother. The anger was deepest at her mother, hence the mother was the first dead parent to appear in her fantasies. The patient and her father were inseparable. Her father was a scientist, and they played together doing math puzzles. As the patient got older, she began to experience sexual feelings toward her father and withdrew from him out of fear and confusion. Neither of them had a close relationship with the mother to provide a balance and allow Elise to sort out her feelings. The father re-acted badly to the loss of his "chum," whom was now a sexual being. He be-gan to drink excessively. She remembers being terrified of him in his drunken states. As the story unfolded, her repressed sexual feelings became conscious and she fantasized sexual play and frolic with him in their flower garden. She became deeply saddened by the loss of her father and experienced acute grief. She understood that her father had lost her mother to first the children and then to her alcoholism, and Elise was the glue that held her father together. When she pulled away because of her frightening oedipal feelings, his abandonment rage and depression erupted. He joined his wife through mutual drinking. Elise began sobbing over the feelings of guilt at her abandonment of him. The unconscious belief that she had destroyed him by becoming sexual became shockingly conscious.

It is noteworthy that her ability to access her sexual feelings blossomed following this breakthrough in our therapy and she began an active sexual relationship with her fiancée. She dressed sexier and began to lose weight. In her next IS-TDP session, she de-repressed an actual sexual molestation by her older brother, who entered her room while she was sleeping and put his hand in her vagina. She awoke but pretended to be asleep, and passively accepted the masturbatory pleasure. I made a link to her unconscious guilt over her sexual feelings toward her father, and she realized that her withdrawal from her father occurred because of the shame over her intense sexual feelings for him and her complex, powerful death wishes for her mother.

The patient interrupted therapy with me, ostensibly to work with a woman therapist whom she felt would help her access "womb and separation trauma." A few months later she returned and shared the insight that she left because she was frightened by the intensity of the anger she was feeling toward me and also by worsening anxiety about the sessions. In the interim her father had died from alcoholism and she had attended his funeral. Her projective/introjective defenses had returned, and I took this opportunity to crystallize her character defenses in the transference. We both acknowledged that she at times dissociated and put on a "mirage defense," which was that of cooperative, in-control, capable person, when, in fact, she was flooded with anxiety and sadistic impulses. This transference exploration led to fantasies of strangling me. Once she held my corpse in her arms, I metamorphosed into her father in his coffin. The pathologic bereavement converted to acute grief in front of me. She sobbed in the deepest way yet. She was racked with sadness that she actually had allowed him to die alone and unattended.

In a moving fantasy, she asked for his forgiveness at her abandonment of him. I commented that he in fact had abandoned himself a long time ago, and that the tragedy was that he had never received help for his emotions. He instead sentenced himself to the worst of all punishments, self-isolation. She saw the connection to her abandoning the therapy and continuing her self-isolation through food addiction and habitual false-self formation. She wept profusely for her mother, whom she was able to nurse through a terrible death from cancer. She saw that her mother went through treatment, sobered up, and engaged in a process of making amends. In fact, when Elise was suicidal and reached out to her mother for help, she responded in a genuine and helpful fashion.

Childhood fantasies of a close interaction with her mother ensued. In these her mother became her mentor in the art of sexuality and in an empathic way tutored her in the art of lovemaking. Her anxiety began to lessen after the breakthrough. She had a core session in which she was reviewing her attachment to her maternal grandfather. She remembered deep feelings for him and deep anger toward her grandmother. She fantasized murdering her grandmother. She de-repressed a memory in which her grandfather promised to always care for her. To ensure this he gave her a duplicate wedding ring to her grandmother's. Rage at her grandfather exploded as she realized the mutual seduction and conspiracy to exclude the grandmother. She remembered his death and grieved his loss. In a vivid fantasy she gave him back the ring in his coffin and told him that it rightly belonged to his wife, not to her. She then could grieve equally for both grandparents, not just one. Therapy began to wind down. Elise had become free of anxiety in our relationship. She had gained promotion and recognition at work, and then resigned when her boyfriend took a position back east. Elise decided to terminate with her group and me before joining him on a farm they had bought together.

Termination was hard for her. She had become close to me and I to her. She was also close to her group members, as her rivalrous feelings had gone away. She now had friends for the first time in her adult life.

Our last session dealt with the memory of her father. She was troubled that she could not put the ambivalence toward him to rest. Somehow, the idea occurred to her that she could forever honor and cherish the gifts that he bestowed on her: her love of science and math, her love of his sense of humor and sexuality, and her love of the garden where they sunbathed together as a family.

The ambivalent insecure attachment seemed to be now secure and loving. Anxiety and depression were gone. Elise and her boyfriend mutually decided not to have children. They are happily together, both in excellent careers, intimately attached to each other, their cats, and their farm.

Insecure Attachment: Disorganized Style—The Ozark Executive

Sally was a bubbly, seductive woman who was referred to me for treatment of "bipolar depression." She had had a series of only partially effective therapeutic interventions. She first felt clinically depressed when she was 42. A high-powered executive, she found herself in a conflict of interest situation at her work. Her boss asked her to do something that she felt was in his interest professionally, but not in the interest of the company. She could not resolve the loyalty conflict and felt anxious, depressed, suicidal, and "crazy." Eventually she saw a family practitioner who placed her on venlafaxine (Effexor) 37.5 mg twice a day. She subsequently gained 40 pounds on this drug. On Christmas day of that year her grandmother, to whom she was attached, died in her arms. Later the drug was changed to Prozac 40 mg per day. At this time she began psychotherapy. A month later she and her husband were forced to declare personal bankruptcy due to the failure of a business deal involving his professional practice.

Her personal financial life was in disarray, but at least she had the security of her career. Frank, her husband, asked her to move to another city where he had a practice opportunity with a friend. Her boss authorized her to move, leading her to believe that she could work on-line. Later, he denied saying this. So suddenly, to her shock and dismay, she found out she had no employment. She was still on Prozac, but even this became ineffective. Another psychiatrist upped her Prozac to 60 mg, added desipramine 75 mg, and recommended day hospitalization, marital therapy, psychotherapy for her child, and a grief support group. She lost confidence in her psychiatrist, stopped her medications on her own, and sought out a new psychiatrist on referral from her internist. She was deteriorating further and at the time of my evaluation, was experiencing auditory hallucinations attacking her self-worth and decision-making abilities. She reported suicidal impulses with fantasies of driving over a cliff or overdosing on drugs and was in severe psychiatric distress.

After a thorough assessment, it was noted that she wanted to try intensive psychotherapy alone. I told her about Davanloo's technique of therapy, and we agreed to use the trial model to determine her suitability for this approach.

We began the process by exploring her feelings toward her husband, Frank. It became clear that there was a triangle of people immediately behind Sally, Frank, and their son Adam. The marriage was of the narcissistic-sadistic, alternating variety described by Solomon in chapter 6. The focus of the interview revolved around using Davanloo's method of restructuring the ego. I constantly pressured Sally to experience her angry feelings toward Frank. She felt anxious, congested in her chest, shortened her breathing, and behaved like a "goody-goody girl." I gave her immediate feedback about her defenses—how she avoided her true emotions with anxiety, how she internalized her anger in depression, how she acted helpless and seductive. I further challenged her that if she wanted to overcome her difficulties she would have to relinquish both her anxiousness and her characterologic ways of avoiding true emotion. She rallied to the challenge with a rise in symptoms. With persistent clarification of the triangle of conflict, she had a partial breakthrough of the unconscious. She visualized herself "smashing out Frank's brains." This primitive image led her to understand that the anxiety and depression were regressive defenses against a deeper quality of emotion.

After a break we began to explore the transference anger and how it felt to her. She began to experience impulses to stab me. Eventually, my corpse transformed into her grandmother, which was a shock to her. In her conscious mind her grandmother was a source of support and comfort to her. She was perplexed as to why she felt so angry with her grandmother, who was her supporter. She then felt a rush of adrenalin-based rage against her own mother, whom she strangled and, along with her grandmother's corpse, threw into a lake. She then thought of her stepfather, George. She began to feel a funny combination of fear and rage. She had a vivid image of a red dress—what she wore the first time that George molested her. Her mother married George in Sally's mind in order to give Willie, her younger brother, a secure family. Sally was the sacrificial lamb for her mother's and Willie's happiness. She remembered multiple episodes of molestation, mainly forced oral copulation. One of the worst aspects of the memory was George's taunting her that she was powerless, that she could not escape him, tell her mother, or otherwise evade his assaults. She was flooded with images of her rage at George. She particularly focused on destroying his eyes and genitals. There were prolonged torture fantasies. She next faced the most shame-producing images, which were her torturously angry impulses toward her brother, Willie. Once the anger phase of the therapy passed, the patient was able to feel the pain of her lost relationship with her mother and grandmother. She realized that the core of her rage was at the pain of being raised as a second-class person to men. Her mother's and grandmother's lives were defined by catering to the needs of men. All the men in her life had been a bitter disappointment. Her father abandoned her before birth, and her only role models were women who survived by being taken care of by men. She was convinced that her mother knew George was molesting her and that she gave tacit permission for the molestation in order to give Willie a secure home under George's roof. Eventually, she left and moved into her grandmother's home.

Sadly, her idealized grandmother, the most competent female of the family, did nothing about the allegations. The patient was seething with anger. She remembered at age 11 her mother's psychotic attack on her grandmother. She realized that she was confused. In part she felt responsible for her mother's decompensation, and in part she felt frightened for her mother's well-being. In therapy I proceeded to make links with the present. She realized that despite all conscious precautions to the contrary, she had married a predatory "King Baby"—just like her stepfather, George. She was reenacting her childhood role as servant to men through her relationship with Frank and her son, Adam. She sobbed profusely at the insight. She realized she was fomenting with self-hatred, and understood for the first time her attacking auditory

hallucinations. She felt pain and remorse at the harm she had done in rais-
ing her own daughter, who was now pregnant and abandoned. She vowed to
stop the transgenerational process in her marriage and with her son.

It took a little over a year—50 visits and 60 hours—to complete the vow.
During that time we were able to rebuild from the ground up her genuine es-
teem for herself. She returned to college to complete her degree, lost 60
pounds, and divorced Frank. She filed and won a breech of contract suit
against her former employer, and at one-year follow up she was an actively
involved single parent for Adam. She separated her finances completely from
Frank's and became a financial officer of a medium-sized company. While co-
parenting Adam with Frank, she attempted to educate him about equality, respect, and love for a woman. She remained off all medication, was symptom
free, and her character change was intact.

The above three cases show three distinctly different attachment styles, and
IS-TDP technique was applied differently for each style. Hopefully, this adds
credence to Davanloo's (1995a) observation that this system of therapy is applicable to a broad spectrum of psychopathology (see chapter 2, Tables 2.1, 2.2).

Universal Manifestations of Unconscious
Psychopathology in Human Neurosis

Siegel (1999) states that complexity (chaos) theory is helpful in understanding
the human brain and its ultimate organization and is also helpful to understanding
psychopathology. It may help us establish scientifically valid models for understanding how dynamic psychotherapy works. Complexity theory is also known
as non-linear dynamics. The theory states that these systems (living as well as
nonliving) have self-organizational properties, are non-linear, and have emergent patterns with recursive characteristics (Boldrini et al., 1998).
Applying this theory to psychological development, tied as it is to brain development, we might say that within each of us there is an inherent drive from
simplicity towards complexity. Siegel argues, and we agree, that stability of a
system is achieved by maximizing complexity. *A balance between continuity and flexibility achieves complexity* (Figure 7.2). Continuity is, of course, memory, which is
a direct function of the quality of the experiences the individual has had. Flexibility lies between the two extremes of rigidity and randomness or chaos.
Human neurosis can be seen as an imbalance between the poles of continuity
and flexibility.

Emotional and cognitive systems are also non-linear. This means *small*
changes deep within the system may result in large changes in behavior. This

is an essential scientific principle supporting the results we see in intensive short-term therapies. Emergent and recursive patterns can enhance life or result in the patient's living an arid emotional life. Siegel writes

> This recursive quality reinforces patterns of representational response learned from earlier encounters with the world. This quality can be adaptive in allowing us to respond rapidly to our perceptions of the world. When engrained and restrictive patterns are taken to the extremes, however, the mind can become deadened to the vital and emergent uniqueness of lived experience. (1999, p. 222)

In this theory, the state of the system is determined by *constraints* (factors) that are internal and external to the system. Internal constraint is determined in part by memory. States of the system that are ingrained are called *attractor states*. Elements of implicit memory are embedded in these attractor states that emerge as automatic responses within intensive short-term therapy or psychoanalysis as transference resistance.

Siegel writes

> Adaptation occurs through modification of constraints. Self-organization is dependent upon the modification of constraints in an effort to

FIGURE 7.2
NON-LINEAR DYNAMICS
Complexity Theory and Psychologic Development—Constant Movement
Toward Self-organization

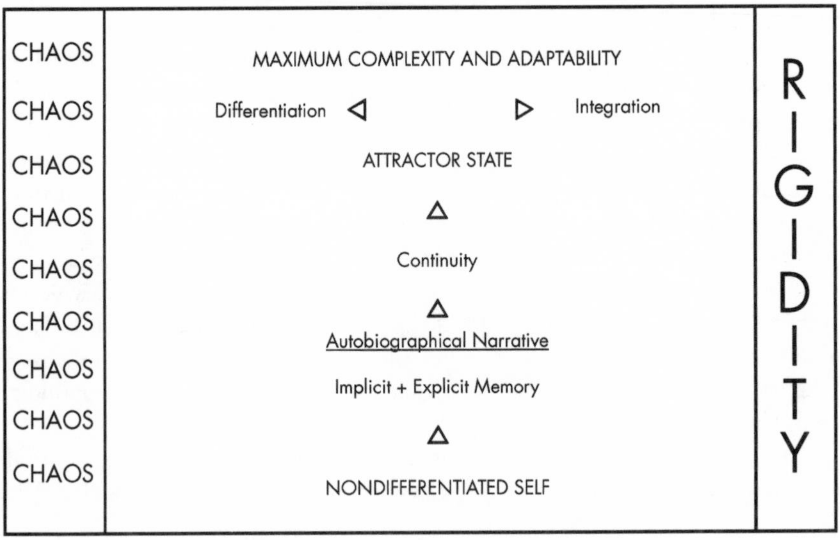

CHAOS	MAXIMUM COMPLEXITY AND ADAPTABILITY	R
CHAOS	Differentiation ◁ ▷ Integration	I
CHAOS	ATTRACTOR STATE	G
CHAOS	△	I
CHAOS	Continuity	D
CHAOS	△	I
CHAOS	Autobiographical Narrative	
CHAOS	Implicit + Explicit Memory	T
CHAOS	△	
CHAOS	NONDIFFERENTIATED SELF	Y

achieve maximum complexity. Dysfunctions in self-organization can be conceptualized as due to any pattern of constraint modification that does not permit movement toward such complexity. (1999, p. 223)

Complexity theory and its implications explain both successful and non-successful therapeutic intervention. If the resistance barrier is breached, set points or attractor states are changed. The breach of resistance liberates non-verbal memory, causing increased continuity. Flexibility is bounded by the extremes of chaos or rigidity. Avoidant insecure attachments (Tin Man) are rigid; the warmth of the intersubjective relationship is rejected for the quasi-security of isolation and stable suffering. Individuals with ambivalent insecure attachments (Guilty Scientist) are compromised by uncertainty in the stability of their relationships; they cannot soothe themselves and their capacity for self-regulation is sorely compromised. Their intimate relationships vacillate between intense overinvolvement and withdrawal into self-absorbed misery. Disorganized insecure attachments (Ozark Executive) vacillate between a sense of inner chaos and outer terror. These individuals have meager internal means to regulate their chaotic emotions; they consciously seek intimate relations to create order out of their inner chaos but inevitably recreate in those very relationships the terror that they felt with their primary attachment figures.

Anger as the Hallmark Symptom of Rigidity

One form of rigidity seen in insecure attachments is the pervasiveness of anger in the unconscious process. Table 7.2 shows the devastating consequences of this anger to the mindbody-important other relationship in these individuals.

TABLE 7.2
Effects of Rigidity (Anger) on the Unconscious

PROCESS	RESULT
Internalization	Depression
Somatization	Organ destruction
Projection	Turns the environment into a more hostile place
Anxiety	Demands reality-altering or self-suppressing defenses; catastrophic thinking
Turning against self	Self-mutilation
	Self-isolation
	Seducing anger out of the other for punishment
	Self-sabotage (self-defeat)
Turning against other	Sadism
	Commingling of sexual and aggressive drives

In case after case, in neurotic individuals, the repressed anger dominates the psychic process. (Davanloo reports that over 600 videotaped interviews demonstrate this unconscious rage.) This anger appears to be the direct result of the types of trauma outlined in Table 7.1.

Etiology of Human Neurosis

A Transgenerational Process

It is important to consider the research findings of Mary Main (1996). The incoherent narrative in the caregiver as a predictor of later patterns of attachment in the child is an intriguing finding. This supports findings from our own clinical research in individuals and couples. The transmission of neurosis is transgenerational. The unconscious of neurotic patients contains a wealth of nonrepresentational data about the psychologic makeup of the grandparents. Whether the patients knew them or not, these grandparents raised the insecurely attached parent. Insecurely attached mothers raise insecurely attached children. The male children will over time recreate the unconscious traumatic attachment process with their families. The females will directly transmit the disorder to their own children despite conscious intent to do everything but. The vehicle for this transmission is, of course, the impairment of empathy for a particularly troublesome set of emotions. The emotions can revolve around rivalry, autonomy, sexuality, power, obedience and dependence—whatever the trigger for reactivation of the parent's PASO. In other words, without therapy that brings these experiences into consciousness and allows them to be incorporated into an authentic narrative, the patient has no awareness of what is missing. This deficiency then creates reciprocal attunement trauma, and so the baton is handed down to the next generation.

The role of the father is essential. He offers a compensatory attunement system, which can neutralize the transmission of trauma. However, all too frequently in systems in which there is severe attachment trauma both parents are part of the disturbed system, so the father's ability to mitigate is impaired as well. Dynamic psychotherapy can then be seen from a public health perspective as a treatment to prevent the spread of the world's most prevalent pandemic disease: neurosis.

Time and the Unconscious

We have established the idea of attachment and trauma and its centrality to the existence of suffering over time. It is worthwhile to examine the issue of the presence of a sense of time in each of us. It is encoded in a form within implicit memory that doesn't feel like a recollection when retrieved (Siegel, 1996). Implicit nonverbal memories are in the form of emotions and pictures without a sense of time.

There is evidence that at least mild states of dissociation occur during trauma, and explicit memory is cleaved from implicit memory by the loss of focal attention. Explicit autobiographical memory is an autobiographical sense of oneself over time—past, present, and projection into the future. Very generally, it is a direct function of the coherency of the autobiographical narrative. Implicit memory is the memory of emotional reaction to events, which may or may not be connected to explicit memory. Explicit memory begins to form during the second year of life, while implicit memory is with us from the beginning of life. Our studies of the unconscious reveal that the pain of loss and grief and the reactive aggressive part of the memory are uniformly cleaved from awareness and exist in a state of "suspended animation" in the unconscious. This information is stored in nonverbal thought. However, in each and every patient it is being acted out in some fashion or other in relationships. This split-off piece is kept out of the autobiographical narrative until crisis or therapy activates it. While it is refused access to the overall integrated autobiographical narrative, it is acted out in behavior (narrative reenactment). So the trauma is in fact always present, but out of awareness of it's orgins in the past. The techniques of therapy described in this book show various ways to access and process this memory system.

Common Areas in "Dissimilar" Short-Term Therapies

This book describes various systems of short-term therapy with individuals and couples. Francine Shapiro describes EMDR as "non-intrusive" because the therapist does not interject his/her psychic organization into the process. She allows patients to do their own integration of the affective memories that the technique brings into consciousness. So on a continuum, at the most nonintrusive end is EMDR. Although the therapist is completely nonintrusive, he or she is implicitly relentless in pursuit of the client's encounter with truth. Next along the spectrum is Michael Alpert's AET. He relentlessly insists that the patient stay in contact with the caring aspects of the therapist. Pleasantly intrusive, he causes patients to experience their emotions in a new context, that of a close accepting environment. In the middle ground is Leigh McCullough's anxiety-regulating therapy, in which she banters with patients' methods of disengagement until they no longer resist an encounter with their emotional truth. Solomon uses empathic resonance to enhance each partner's contact with the unconscious system at play in the dyad. Lastly, there is Neborsky, who practices Davanloo's method of enforced paradox. In this method, he constantly interweaves confrontation of maladaptive defense with patients' motivation for treatment, imploring them not to (self) defeat attempts to help them with their rigid, habitual responses to their emotions. This technique uses confrontation in an active way, in order to repair the insecure attachment (Table 7.3).

In each of the above therapies, with appropriate selection of candidates, eventually the old PASO withers on the vine, and a new MASO (mature adaptive self-organization) replaces it. The new MASO is created by the internalization of the unconscious qualities of the therapist, who has lent himself to the patient as a guide to emotional reintegration. This change results in a decrease in symptom formation, increased ability to maintain boundaries, increased freedom to feel emotion within the self, and increased self-directed compassion and empathy for others. Ultimately, the new adaptive self-organization allows patients to take in information from their intimate partners without the immediate shift into defensive operation. This enhances collaborative communication and conflict resolution, allowing intimacy to blossom. An environmentally acquired insecure attachment or a dormant one from childhood is thus transformed into a secure attachment in a lasting way (Pearson, 1994). In this way the love imprint is changed.

TABLE 7.3
Proposed Way in Which IS-TDP Changes the Love Imprint

INITIAL LOVE IMPRINT FROZEN BY PASO

The attractor state (resistance) exists at the edge of chaos (unconscious affect, anxiety).

The IS-TDP technique (CDS) overwhelms the rigidity (neurotic balance) and puts the system into momentary chaos.

The unblocking of defenses release the attachment system.

The superego melts, revealing the id, which liberates ego.

Rapid hemispheric shifts occur, creating openings to new neural networks.

This causes a psychologic "paradigm shift."

A new personality organization emerges as the system moves to a new self organization (MASO—mature adaptive self organization).

References

Ainsworth, M. D. S., Blehar, M. C., Waters, E., & Wall, S. (1978). *Patterns of attachment: A psychological study of the Strange Situation.* Hillsdale, NJ: Erlbaum.

Ainsworth, M. D. S., & Eichberg, C. (1991). Effects on infant-mother attachment of mother's unresolved loss of an attachment figure, or other traumatic experience. In C. M. Parkes, J. Stevenson-Hinde, & P. Marris (Eds.), *Attachment across the life cycle* (pp. 160–186). London: Routledge.

Boldrini, M., Placidi, G. P. A., & Marazziti, D. (1998). Applications of chaos theories to psychiatry: A review and future perspectives. *International Journal of Neuropsychiatric Medicine, 3,* 22–29.

Bowlby, J. (1969). *Attachment and loss: Vol. 1. Attachment.* New York: Basic Books.

Bowlby, J. (1973). *Attachment and loss: Vol. 2. Separation and anger.* New York: Basic Books.

Bowlby, J. (1980). *Attachment and loss: Vol. 3. Loss: Sadness and depression.* New York: Basic Books.

Davanloo, H. (1995a). Intensive short-term dynamic psychotherapy: Spectrum of psycho-neurotic disorders. *International Journal of Short-Term Psychotherapy, 10*(3,4), 121–155.

Davanloo, H. (1995b). Intensive short-term dynamic psychotherapy: major unlocking of the unconscious. Part II. The course of the trial therapy after partial unlocking. *International Journal of Short-Term Psychotherapy, 10*(3,4), 183–230.

Devereux, G. (1964). *Why Oedipus killed Laius.* New York: Dutton.

Dicks, H. V. (1953). *Marital tension: Clinical studies toward a psychological theory of interaction.* London: Routledge and Kegan Paul.

Emde, R., Gaensbauer, T., & Harmon, R. (1976). *Emotional expression in infancy, Psychological Issues, Monogr. 37.* New York: International Universities Press.

Emde, R. (1983). The prerepresentational self and its affective core. *The Psychoanalytic Study of the Child,* 38:165–192. New Haven, CT: Yale University Press.

Erikson, E. H. (1963). *Childhood and society* (2nd ed.). New York: Norton.

Fairbairn, W. R. D. (1952). *Psychoanalytic studies of the personality.* London: Tavistock.

Freud, A. (1967). Comment on trauma. In S.S. Furst (Ed.), *Psychic Trauma* (pp. 235–245). New York: Basic Books.

Freud, S. (1898). Sexuality in the aetiology of the neuroses. In J. Strachey (Ed. and Trans.), *The standard edition of the complete psychological works of Sigmund Freud* (Vol. 3, pp. 259–285). New York: Norton, 1962.

Freud, S. (1900). The interpretation of dreams. In J. Strachey (Ed. and Trans.), *The standard edition of the complete psychological works of Sigmund Freud* (Vol. 4,5). New York: Norton, 1953.

Freud, S. (1905) Three essays on the theory of sexuality. In J. Strachey (Ed. and Trans.), *The standard edition of the complete psychological works of Sigmund Freud* (Vol. 7, pp. 123–245). New York: Norton, 1953.

Freud, S. (1909). Analysis of a phobia in a five-year old boy. In J. Strachey (Ed. and Trans.), *The standard edition of the complete psychological works of Sigmund Freud* (Vol. 10, pp. 1–149). New York: Norton, 1955.

Freud, S. (1911). Remembering, repeating, and working through. In J. Strachey (Ed. and Trans.), *The standard edition of the complete psychological works of Sigmund Freud* (Vol. 12, pp. 150). New York: Norton, 1959.

Freud, S. (1917). Fixation to traumas—the unconscious. In J. Strachey (Ed. and Trans.), *The standard edition of the complete psychological works of Sigmund Freud* (Vol. 16). New York: Norton.

Freud, S. (1918). Introduction to psychoanalysis and the war neurosis. In J. Strachey (Ed. and Trans.), *The standard edition of the complete psychological works of Sigmund Freud* (Vol. 17, pp. 207–210). New York: Norton, 1959.

Freud, S. (1926). Inhibitions, symptoms, and anxiety. In J. Strachey (Ed. and Trans.), *The standard edition of the complete psychological works of Sigmund Freud* (Vol. 20, pp. 75–175). New York: Norton, 1959.

Guntrip, H. (1961). *Personality structure and human interaction.* New York: International Universities Press.

Jones, J. M. (1995). *Affects as process.* Hillsdale, NJ: Analytic Press.

Kahn, M. (1963). Cumulative trauma. *Psychoanalytic Study of the Child, 18,* 286–306.

Klein, M. (1932). *The psychoanalysis of children.* London: Hogarth.

Konzelmann, C. (1995). Head on collision with resistance against emotional closensss in intensive short term dynamic psychotherapy. *International Journal of Short-Term Psychotherapy, 10,* 35–51.

Main, M. (1991). Metacognitive knowledge, metacognitive monitoring, and singular (coherent) versus multiple (incoherent) models of attachment: Findings and directions for future research. In C. M. Parkes, J. Stenson-Hinde, & P. Marris (Eds.), *Attachment across the life cycle* (pp. 127–159). London: Routledge.

Main, M. (1993). Discourse, prediction, and recent studies in attachment: Implications for psychoanalysis. *Journal of the American Psychoanalytic Association, 41,* 209–244.

Main, M. (1995). Attachment: Overview, with implications for clinical work. In S. Goldberg, R. Muir, & J. Kerr (Eds.), *Attachment theory: Social, developmental and clinical perspectives* (pp. 407–474). Hillsdale, NJ: Analytic Press.

Main, M. (1996). Introduction to the special section on attachment and psychopathology: 2. Overview of the field of attachment. *Journal of Consulting and Clinical Psychology, 64,* 237–243.

Main, M. (in press). The adult attachment interview: Fear, attention, safety and discourse processes. *Journal of the American Psychoanalytic Association.*

Main, M., & Goldwyn, R. (1984). *Adult attachment scoring and classification system.* Unpublished manuscript, University of California at Berkeley.

Main, M., & Goldwyn, R. (1998). *Adult attachment scoring and classification systems* (Version 6.3). Unpublished manuscript, University of California at Berkeley.

Main, M., & Hesse, E. (1990). Parent's unresolved traumatic experiences are related to infant disorganized status: Is frightened and/or frightening parental behavior the linking mechanism? In M. T. Greenberg, D. Cicchetti, & E. M. Cummings (Eds.), *Attachment in the preschool years: Theory, research, and intervention* (pp. 161–182). Chicago: University of Chicago Press.

Main, M., Kaplan, N., & Cassidy, J. (1985). Security in infancy, childhood, and adulthood: A move to the level of representation. In I. Bretherton & E. Waters (Eds.), *Growing points of attachment theory and research. Monographs of the Society for Research in Child Development, 50* (2–3 Serial No. 209), 66–104.

Main, M., & Morgan, H. (1996). Disorganization and disorientation in infant Strange Situation behavior: Phenotypic resemblance to dissociative states. In L. K. Michelson & W. J. Ray (Eds.), *Handbook of dissociation: Theoretical, empirical, and clinical perspectives* (pp. 121–160). Chicago: University of Chicago Press.

Main, M., & Solomon, J. (1986). Discovery of an insecure-disorganized/disoriented attachment pattern. In T. B. Brazelton & M. Yogman (Eds.), *Affective development in infancy* (pp. 95–124). Norwood, NJ: Ablex.

Main, M., & Solomon, J. (1990). Procedures for identifying infants as disorganized/disoriented during the Ainsworth Strange Situation. In M. T. Greenberg, D. Cicchetti, &

E. M. Cummings (Eds.), *Attachment in the preschool years: Theory, research, and intervention* (pp. 121–160). Chicago: University of Chicago Press.

Miller, A. (1996). *Prisoners of childhood: The drama of the gifted child and the search for the true self* (reissue). New York: Basic Books.

Neborsky, R. (1998). The role of the sibling in the unconscious. In B. S. Mark & J. A. Incorvaia (Eds.), *The handbook of infant, child, and adolescent psychotherapy* (Vol. 2). Northvale, NJ: Aronson.

Neborsky, R. (2001, May). *Perinatal trauma and resistance to emotional closeness.* Presentation at conference on Core Factors for Effective Short-Term Dynamic Psychotherapy, Milan, Italy.

Pearson, J. L., Cohn, D. A., Cowan, P. A., & Cowan, C. P. (1994). Earned and continuous security in adult attachment: Relation to depressive symptomotology and parenting style. *Development and Psychopathology, 6,* 259–373.

Scharff, D. & Scharff, J. (1990). *Object relations couple therapy.* Northvale, NJ: J Aronson.

Schore, A. N. (1994). *Affect regulation and the origin of the self: The neurobiology of emotional development.* Hillsdale, NJ: Erlbaum.

Schore, A. N. (1996). The experience-dependent maturation of a regulatory system in the orbital prefrontal cortex and the origin of developmental psychopathology. *Development and Psychopathology, 8,* 59–87.

Schore, A. N. (1997). Early organization of the nonlinear right brain and development of a predisposition to psychiatric disorders. *Development and Psychopathology, 9,* 595–631.

Schore, A. N. (1998). The experience-dependent maturation of an evaluative system in the cortex. In K. H. Pribram & J. King (Eds.), *Brain and values: Is a biological science of values possible?* (pp. 337–358). Mahway, NJ: Erlbaum.

Schore, A. N. (in press). Clinical implications of a neurobiological model of projective identification. In S. Alhanti (Ed.) *Primitive mental states, Vol. III. Pre- and peri-natal influences on personality development.* ESF Publishers.

Siegel, D. J. (1999). *The developing mind.* New York: Guilford.

Siegel, D. J. (1995). Memory, trauma, and psychotherapy: A cognitive science view. *Journal of Psychotherapy Practice and Research, 4,* 93–122.

Solomon, M. (1989). *Narcissism and intimacy: Love and marriage in an age of confusion.* New York: Norton.

Solomon, M. (1994). *Lean on me.* New York: Simon and Schuster.

Spitz, R. A. (1945). Hospitalism; An inquiry into the genesis of psychiatric conditions in early childhood. *Psychoanalytic Study of the Child, 1.*

Spitz, R. A., & Wolf, M. (1946). Anaclitic depression: An inquiry into the genesis of psychiatric conditions in early childhood, II. *Psychoanalytic Study of the Child, 2,* 313–342.

Stern, D. N. (1985). *The interpersonal world of the infant.* New York: Basic Books.

Sroufe, L. A., Egeland, B., & Krentger, T. (1990). The fate of early experience following developmental change: Longitudinal approaches to individual adaptation in childhood. *Child Development, 54,* 1615–1627.

Tomkins, S. (1962). *Affect, imagery, consciousness, Vol I.* New York: Springer.

Tomkins, S. (1963). *Affect, imagery, consciousness, Vol II.* New York: Springer.

Winnicott, D. W. (1951/1975). *Through paediatrics to psycho-analysis.* New York: Basic Books.

8

The Way Ahead

David Malan

IN THIS CHAPTER I shall touch on four main themes:

1. The current position of short-term psychotherapy and how it has been reached.
2. The use therapists can make of this, adapting the basic principles to their own personalities.
3. Whether the effectiveness of short-term psychotherapy can be increased.
4. That dynamic psychotherapy is a valid treatment and how this can be conveyed to the world.

The Current Position of Short-Term Psychotherapy

An understanding of the present position in short-term psychotherapy depends on seeing it in its historical perspective. The development of short-term therapy has gone through a number of stages, beginning with the psychoanalytic view.

The Psychoanalytic View

Until the Second World War psychoanalysis was the only form of psychotherapy that was thought to be truly effective. All briefer methods were subject to "the hypothesis of superficiality," which states that only superficially ill patients can be treated briefly, the technique should be superficial and should avoid the transference, and the results can be only superficial and are usually transient.

Alexander and French

In 1946 these two authors, working in Chicago, published their book *Psychoanalytic Therapy*, which contains an account of 21 successful therapies ranging from 2 to 57 sessions. Two important principles that they used consisted of planning therapy in terms of what we would now call a focus and active pursuit of the focus by the therapist.

Alexander and French's most striking therapy, from among many, was "Case P." The patient was a young man of 19 suffering from severe depression, who was treated by a woman therapist in 35 sessions of 20 minutes, which was all he could come for. In the main part of therapy he was extremely resistant to talking about his mother, who had died in a terrible accident when he was three; however, he completely recovered after derepressing his grief about her death, which hitherto had been deeply unconscious. The therapy culminated in an intensely moving transference experience, in which the man put the therapist in the position of his mother and symbolically reincorporated her into himself. Follow-up was two years since termination.

Taking this result together with several others, these authors demonstrated unequivocally that *with certain patients* all three aspects of the "hypothesis of superficiality" were false: i.e., (1) certain relatively severe and chronic conditions can be treated with short-term psychotherapy in under 40 sessions; (2) the technique used should be active and can contain all the essential ingredients of psychoanalysis, including interpretation of resistance, the use of the transference, and the link between the transference and the past; and (3) the resulting changes can be profound and lasting.

However, the trouble is that the Chicago team treated over 500 patients, and nobody knows what happened to the other 480-odd. The overall effectiveness of their methods therefore remains unknown. This book brought down a storm of hostility from psychoanalysts, most of whom, it seemed, had never been trained in the elementary scientific principle of checking preconceptions against experimental evidence. A review by Ernest Jones (1946) ends with the following passage, which shows the almost infinite capacity for denial in some prejudiced people: "The word 'unconscious' is not mentioned in the index, nor have we been able to find it in the text itself. Perhaps indeed it is not germane to the content of the book." It is difficult to see exactly how this remark applies to therapies like the one described above.

Nevertheless, as a consequence of this hostility the work of Alexander and French was ignored and virtually forgotten.

The Tavistock Clinic: Balint and Malan

In 1955 Michael Balint got together a small team of well-trained analysts, of which I was one, with the aim of investigating the whole question of short-term therapy from the very beginning. Interestingly, in spite of the fact that he knew both Franz Alexander and Thomas French personally, Balint seemed to have shared other analysts' dismissal of their observations, which were never mentioned in our preliminary discussions.

The results of several years' work were published in 1963 in my book, *A Study of Brief Psychotherapy*, and a replication was published in two further books in 1976.

Our work had the following characteristics:

- The technique used was purely interpretative.
- We published details of a continuous series of therapies, both successful and unsuccessful.
- We confirmed unequivocally Alexander and French's refutation of all three aspects of the hypothesis of superficiality.
- We showed not merely that interpretation of the transference together with the link with the past *could* be used successfully, but that the more effectively it was used the better were the therapeutic results.

Many years later, we demonstrated the extremely important observation that similar results could be obtained by trainees under experienced supervision (Malan & Osimo, 1992). However, we also showed that this kind of work depended on the selection of patients who were *highly motivated and responsive*. With more resistant patients we were defeated. Suitable patients represented only about 5% of the psychotherapeutic population.

This brings us to the most important development of all.

The Work of Davanloo

Like Balint, Davanloo started investigating this problem in the 1950s. He worked virtually in secret—secure, like Freud, in the knowledge that no one would pre-empt him. After 20 years he finally began to publicize his results in a series of international conferences starting in Montreal in 1975.

His main finding was that a highly active, challenging technique could break through even the most stubborn resistance and achieve "total resolution" of the patient's neurosis. Although some of his claims may be exaggerated, no one can deny the effectiveness of his technique in those many patients whom he has shown on videotape. Thus, he was able to bring a far higher proportion of patients into the field of short-term therapy, overcoming the major disadvantage of our own work (see Davanloo, 1978, 1980, 1990). However, this work suffers from another disadvantage, which is almost equally unfortunate from a practical point of view: Whereas our technique is only applicable to a limited proportion of *patients*, his somewhat abrasive style does not suit the majority of *therapists*, and therefore it is very difficult to learn and transmit. (Robert Neborsky, an author of this book and presenter at two conferences that I attended in 1998 and 2000, has notably shown himself able to overcome this problem.)

Developments from Davanloo's Technique

The result has been that a number of therapists who have had some training from Davanloo have set about adapting his technique to their own personalities. Notable among these are Leigh McCullough in Boston, who has shown her work at these conferences and has written it up in a monumental book called *Changing Character* (1997), and Patricia Della Selva, in Albany, New York, who has shown videotapes at Michael Alpert's Conferences, and is the author of an important book called *Intensive Short-term Dynamic Psychotherapy* (1996). Both these therapists have been able to get some striking therapeutic results by means of a softened technique, which nevertheless uses the most important of Davanloo's basic principles. A third school of short-term therapy, also demonstrated at these conferences, has been developed by Michael Alpert and his colleagues in New Jersey and is called accelerated empathic therapy (AET). Their technique lies at the very opposite end of the spectrum of challenge, since they deliberately offer the patient great warmth and empathy. Because most patients are afraid of emotional closeness, this brings its own kind of resistance, which then has to be dealt with in its turn (see Alpert, 1992).

How May Therapists Make Use of This Work?

First of all one must ask, what are the essential principles of a technique of short-term therapy that can be effective with relatively resistant patients? The answer seems to lie in the following:

1. Therapists must start by concentrating on the *resistance* (defined as defenses used in the therapeutic situation) to the exclusion of all else, until this is resolved.

2. They must pay the strictest attention to detecting *transference* and must bring it into the open wherever it is found.

3. They must bring patients to the *direct physical experience* of their hitherto buried feelings and must accept nothing less than this.

I would encourage you to experiment with these three principles, and as long as you adhere to them you may find that you can develop an effective technique that suits your own personality.

How Might the Effectiveness of These Techniques be Increased Even Further?

The Importance of a Continuous Series

The first question that must be asked is an obvious one, which unfortunately is usually neglected: How effective are they already? The situation must not be allowed to suffer from what may be called the "Alexander and French fallacy," namely that books are written and videotapes shown illustrating a number of strikingly successful therapies, without any mention of what happened in all the others. Essential above all else is the publication of at least some details from a *continuous series*. In this connection Davanloo has made a stupendous claim (personal communication): of 617 successive general psychiatric patients referred to the outpatient department of the Montreal General Hospital, he personally treated 172 (28%). He stated that 83% of these gave successful therapeutic results, defined as "total resolution" of their neurosis, and that more than half were followed up for two to nine years. Unfortunately, there are no details to support these figures.

However, I am very pleased to be able to say that—apart from our own work—there are three notable exceptions or potential exceptions to the Alexander and French fallacy, two of them Norwegian:

1. A group of therapists working in Oslo have studied a form of short-term dynamic psychotherapy similar to that used by Balint's team, and have already published a series of papers (e.g., Hüsby, 1985). The results of the continuous series, with a five-year follow-up, were written up in a thesis by the same author, but unfortunately this has not been published (Hüsby, 1982).

2. In Boston Leigh McCullough has for some years been leading a research team working with her own form of post-Davanloo therapy. She will

be in a position to publish details of a continuous series, which she intends to do.

3. The same is true of a team working under McCullough's leadership in Trondheim, who are in process of completing a two-year follow-up of a comparison of post-Davanloo therapy with cognitive-behavioral methods.

The Length of Therapy

Another crucial question, which in the relative absence of continuous series remains unanswered, is: In general, how many sessions do these forms of therapy require? The last thing one wants is for therapists to get into a competitive situation ("My therapy is shorter than your therapy") and yet, as far as practical usefulness is concerned, particularly in the current atmosphere in the U.S. and Canada, there is a world of difference between 20 sessions and 60 sessions. Therapists who are regularly exceeding 40 sessions might well try to tighten up their work by paying even stricter attention to the three basic principles listed above.

Training

I would also be concerned not only with increasing the effectiveness of techniques, but also with increasing the number of therapists who can use them. This means more emphasis on training, which of course is a major undertaking.

The Use of Non-dynamic Techniques

Are there other techniques that could be usefully incorporated into our work? Here I believe we need to consider developments in non-dynamic forms of therapy, particularly cognitive-behavioral therapy. Leigh McCullough, whose original training was in behavior therapy, already deliberately uses such methods as desensitization to disturbing feelings, encouragement to face phobic situations, guided fantasy, and the two-chair technique. Other therapists could well make use of these methods, in ways that suit their own personalities.

It is one of the tenets of dynamic psychotherapy that therapists need do no more than resolve patients' underlying conflicts, and not only do symptoms disappear completely, but patients also discover for themselves how to replace maladaptive with adaptive patterns of behavior in their life outside therapy. Is this as true as we would wish?

We need to remember that the direct attack on symptoms and certain other disturbances may well be more quickly effective than the dynamic approach. In particular, where the relief of symptoms is a matter of urgency, then we ought to consider such techniques as exposure and response prevention for severe compulsions, cognitive-behavioral therapy for panic disorder, and assertive training for problems of aggression. After the symptoms have been relieved, dynamic therapy can follow.

This applies also in the reverse order. One of my very important observations—repeatedly made—is that, even when the patient's core conflict has apparently been truly resolved, some symptoms often remain in an attenuated form. I once tried to get such a patient taken on by a behavior therapist, who refused, saying that this was exactly the kind of state in which patients tended to be left after successful behavior therapy—something that does not receive much emphasis in the literature! Nevertheless, it may be much more effective to relieve a symptom by behavioral methods than to just wait for it to disappear.

Dynamic Psychotherapy by Behavior Therapists

Some of the ideas expressed above involve the use of behavioral methods by dynamic psychotherapists. What about the other way round? One of the fascinating developments of recent years is that some of the most polemically anti-dynamic behavior therapists, including especially both Joseph Wolpe and Arnold Lazarus, have become—without overtly admitting it—highly skilled dynamic psychotherapists. At the Second Conference on the Evolution of Psychotherapy, which was held in Anaheim, California, in 1990, Wolpe reported the following vignette (see Zeig, 1992, pp. 138–9): The patient was a married woman complaining of depression for 10 years, who had failed to respond to previous psychoanalysis. Wolpe quickly traced her symptom to severe loss of self-esteem caused by her inability to achieve orgasm in sexual intercourse, though she could in masturbation by herself. This relieved her depression permanently within three sessions. He then traced her sexual problem to her fear of trusting other people, and this in turn to her inability to trust her father in her upbringing. So far this was pure dynamic psychotherapy. However, he then took a more direct approach, first getting the patient to achieve orgasm by masturbating in the presence of her husband and then *"desensitizing her to her fear of emotional closeness,"* with the final result that she was able to overcome her symptom completely. Follow-up was 13 years. Unfortunately he didn't say how the desensitization was conducted, but the important point is that he used *behavioral methods* on *psychodynamic phenomena,* and—whatever he did—dynamic therapists need to take this kind of approach seriously.

Concurrent Dynamic Therapy and Behavior Therapy

This is yet another possibility. Segraves (a behavior therapist) and Smith (a dynamic psychotherapist) described the following therapy in 1976: The patient was a young woman of 23 complaining of depression, difficulties in relations with men, and a phobia of birds. Smith took her on for dynamic psychotherapy, but after a few months her therapy seemed to reach a dead-lock. He therefore decided to try and make a direct attack on her phobia by referring her for behavior therapy, while continuing with her psychotherapy. Segraves offered her 12 sessions of *in vivo* desensitization. In the 10th session he brought a live duck into the office and encouraged her to touch it. Suddenly she told him that her fear of touching the duck was like her mixed feelings about having sex with boys when she was in high school—both wanting it and feeling it was wrong. The behavior therapist didn't regard this comment as relevant to his work and continued with desensitization. Eventually, the patient touched the duck and cried with relief. From this point onwards both her depression and her bird phobia permanently disappeared. In the next psychotherapeutic session she recalled that her father was still touching and kissing her when she was 17, and that if she protested he would accuse her of being hysterical. The deadlock in her psychotherapy was broken. Smith continued to treat her for another two years, which resulted in a major improvement in her ability to relate to men.

A fascinating question raised by such a patient is: What on earth is the connection between oedipal anxieties and a phobia of birds? Unfortunately it remains unanswered. The important observation illustrated by this clinical story is that the direct attack on a symptom with behavior therapy may some-times *activate a patient's unconscious* and thus have a major facilitating effect on dynamic psychotherapy.

The Validity of Dynamic Psychotherapy and How This can be Conveyed to the World

Here I would like to start by describing some aspects of an exceedingly well-designed study comparing brief dynamic psychotherapy and behavior therapy (14 sessions of each), which was conducted in Los Angeles (Sloane, Staples, Cristol, Yorkston, & Whipple, 1975). As usual, *on average* behavior therapy did better than psychotherapy, though the difference was not statistically significant. However, there were also the following three observations, the first two of which were mentioned by the authors, though not emphasized, while the third emerges now from an examination of their clinical examples:

i. "... the results of psychotherapy were more variable [than those of behavior therapy]: more patients showed greater improvement and more showed less improvement than in behavior therapy.

ii. "Given the right combination of patient and therapist, psychotherapy was as effective, or *more effective*, than behavior therapy. With the wrong combination it was less effective" (my italics).

iii. The authors published clinical vignettes on six patients who gave good therapeutic results. Of these, *five came from psychotherapy and only one from behavior therapy.*

These three observations show how important it is to examine each individual therapeutic result in detail, rather than simply to report averages. They also tend to confirm a conjecture that I have held for many years: that although many of the results of psychotherapy are no more than *moderately* favorable, and are indistinguishable from those given by non-dynamic methods, the best results possess qualities that are specific to dynamic psychotherapy and are superior to those of other methods.

It seems to me that there are two reasons why this observation—if it is true—has never been reported in the literature. The first is that, like the Sloane study, every single controlled study in the literature is concerned only with averages and these best results represent only a small proportion of the total. Consequently, they do not significantly influence the overall statistics, and psychotherapy appears to do no better—or indeed appears to do worse—than more direct methods such as behavior therapy.

The second follows from a problem that has bedeviled outcome studies of psychotherapy from the beginning, namely that the qualities that I postulate as evidence for the effectiveness of dynamic psychotherapy represent the *ultimate in subjectivity*. To this problem there are two main kinds of reaction. Those therapists who value such qualities throw up their hands in despair at the prospect of trying to study them, while the "scientists," preoccupied with objectivity, reliability, and so-called validity, do not regard them as suitable for scientific study at all.

You may ask, what are these qualities, and how can they be studied? Strangely, I find both questions easy to answer. The main qualities that I seek in a true therapeutic result can be stated in a single comprehensive sentence: *inhibition* or *compulsiveness* replaced by *emotional freedom, intensity,* or *depth.*

(Obviously, these qualities must be appropriate—it would be no good converting an inhibited man into a potential murderer.) But how can such imponderables be studied? Easy. By reporting verbatim what patients say at follow-up, and allowing readers to judge these qualities for themselves. Below are some examples, taken from short, medium, and long-term treatment. (The ages given apply when the patient first asked for help; the length of follow-up is measured from the date of termination.)

THE INDIAN SCIENTIST, age 29
(12 sessions, follow-up 7 years. See Malan, 1976a, pp. 157–164).
Inhibition replaced by emotional freedom and intensity

One of the things that worried him when he first came was that he was so little involved in love-making that, as he said, "If someone gave me a complicated calculation to do at the time, I could perfectly well do it."

At follow-up, now married, he wrote, in his touching Indian English: "The insatiable physical want that I had to begin with, these resulted to satisfaction of both the partners, gave way after marriage to more limited but regular intimacies ..."

THE PERSONNEL MANAGER, age 40
(62 sessions, follow-up nearly 7 years. See Malan, 1976a, pp. 185–197).
Inhibition replaced by emotional intensity, freedom, and depth

This extremely competent unmarried woman had panicked in her early twenties when a man for the first time paid attention to her. She had kept away from men ever since, apparently denying to herself that she had any interest in them. At follow-up she spoke of having formed a relation with a man, which had developed into an affair. "I have also had an experience of sex, the absence of which was always a loss to me—as, if I had to go to my grave without having been to bed with a man, I had missed out on something. It was something I felt was my birthright, just the same as that I feel, if I really let myself, that I am going to have a child. In fact, *if I can only hold this man's child in my arms I would be quite happy.* I would take whatever came, even if we were not married."

THE INTERNATIONAL FENCER, 19
(58 sessions, follow-up 6 years)
Compulsiveness replaced by emotional freedom and depth

"All my masculinity went into that foil, and holding a foil was my only way of expressing it. Now I'm a man at all times and not just when I'm holding a foil; and if I do lose a match I lose without feeling annihilated. I realize that all my competitiveness and sexuality had been channeled into my fencing. Now I enjoy it, which I didn't really before— and I'm not prepared to put more of myself into it, because I've got a lot of other things going for me as well, and it no longer has the same significance. It's just a pleasant hobby. I refuse to return to competitive fencing.

THE TRAINING ANALYSAND, 22
(960 sessions, follow-up 2 years)
Inhibition replaced by emotional freedom, intensity, and depth

Now married, she spoke as follows: "I used to be frigid and promiscuous at the same time. I went through the motions. I occasionally enjoyed it and might get orgasm in a kind of mechanical way. Now orgasm itself is not the point, it's what I feel the whole way through. It's very flowing, close, all over, not just in my head. I want it to go on and never stop, and then I don't mind knowing that it's going to build up and then stop. It has the effect of bringing us closer together—in the past with my husband it sometimes didn't."

I have many other examples, but to quote them would make this chapter too long. How might these concepts be used? These vignettes make it clear how the qualities that are observed in really good therapeutic results are both extraordinarily subtle and yet unmistakable. I am not saying that such qualities do not occur in other forms of therapy. I suggest only that they tend to occur more often when a patient's neurosis has been truly resolved, and that it is dynamic psychotherapy that is most likely to achieve this. These considerations suggest very clearly a way of comparing dynamic psychotherapy with other forms of therapy, which could be used retrospectively, without modification, in any controlled study that has been carried out—of which Leigh McCullough's Norwegian study of dynamic psychotherapy and cognitive-behavioral therapy is a prime example.

By far the simplest would be a purely qualitative study, which could be carried out as follows: The best ten (or any other arbitrary number) of the results are chosen from each form of therapy. The study then requires no more than that a trained researcher should extract, from transcripts of the follow-up interviews, those passages that fulfill the above criteria to the greatest degree. These are then published for readers to judge for themselves. The study can of course be made more "scientific" if all clues about the nature of the therapy are removed from the transcripts, which are then submitted "blind" to trained judges, who assess on some appropriate scale the degree to which the above qualities are present in each therapeutic result.

Final Summary

The history of short-term psychotherapy shows that Davanloo's challenging technique is effective with even some of the most resistant patients, but this technique needs to be modified and softened if it is to be acceptable to the majority of therapists. The essential principles of any truly effective short-term psychotherapy are:

- concentrating on the *resistance* to the exclusion of all else;
- attending to *transference* and bringing it into the open whenever it is detected; and
- persisting until patients are brought to the actual *physical experience* of their buried feelings.

Then, we must establish an accurate baseline of what our current methods can and cannot actually accomplish. Essential to this is the publication of results from continuous series.

In order to improve the efficiency further we need to pay even stricter attention to the three principles listed above. Then we need to explore further the use of non-dynamic methods, such as those derived from cognitive-behavioral therapy, and make more training available for clinicians who wish to undertake this kind of work.

Finally, we must convey the validity of dynamic psychotherapy to the world. To accomplish this, we need to consider certain qualities of a therapeutic result that indicate that a patient's neurosis has been truly resolved. Such qualities are highly subjective, but they can be named, and the evidence can easily be confirmed. This confirmation comes from publishing the material and allowing readers to judge it for themselves. This can be applied retrospectively to any studies where transcripts of initial assessment and follow-up interviews are still available, especially those in which dynamic and non-dynamic forms of therapy have been compared.

The painstaking work of the clinician-scientists and researchers of the past half-century has shown us the essential principles underlying the best in patient care; it's now up to the next generation to refine and apply them. Hopefully they will glean yet better techniques to help neurotic patients conquer their self-imposed misery. It is my further hope that the techniques described by the authors in this volume will facilitate that process.

Addendum

It is important to note that this chapter was written before I became acquainted with EMDR, the significance of which is described by Francine Shapiro in chapter 5.

References

Alexander, F., & French, T. M. (1946). *Psychoanalytic therapy.* New York: Ronald Press.

Alpert, M. C. (1992). Accelerated empathic therapy: A new short-term dynamic psychotherapy. *International Journal of Short-term Psychotherapy, 7,* 133–156.

Davanloo, H. (1978). *Basic principles and techniques in short-term dynamic psychotherapy.* New York: Spectrum.

Davanloo, H. (1980). *Short-term dynamic psychotherapy.* New York: Aronson.

Davanloo, H. (1990). *Unlocking the unconscious.* Chichester: Wiley.

Della Selva, P. C. (1996). *Intensive short-term dynamic psychotherapy.* New York: Wiley.

Hüsby, R. (1982). *Effect of short-term dynamic psychotherapy.* Unpublished thesis for the University of Oslo.

Hüsby, R. (1985). Short-term dynamic psychotherapy. III. A 5-year follow-up of 36 neurotic patients. *Psychotherapy and Psychosomatics, 43,* 17–22.

Jones, E. (1946). Review of *Psychoanalytic Therapy* by Alexander and French. *International Journal of Psychoanalysis, 27,* 162.

Malan D. H. (1963). *A study of brief psychotherapy.* London: Tavistock. Reprinted by Plenum, New York, 1975.

Malan, D. H. (1976a). *The frontier of brief psychotherapy.* New York: Plenum.

Malan, D. H. (1976b). *Toward the validation of dynamic psychotherapy.* New York: Plenum.

Malan, D. H., & Osimo, F. (1992). *Psychodynamics, training, and outcome in brief psychotherapy.* Oxford: Butterworth-Heinemann.

McCullough Vaillant, L. (1997). *Changing character.* New York: Basic Books.

Segraves, R. T., & Smith, R. C. (1976). Concurrent psychotherapy and behavior therapy. *Archives of General Psychiatry, 33,* 756–763.

Sloane, R. B., Staples, P. R., Cristol, A. H., Yorkston, N. J., & Whipple, K. (1975). *Psychotherapy versus behavior therapy.* Cambridge, MA: Harvard University Press.

Zeig, J. K. (1992). *The evolution of psychotherapy: The second conference.* New York: Brunner/Mazel.

About the Authors

Michael Alpert, M.D., M.P.H., received his psychiatric training at the University of Colorado, after which he obtained a degree in Public Health in the Behavioral Sciences at Harvard University. He became interested in brief psychotherapy in the late 1970s and subsequently introduced an IS-TDP training program at Saint Clare's Hospital, where he was Chairman of the Department of Psychiatry. Attempts to make IS-TDP more effective led to the development of accelerated empathic therapy (AET), a model that emphasizes the discussion of the empathic interaction and relationship between therapist and patient. Dr. Alpert is currently the Director of the STDP Institute of New York and New Jersey and Medical Director of the St. Clare's Behavioral Health Services. Recently he co-founded the STDP Discussion List and the International Experiential STDP Association (IESA) to advance brief therapies. He is married to a public health physician and has two children.

David Malan: At the age of 25, Dr. Malan gave up his career as a research chemist and undertook simultaneous training in medicine and psychoanalysis, eventually becoming a psychotherapist at the Tavistock Clinic in London. In 1955, he was a founding member of Michael Balint's team investigating brief psychotherapy, the results of which he reported in three books. He has specialized in the long-term follow-up of various forms of psychotherapy, and, because of his background in the physical sciences, he has always tried to introduce as much science into the study of psychotherapy as the subject will allow—no more and no less.

In the 1970s, Dr. Malan was commissioned by Butterworth-Heinemann to write a textbook of dynamic psychotherapy, which appeared in 1979 under the title *Individual Psychotherapy and the Science of Psychodynamics*. In the 1980s he wrote a number of articles in collaboration with Davanloo, with the aim of helping to publicize the latter's work, the importance of which he was quick

to recognize. Since then he has been almost entirely concerned with publishing detailed outcome studies with many years' follow-up using psychodynamic outcome criteria of patients treated with dynamic psychotherapy—believing that this is the only practical way in which the validity of this form of
therapy can be demonstrated. The result has been two published books and
one in preparation: *Psychodynamics, Training, and Outcome in Brief Psychotherapy*
(written in collaboration with Dr. Ferruccio Osimo); *Anorexia, Murder, and Suicide*, a 20-year follow-up of three remarkable patients whose problems are
enumerated in the title; and currently he is collaborating with Dr. Patricia
Della Selva in a book provisionally titled *Lives Transformed.*

Leigh McCullough, Ph.D., is Clinical Assistant Professor and Director of the
Short-term Psychotherapy Research Program at Harvard Medical School. She
has published extensively on therapy, training, and research in short-term
dynamic psychotherapy and gives training seminars worldwide. She has
served as Research Director of Beth Israel Medical Center's Short-term
Psychotherapy Program, is a Visiting Professor at the University of Trondheim
in Norway, and has a clinical practice in Dedham, Massachusetts. She is the
author of *Changing Character.*

Robert J. Neborsky, M.D., is a psychiatrist in private practice in Del Mar,
California. He is a Clinical Professor of Psychiatry at UCSD School of
Medicine, Medical Director of Lifespan Learning Institute, and Director of
the Lifespan Foundation for Research and Training in Psychotherapy. He
is on the editorial board of the *International Journal of Short-term Dynamic
Psychotherapy.*

After training at the University of Maryland School of Medicine and undertaking his psychiatric residency at Emory University School of Medicine,
Dr. Neborsky served in the United States Navy as director of inpatient psychiatry at Balboa Naval Hospital. From there he joined the full-time faculty
of UCSD School of Medicine as an assistant professor of psychiatry in charge
of emergency services and the medical student clerkship. With David
Janowsky, he published significant research on the treatment of acute psy-
chosis with high-dose/low-dose haloperidol, and wrote articles on the com-
bined use of pharmacotherapy and psychotherapy in the treatment of
depression. In 1979, while at UCSD, he met Habib Davanloo and David
Malan, and in 1981 he co-founded the San Diego Institute for Short-Term
Dynamic Psychotherapy while in training with Dr. Davanloo.

Dr. Neborsky's professional activities include teaching IS-TDP technique,
writing about the unconscious, and presenting at local, national, and international symposia. He is married and the father of four daughters.

Francine Shapiro, Ph.D., the originator and developer of EMDR, is a senior research fellow at the Mental Research Institute in Palo Alto, California. She is the founder and President Emeritus of the EMDR Humanitarian Assistance Programs, a nonprofit organization that coordinates disaster response and pro bono trainings worldwide. She has served as advisor to a wide variety of trauma treatment and outreach organizations and journals. Dr. Shapiro has been an invited speaker on EMDR at many major psychology conferences, including two divisions of the American Psychological Association and the American Psychological Society Presidential Symposium on PTSD. She has written and coauthored numerous articles, chapters, and books about EMDR, including *Eye Movement Desensitization and Reprocessing*, *EMDR*, and *EMDR and the Paradigm Prism*. She is a recipient of the Distinguished Scientific Achievement in Psychology Award presented by the California Psychological Association.

Marion F. Solomon, Ph.D., is Director of Clinical Training for the Lifespan Learning Institute and coordinator of continuing education seminars, Department of Humanities, Sciences, and Social Sciences, UCLA Extension, Los Angeles. She is co-director of the "Cutting Edge" conference series, Department of Psychiatry, University of California, San Diego. Dr. Solomon is the author of *Narcissism and Intimacy: Love and Marriage in an Age of Confusion* and *Lean on Me: The Power of Positive Dependency in Intimate Relationships*, and co-editor of *The Borderline Patient: Emerging Concepts in Diagnosis, Etiology, Psychodynamics and Treatment* and *Countertransference in Couples Therapy*. She has written ten articles and chapters in five books on the subject of couples therapy.

INDEX